Military Money

Military Money

A Fiscal History of the U.S. Army
Overseas in World War II

By WALTER RUNDELL, JR.

Texas A&M University Press
COLLEGE STATION & LONDON

Library of Congress Cataloging in Publication Data

Rundell, Walter.
    Military money.

    Bibliography: p.
    Includes index.
    1. United States. Army—Finance—History.
    2. World War, 1939–1945—Finance—United States.
    I. Title.
    UC23 1941–45.R86   355.6′22′0973   79–7408
    ISBN 0-89096-079-8 (cloth) ISBN 1-58544-031-0 (pbk.)

Manufactured in the United States of America
FIRST PAPERBACK EDITION

For Stanley L. Falk
Friend and scholar

Contents

Illustrations

Preface

THIS study began in March 1953 when I arrived at the Kansas City Records Center to initiate research on the army's overseas fiscal activities in World War II. I had just graduated from the army's finance school, so presumably I knew something about military finance. My assignment as a second lieutenant in the Finance Corps was to research and write on the prescribed topic. Immediately I was immersed in vast quantities of raw data constituting the army's field records from World War II. With only the crudest of finding aids, I learned to locate the fiscal records and began my work. The staff there and at the Departmental Records Branch in Alexandria, Virginia, where I did subsequent research, allowed me to do my own searching, which presented an opportunity to obtain the kind of invaluable archival training largely denied graduate history students currently.

In the 1950's, when I did the original research for this volume, army records were under the jurisdiction of the Adjutant General. The following decade saw them transferred to the National Archives and Records Service. All the primary sources I examined at the Kansas City Records Center and Departmental Records Branch are now in the General Archives Division, Washington National Records Center, located in Suitland, Maryland.

The historical files in the Office of the Chief of Finance (now defunct) and Office of the Chief of Military History (since 1973 the Center of Military History [CMH]) proved indispensable. Without the full cooperation of these two organizations, research for this book would have been impossible. I warmly acknowledge this assistance and express my thanks. Those sources from the reference files of CMH are so cited.

At the beginning of World War II the Finance Department operated as one of the army's administrative services. The Office of the Chief of Finance was a War Department staff agency, and the Chief of Finance, a major general, reported to the army's Chief of Staff. The Chief of Finance, by virtue of his position, was also the budget officer for the War Department. In addition to serving a staff function, the Office of the Chief of Finance, composed of military and civilian employees, directed activities of the Finance Department in the field. These activities consisted of handling all financial activities on military installations and paying the army's commercial bills. Again, both military and civilian employees staffed field finance offices. Only four months after the outbreak of war, much of the staff authority of the Office of the Chief of Finance was supplanted by that of the newly formed Office of the Fiscal Director, but the Finance Department remained responsible for fiscal services in the field, both at home and overseas. Once Finance began overseas operations, its personnel there were almost exclusively military.

During World War II, the Finance Department disbursed a total of approximately $176 billion—a sum that still staggers the imagination, even considering the immense inflation subsequent to 1945. This total figure included all the army's expenses—although some were quite remote from the actual fighting. This study covers various aspects of the army's fiscal structure and operations connected with that expenditure, treating the most significant topics in overseas fiscal management.

The first chapter deals with the Finance administration—the organization, personnel, and facilities of finance offices, ranging from the Office of the Chief of Finance, through theater fiscal offices, to individual finance disbursing sections, created during the war as separate units to be attached wherever needed. Overseas theaters answered only to the War Department, and each operated within the context of its mission and environment. Consequently, considerable variation existed among the ways theaters and their subordinate organizations handled financial matters. These contrasts had an impact on virtually all phases of fiscal management. Despite the fact that Washington planners imposed the same structure on administrative units in disparate areas of the world, those responsible for fiscal affairs could make some adaptations to the requirements of their locales. These adaptations resulted in fiscal practices that were different from one theater to another.

Subsequent chapters consider the army's fiscal diplomacy in negotiating with other agencies of the U.S. government and foreign powers, as well as budgeting and accounting for public funds. The book also examines the topics of funding—providing currency wherever needed around the world—and of paying GI's, civilians, and prisoners of war. Since they were paid in foreign currencies overseas, soldiers frequently needed their money exchanged. The discussion of currency exchange highlights the inadequate planning that underlay this extensive activity, exemplifying a lack of leadership in the Office of the Chief of Finance. Those who served in the Finance Department shared highly atypical military missions. Because of the technicality of their work and their superior mental abilities, their reactions to army life differed from those of combat soldiers. The final chapter analyzes this difference.

The book's basic argument is that the leadership of the Finance Department, being unprepared for World War II, approached many of its responsibilities unsystematically and without much conceptualization of the kinds of situations it would face. It projected domestic peacetime procedures into foreign theaters, where they often were unsuitable. More realistic planning, either before the war or after its outbreak, could have made finance service far more efficient. But most institutions, especially the military, are addicted to their past and change is painful. It is therefore not really surprising that the army's record of wartime fiscal services was imperfect.

Throughout the war names of organizations and commands changed, reflecting the constant flux of the federal bureaucracy. In the text I employ organizational names that will be most familiar. For example, I use "European theater" rather than ETO, ETOUSA, or USFET. Sometimes, however, the initials are more graceful and as understandable as the full or shortened title. Consequently, I use USAFIME for U.S. Army Forces in the Middle East. The list of abbreviations provides both the abbreviation and the full name for the military initials in both the text and the notes.

Although the war ended officially with V-J Day on 2 September 1945, many of the wartime fiscal problems extended into the immediate postwar period. This study only touches on new situations presented by the occupation, but deals with pay and currency exchange until troops redeployed to the United States.

Portions of three chapters appeared originally as articles in *Military Affairs, The Southwestern Social Science Quarterly*, and *The Historian*. I happily acknowledge the permission of the editors of those periodicals to use the revised material in this volume.

An author inevitably receives much help in preparing such a study, and it is a genuine pleasure to express public appreciation for it. Edith H. Parker first involved me in this pursuit, and I have been in her debt, one way or another, since 1948. Her leadership as chief historian in the Office of the Chief of Finance proved inspiring. Others in that office who gave valuable assistance include her successor, Jonathan Grossman, the late Ann Kannmacher, and Harry W. Crandall. Especially helpful were archivists Erwin Gemmer, Sherrod East, Lois Aldridge, Peggy Liebman, and Hannah Zeidlik. Numismatist C. Frederick Schwan, coauthor of *World War II Military Currency*, graciously supplied the photographs of currency from his extensive collection. I appreciate the criticism of colleagues in economic history at the University of Maryland, John R. Lampe and John J. McCusker, as well as the help of my able research assistants, Richard Hallion and Bruce F. Adams. For Stanley L. Falk's criticism, which has been most pertinent and rewarding, I am particularly grateful. Dorothy Lukens willingly typed drafts of the manuscript. My wife, Deanna, supports my scholarly endeavors with constant interest and genuine enthusiasm. The foregoing naturally have no responsibility for the contents, interpretations, or shortcomings of this volume. That is my own.

WALTER RUNDELL, JR.

University of Maryland

Abbreviations

AAFPOA—Army Air Forces Pacific Ocean Area

ACofS—Assistant Chief of Staff, usually followed by a "G" designation, e.g., G-5

AdSec—Advance Section

AFWESPAC—United States Army Forces in the Western Pacific

AG—Adjutant General

AMET—Africa–Middle East Theater

APO—Army Post Office

AR—Army Regulation

ASF—Army Service Forces

ATC—Air Transport Command

AWOL—absent without official leave

CBI—China-Burma-India Theater

CG—Commanding General

CIC—Counterintelligence Corps

CID—Criminal Investigation Detachment

CinC—Commander in Chief

Cir—Circular

CMH—Center of Military History, formerly Office of the Chief of Military History

CNC—Chinese National Currency

CO—Commanding Officer

CofS—Chief of Staff

COMZ—Communications Zone

CPBC—Central Pacific Base Command

CWO—Chief Warrant Officer

DO—Disbursing Officer

ETO—European Theater of Operations

ETOUSA—European Theater of Operations, United States Army

FDGA—Finance Department General Allotment

FDS—Finance Disbursing Section

FOUSA—Finance Office, United States Army

FY—Fiscal Year

GAO—General Accounting Office

G-1—Personnel

G-2—Intelligence

G-4—Supplies and Equipment

G-5—Civil Affairs and Military Government

GHQ—General Headquarters

Hq—Headquarters

HUSAFPOA—Headquarters, United States Army Forces in the Pacific Ocean Areas

IBT—India-Burma Theater

IG—Inspector General

IND—Indorsement

LST—Landing Ship, Tank

Ltr—Letter

MTO—Mediterranean Theater of Operations

MTOUSA—Mediterranean Theater of Operations, United States Army

NATOUSA—North African Theater of Operations, United States Army

OBASCOM—Okinawa Base Command

OCF—Office of the Chief of Finance

ODB—Office of Dependency Benefits

OFD—Office of the Fiscal Director

OMGUS—Office of Military Government, United States (Germany)

OSS—Office of Strategic Services

PCAU—Philippine Civil Affairs Unit

P&CO—Purchasing and Contracting Officer

PGC—Persian Gulf Command

PGSC—Persian Gulf Service Command

PMG—Provost Marshal General

POW—prisoner of war

PTA—personal transfer account

RG—Record Group

SCAP—Supreme Commander Allied Powers

SHAEF—Supreme Headquarters, Allied Expeditionary Forces

SIPR—Soldier's Individual Pay Record

sop—Standing Operating Procedure
sos—Services of Supply
spbc—South Pacific Base Command
swpa—Southwest Pacific Area
S-2—Intelligence Staff Officer
tag—The Adjutant General
tm—Technical Manual
t/o&e—Table of Organization and Equipment
twx—Military Telegram
usaffe—United States Army Forces in the Far East
usafime—United States Army Forces in the Middle East
usafispa—United States Army Forces in the South Pacific Area
usafmidpac—United States Army Forces in the Middle Pacific
usafpac—United States Army Forces in the Pacific
usafpoa—United States Army Forces in the Pacific Ocean Areas
usarpac—United States Army in the Pacific
usasos—United States Army, Services of Supply
usfet—United States Forces, European Theater
usfip—United States Forces in the Philippines
uso—United Service Organizations
wac—Women's Army Corps
wd—War Department
wdgs—War Department General Staff
wojg—Warrant Officer, Junior Grade
wpbc—Western Pacific Base Command

Military Money

CHAPTER *1*

Finance Administration

MONEY, according to Tacitus, was "the sinews of war."[1] All activities of the U.S. Army Finance Department in World War II related somehow to money. Finance never claimed that it constituted the sinews that held together the American war machine—but then few finance men were classical scholars. A more colloquial aphorism, surely as authoritative as Tacitus, counseled: "Pay the troops and fear nothing." While paying soldiers remained Finance's central mission, military money for all purposes had to be supplied (funded), exchanged, budgeted, and accounted for. The wartime Finance organization developed to meet these varied responsibilities.

The Finance Department accomplished its mission in World War II with surprisingly small numbers of personnel. As the army's fiscal agent, Finance handled all monetary matters and dealt with other government agencies and foreign powers. At the outbreak of war, officers and enlisted men of Finance numbered 3,000 out of a total of 1,686,000, less than one-fifth of 1 percent. In June 1943 the proportion from Finance had increased to nearly one-quarter of 1 percent (17,140 of 6,994,472). By May 1945 when the army's manpower peaked at 8,290,000, Finance claimed 4,000 officers and 10,800 enlisted men; the Finance ratio had receded to the December 1941 figure of less than one-fifth of 1 percent. Throughout the war, then, the army's fiscal management was handled by a miniscule organization.[2]

---

[1] *The History*, Book ii, 84.

[2] Figures supplied by Reference Branch, Center of Military History. The decrease in Finance strength from 1943 to 1945, although small, represents an anomaly, for the records indicate that finance needs grew with the army's numbers and they do not indicate any consistent personnel surpluses. The statistics are admittedly rough, so the small difference may result from their imprecision rather than from an absolute decline in the number of Finance personnel.

Manifold problems faced the Finance Department as it began overseas operations in World War II. When Japan attacked Pearl Harbor on 7 December 1941, this country's military machine was far from ready for global conflict. While there had already been pointed indications that the United States could not escape the maelstrom, the general temper of the population would not sanction preparation for total war. Hence, when war came, the army's Finance Department, along with other components of the armed forces, had to address itself to the task at hand. No time was left for theorizing or planning for the fiscal support of the army, should it become engaged in total warfare. The accomplished fact of the attack on Pearl Harbor dictated immediate service.

The Finance Department, unlike most of the army's technical and administrative services, had never before operated in a war, having been established 15 July 1920. During World War I the Quartermaster Department had handled financial matters. This lack of wartime experience might have been the dominant cause for the insufficient preparation. More likely was a lack of foresight on the part of Finance leadership. The Office of the Chief of Finance, a staff agency of the War Department, had responsibility for disbursing and accounting for funds appropriated by Congress to the army, as well as for administering the Finance Department. Before and during World War II the Chief of Finance was Maj. Gen. Howard K. Loughry. The European war, which began in September 1939, did little to cause General Loughry to anticipate American involvement. Rather than gearing his office for wartime planning, which obviously would have required a larger staff, he actually allowed the loss of one position between 1940 and 1941.[3] Since Loughry had not planned adequately for wartime operations, finance offices had to cope with new situations as best they could, by improvising and muddling through. The War Department realized in early March 1942 that the Chief of Finance offered in-

[3] War Department Justifications, Estimates, FY 1941, as Submitted to Congress, vol. 1, p. #1-1/18/40, Records of the Office of the Chief of Finance (Army) (OCF), Record Group 203, Washington National Records Center. In FY 1940, OCF had 268 civilian employees and 1 less the following year. The Finance Department, at various posts in the United States, employed 903 civilians in FY 1940 and by June 1941, only 868 (ibid., vol. 2, p. #4-1/18/40).

adequate leadership, and so supplanted his authority in the areas of policy and planning by organizing a superior Office of the Fiscal Director in the Army Service Forces. The new Fiscal Director was Arthur H. Carter, a senior partner in the accounting firm of Haskins and Sells, appointed as a major general. Loughry continued as Chief of Finance through the war, but operated on a circumscribed technical plane.[4] Wartime activities of the Finance Department overseas were prescribed largely by the Office of the Fiscal Director and monitored by the Office of the Chief of Finance. The latter was so clearly subordinate that there was scarcely any conflict between the two agencies.[5]

The Office of the Fiscal Director bore responsibility for establishing broad policies relating to military money throughout the war. These included preparation and administration of the army's budget, as well as supervising fiscal operations overseas. The Office of the Chief of Finance paid millions of commercial bills to vendors and contractors. These two offices, in addition to setting policies, performed operational tasks such as sending monthly checks to dependents of servicemen, promoting and selling war bonds to the military and civilians in the War Department through payroll deductions, and auditing the army's mammoth expenditures. They likewise established the mechanism by which soldiers could pay premiums for National Service Life Insurance through payroll deductions.

Because of the nature of military operations abroad, financial administrative procedures overseas were never as stable as in the Washington headquarters. Combat operations dictated shifting command structures and organizations, which meant that no one set of policies or procedures remained constant throughout the war. Some examples will be cited as typical of overseas fiscal operations, but change rather than stability characterized the administrative apparatus.

Three basic administrative problems arose concerning financial services in foreign areas: the organizational structure of finance

[4] John D. Millett, *The Organization and Role of the Army Service Forces*, pp. 349–350.
[5] Walter Rundell, Jr., *Black Market Money*, pp. 4–5.

units, personnel requirements, and office facilities and equipment. This chapter describes and analyzes the administrative foundation on which the Finance Department operated overseas.

Finance Organizations

To handle its varied assignments abroad, Finance had both administrative and tactical units. Each major overseas theater had an office of the fiscal director that coordinated all aspects of fiscal service in its area. The army's overseas administrative structure placed theaters at the top and gave them responsibility for activities within their domain. Theater fiscal directors and their offices supervised all financial operations beneath them. Among the most active combat areas were the North African, European, and Pacific. An examination of these three fiscal offices reveals differences and similarities and shows the nature of their concerns.

America's first sustained ground combat involvement in World War II came in the North African Theater of Operations, U.S. Army (NATOUSA), later redesignated the Mediterranean Theater of Operations (MTO). Its fiscal office had the following duties: to formulate and recommend to the theater commander policies for financial administration; to advise on rates of exchange, currency problems, and the impact of military expenditures within the area; to advise on lend-lease and reciprocal aid; to coordinate with the British; to promote the sale of war bonds; to supervise the work of disbursing officers; to supervise the processing of allotments; and to review reports of survey and board proceedings. The last involved assessments of responsibility for the loss of army property or funds.

To perform the foregoing duties, the NATOUSA fiscal office relied on five branches: special fiscal services, administrative, audit, receipts and disbursements, and accounts. The special fiscal services branch planned new operations, studied foreign currencies and currency control, handled depository problems, and maintained liaison with the Allied Forces Headquarters. The administrative branch dealt with office procedures, personnel, and equipment. The audit branch reviewed disbursement and collection vouchers, reviewed proceedings of boards of officers, examined payments of native civilian employees, and developed audit procedures for non-appropriated funds. The receipts and disbursement branch prepared statistical reports reflecting the disbursing activities within the theater, performed research for finance circular letters and theater directives, supervised personnel, and allocated work loads. Its last two functions clearly duplicated those of the administrative branch, reflecting the imprecision and waste inevitably connected with hastily erected administrative organizations. Such overlapping was, moreover, bound to occur throughout the war as commands phased in and out, corresponding to the ebb and flow of combat. Prewar planning might have mitigated some of the difficulties, but the Chief of Finance had not projected operations into foreign areas.

Principal duties of the accounts branch were to receive accounting documents from disbursing officers, to classify collections and expenditures, to post each disbursing officer's ledger, to prepare accounting reports for the Office of the Fiscal Director in Washington, to reconcile accounts current, to forward original accounting documents to the army audit branch of the General Accounting Office (GAO), to receive reports on lend-lease and reciprocal aid, and to control and account for funds allotted under the Finance Department General Allotment (FDGA) for the theater. The FDGA plan was initiated to disencumber accounting procedures during wartime.[6]

By the time the North African theater had been transformed into the Mediterranean theater, the fiscal director's office had added two additional branches, a war bonds and savings branch and a British liaison branch, as the following page shows.

When the European theater was activated on 8 June 1942, Col. Nicholas H. Cobbs became the chief finance officer, as well as the finance officer for the Services of Supply (SOS), the theater's support echelon. On 22 August 1943 the theater redesignated his primary office as that of fiscal director and enunciated his duties: to develop and supervise special financial services; to supervise the

[6] Cir ltrs, Office of Fis Dir, Peninsular Base Sec, NATOUSA. Records of United States Army Commands, 1942– , Record Group 338, Washington National Records Center, hereafter referred to as RG 338. See the discussion of FDGA on pp. 71–73.

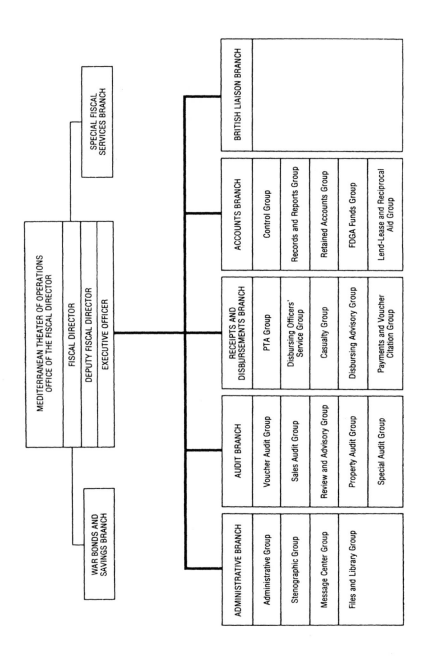

MEDITERRANEAN THEATER OF OPERATIONS
OFFICE OF THE FISCAL DIRECTOR

FISCAL DIRECTOR

DEPUTY FISCAL DIRECTOR

EXECUTIVE OFFICER

WAR BONDS AND SAVINGS BRANCH

SPECIAL FISCAL SERVICES BRANCH

ADMINISTRATIVE BRANCH
- Administrative Group
- Stenographic Group
- Message Center Group
- Files and Library Group

AUDIT BRANCH
- Voucher Audit Group
- Sales Audit Group
- Review and Advisory Group
- Property Audit Group
- Special Audit Group

RECEIPTS AND DISBURSEMENTS BRANCH
- PTA Group
- Disbursing Officers' Service Group
- Casualty Group
- Disbursing Advisory Group
- Payments and Voucher Citation Group

ACCOUNTS BRANCH
- Control Group
- Records and Reports Group
- Retained Accounts Group
- FDGA Funds Group
- Lend-Lease and Reciprocal Aid Group

BRITISH LIAISON BRANCH

receipt of and accounting for funds due the War Department; to supervise the disbursement of and accounting for all appropriated funds in the theater; to audit disbursements; to secure local adjustments and corrections of errors; to prepare summary accounts of receipts and disbursements monthly to send to Washington; and to establish bank credits for all disbursing officers in the theater. In addition, the European theater fiscal director had the same responsibilities as his NATOUSA counterpart in the areas of foreign banking, exchange, currency, the study of the impact of soldier spending on local economies, lend-lease and reciprocal aid, and the sale of war bonds (see following page for ETO fiscal organizational chart).[7]

Since the European theater became considerably larger than the North African and the Mediterranean, its fiscal office had a more complex organization. Rather than having five basic branches, it consisted of eleven divisions: adjusted accounts; fiscal; sales audit; personnel and control; reciprocal aid and lend-lease liaison; reciprocal aid and lend-lease reports; administrative; currency, planning, and redeployment; war bonds and insurance; receipts, disbursements, and allotments; and reports of survey. The receipts, disbursements, and allotments division included branches similiar to those in other theaters—allotments, accounts, audit, and retained accounts. A comparison of the responsibilities of the fiscal directors' offices in the two theaters reveals that they were almost identical. Yet the larger magnitude of operations in the European theater resulted in more individual functions being handled by a division established just for this purpose than in the North African theater, where fewer branches handled a greater variety of chores.

Both these theaters were geared for land operations, with supporting air power, including large concentrations of men within fairly well-delimited geographical areas. In this regard they differed considerably from Pacific operations, where smaller units were scattered over that huge ocean. That notwithstanding, the organization of the fiscal office of the U.S. Army Forces, Pacific Ocean Area (USAFPOA) was exactly the same as that of NATOUSA. Apparently, the Office of the Fiscal Director in Washington did not perceive that the needs of the two highly disparate geographical operations

[7] Circ 63, Hq SOS, ETO, 23 Nov 43. RG 338.

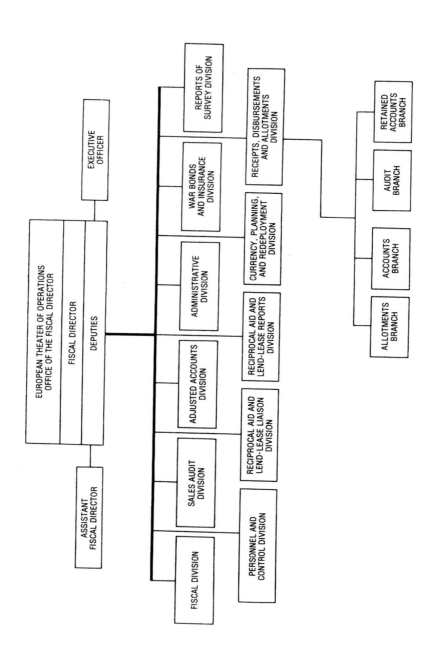

would call for different alignments in the theater fiscal offices. Responsibilities of these two offices were practically the same, indicating again the influence of the Washington blueprint. The only duties of the Pacific office that were not prescribed for NATOUSA were that (1) its accounts branch received notices of exception (indications of irregular payments) from the GAO and cleared the exceptions; (2) the chief of the receipts and disbursements branch acted as the central funding officer for the Pacific theater; and (3) the special fiscal services branch dealt with allotments, insurance, and savings promotion.[8]

The creation of USAFPOA illustrates a major administrative problem faced by the army during the war. This theater came into being in July 1944, superseding the Central Pacific Area. Simultaneously, the Central Pacific Base Command (CPBC) was established on a subordinate level, with each of the new commands getting a part of the old Central Pacific Area fiscal office. The broad responsibilities of the USAFPOA fiscal office were practically identical with those of its predecessor command. But the intention had been for the USAFPOA fiscal office to make policy, while CPBC handled operations. Although CPBC dealt with smaller details, such as auditing nonappropriated funds and processing final pay accounts for those killed and missing in action, the similarities in functions and responsibilities obscured any real differentiation of responsibilities between the two commands. Since the commanding officer of the CPBC fiscal office, Lt. Col. Robert J. Irish, was under the supervision of the USAFPOA fiscal director, Col. Bickford E. Sawyer, he was in no position to reduce the duplication.[9] Any moves toward such a reduction would have had to come from Sawyer, who was apparently satisfied with the overlapping. Frequent reorganization of command structures during the war resulted in similiar administrative inefficiences. In fluid wartime situations, however, such problems were understandable. The elements of chance and uncertainty played practically as large a part in military administra-

[8] "History of Fiscal and Finance Activities in the Middle Pacific from 7 Dec 1941 to 2 Sep 1945," pp. 33, 49–60. Center of Military History (CMH). Hereafter referred to as "History of Fiscal Mid Pac."

[9] Ibid., p. 32. On 1 July 45 USAFPOA was redesignated U.S. Army Forces, Middle Pacific (USAFMIDPAC).

tion as in tactical operations. Under wartime conditions, textbook efficiency remained a fiction.

In the army's hierarchical structure, below theater commands were army groups, air forces, armies, corps, and divisions. The table of organization and equipment (T/O&E) for each of these provided organic finance service. Except for divisions, the financial needs of these administrative units were limited, since they involved few personnel. Consequently, they had small finance units. For an infantry division, the basic building block in the command structure, the T/O&E prescribed a finance section consisting of two officers, one warrant officer, and seventeen enlisted men.[10] Usually six to eight additional men on special duty or detached service supplemented the section's strength, since it was insufficient to provide complete finance service for the 15,000 men in a division. The principal duties of division finance offices involved paying troops, exchanging currencies, and handling deductions for dependency benefits, war bonds, and other savings programs. The division finance officer, like any other accountable disbursing officer, i.e., one who had direct access to Treasury funds and who was responsible to the GAO for the expenditure of these public funds, performed budgeting and accounting functions. To service unattached units, the War Department created separate, numbered finance disbursing sections (FDS)—as a somewhat harried afterthought.

Finance Disbursing Sections

Soon after the war began, it became apparent that there had been a serious omission in mobilization planning in the Finance Department. No one had foreseen need for finance service to troops that were not an integral part of a division, corps, army, or air force. Men in regular combat organizations, such as the division, were paid by the finance section included in the T/O&E. When it became recognized in June 1942 that troops outside a combat component, as well as those in the Services of Supply, required the same financial support as soldiers in tactical organizations, the War De-

---

[10] A unit formed under a table of organization and equipment theoretically had all the personnel and equipment authorized to perform its mission. Men were usually assigned permanently to such outfits and given specific jobs. T/O&E infantry divisions were considered self-sufficient.

partment recommended that separate finance disbursing sections be formed under T/O&E 7-1. The first two sections arrived 5 October 1942 in England, where need for their service was urgent. Until that time, service troops had been paid by the most available disbursing officer.

In determining the number and size of separate FDS's required in the European theater, the Finance Department decided that the infantry division finance section was too small to service non-divisional troops spread over a wide area, both in the United Kingdom and on the Continent. For as dispersion increased, more finance men would be required. Also, those served were in individual small units without unified command. Consequently, they would need more assistance from the finance units paying them. Original requisitions were submitted on the basis of one disbursing unit for each 10,000 servicemen without organic finance service. The War Department, however, had prescribed the division finance unit to serve 15,000 and, in addition, had limited the number of troops in the Services of Supply[11] to a percentage of the ground forces. To stay within these restrictions, the basis for requisitioning separate finance units had to be revised to 1 for each 12,500 ground and service troops without organic finance service. Hence, an FDS of 2 officers, 1 warrant officer, and 17 enlisted men served 12,500 such troops. Repeated efforts to obtain one unit per 10,000 were disapproved. No precedent T/O&E for the air forces or Air Transport Command finance units existed, and their personnel requirements were therefore met more according to their needs than those of the Services of Supply.

The European theater fiscal director's office assisted in organizing disbursing offices and devised training procedures for new FDS's. Many officers and men had completed a course in the finance school at Fort Benjamin Harrison, Indiana, but practically none had had any disbursing experience. The theater fiscal director, Brig. Gen. Nicholas H. Cobbs, immediately instituted a training program to surmount this handicap. He prescribed a system of combining offices, whereby arriving units would work with established ones

---

[11] The SOS consisted of the nontactical support troops, such as finance, quartermaster, adjutant general, ordnance, transportation, and the like.

for a fortnight, or as long as they could be spared before assuming full responsibilities. Working alongside the old unit, the newer one would learn the field methods of the European theater. When the new section moved from its training location, a cadre of four enlisted men was attached to work with it until it could operate unassisted. As new units received invaluable instruction during periods of combined operations, finance men developed an esprit de corps equally as valuable as the technical proficiency acquired. A section that received help upon its arrival in the theater was then happy to assist another. The spirit of cooperation existing among all echelons of finance units led General Cobbs to specify that disbursing sections, wherever located, could serve any troops within their area.[12]

Several unforeseen duties devolved on finance sections and emphasized the inequity of their work load. The necessity for submitting final requisitions for finance men early in 1943 proved a hindrance, since the Finance Department did not know at that time that it would distribute invasion currencies. That decision came only in March 1944. Inauguration in the European theater of both personal transfer accounts (PTA) in March 1943[13] and the spearhead

---

[12] Brig Gen N. H. Cobbs (Ret), "Finance Department, European Theater of Operations," Jan 46, pp. 3–4. RG 338.

[13] The chief finance officer of the European theater devised the personal transfer account (PTA) system, which enabled servicemen to send surplus cash home; the War Department approved its use in all theaters. This system, which involved no expense to the transmitter, was merely a matter of trust fund accounting, i.e., crediting collections to one account and charging payments to another. Only the New York and San Francisco Finance Offices, U.S. Army (FOUSA's) paid recipients in the United States. (FOUSA's were large organizations located in several American and foreign cities. They dealt with commercial and specialized fiscal activities—such as PTA's—that they could handle more efficiently than offices in the field.) When a soldier wanted to send money home via the PTA plan, he took the sum to his unit personnel officer, who gave him a receipt. A PTA collection could also be made from the payroll. After the personnel officer had collected all the PTA money from his unit, he took it to the finance officer, who would acknowledge receipt by signing the necessary forms. The disbursing officer then credited the collection to the proper trust fund account. Next, a list of collections and recipients went to the New York or San Francisco FOUSA by cable or air mail. When the latter means was used, the information was recorded on microfilm. The stateside FOUSA's paid recipients by check. The minimum PTA transmission was

deposit (a pre-invasion non-interest-bearing deposit)[14] in May 1944 placed an additional burden on already overworked finance disbursing sections, organic and separate, but no additional men could be obtained.[15]

The work load of the division finance section usually seemed lighter than that of a separate, or numbered, finance disbursing section. This inequality produced some jealousy. T/O&E 14-500 of 2 April 1944 had made the grades of members of numbered FDS's commensurate with those of the division finance unit. In December 1944 this T/O&E was revised so that both officers and enlisted men in separate FDS's were one grade lower than those performing the duties in a division. Naturally, such discrimination was unpopular

---

ten dollars. Any larger amount had to be sent in round dollars (WD Cir 215, 1 Jun 44. RG 338).

Studies on the use of PTA's revealed several interesting facts. Finance records have always disclosed significant information about the army's morale. Absences without leave, desertions, losses and destruction of government property, and court-martial fines were reflected in pay records. Before the invasion of Normandy, soldiers in the United Kingdom used a "surprising" number of PTA's to repay loans from Army Emergency Relief and college student loan funds. Had morale not been good, soldiers would have scarcely been concerned with repaying small loans. PTA's became a gauge, not only of morale, but also of military activity. After the plan had been in operation for several months, weekly receipts averaged between $1 and $2 million. When, during the week ending 24 May 1944, the European theater figure catapulted to $18,064,333, it became manifest that the invasion was imminent. Another sizable operation was foretold by the receipts for the last week in October 1944, when a total of $25,182,358 was sent home. The warning given by the PTA's preceded the Battle of the Bulge. American intelligence had sufficient indications of the German counterattack to urge soldiers to divest themselves of surplus cash (Maj Wendell J. Van Riper, "Logistical Support by the Army Finance Corps, 1940–1945").

[14] The spearhead deposit was one of the series of innovations made in the European theater. Finance officers realized there was no need for soldiers going into combat to carry any large amount of currency with them. To provide safekeeping for individual and unit funds through the initial phases of an invasion, the chief finance officer devised this non-interest-bearing deposit. Disbursing officers carried spearhead deposits in a trust fund receipt account. When the individual or unit needed money again after the initial rigors of combat, they could reclaim it from the nearest disbursing officer. Enlisted men were repaid on payrolls, and officers on separate vouchers (WD Cir 256, 22 Jun 44. RG 338).

[15] Cobbs, "Finance Department," pp. 4–5.

with those who were adversely affected. Complaints appeared consistently in FDS's unit histories, the periodic reports required of all separate organizations. The "unfair" revised T/O&E called for a major and a first lieutenant, while that of the division listed a lieutenant colonel and a captain. "The duties and responsibilities of a finance disbursing section," declared the unit historian of the Ninetieth FDS, "are much greater than those of a division finance office." This particular section had serviced over 40,000 officers and men in one month, the equivalent of enough work for three divisions.[16]

A special T/O&E designed toward the end of the war and consisting of one officer and two enlisted men, filled the need for small disbursing units for hospitals. The 253d FDS was activated in England on 21 March 1945 to pay patients at U.S. Army station hospitals. As a secondary function, the section handled the pay and allowances of the officers, nurses, and enlisted staffs of the hospitals it served. Inasmuch as most hospitals were situated at some distance from a finance office, it was expected that problems of personnel officers would be materially reduced and that the finance needs of all could be dispatched with greater efficiency and economy by this type of disbursing section. The record the 253d made during its five-month life justified this expectation. The commandant of a hospital served by the section enthusiastically commended both the idea of a small finance agency for hospitals and the 253d's superior performance.[17]

Agents

In both prewar and wartime operations, an important administrative link in the Finance Department's chain of service was the agent system. At the top of the disbursing network was the accountable disbursing officer, who paid out public funds in his own name. A class B agent, either a commissioned or warrant officer, had virtually the same powers of payment as his superior, but did not have direct access to Treasury funds. Rather, he disbursed and collected public funds in the name of an accountable disbursing officer. The scope of class B agents was enlarged considerably early in the war when they were given, first in England and later on the

---

[16] CWO Elve T. Westgaard, "Unit History."
[17] 2d Lt W. J. O'Brien, "Historical Report," pp. 1–2.

Continent, limited depositary accounts over which they had full control. Banks welcomed this innovation, since they would receive full acknowledgment for their transactions with agents. Under the old system, agents banked in the names of their accountable disbursing officers and the depositaries had not received such credit.[18] Class B agents were a key part of the concept of area finance. Instead of each small installation having an accountable disbursing officer, there would be one such central officer and as many class B agents as necessary.

Frequently in the Pacific, agents on islands had to be at great distance from their accountable disbursing officers and depositaries. One agent officer was 1,800 miles from the nearest depositary. In such cases, agents could keep much more cash on hand than usual; possibly the largest amount any agent in the Pacific ever had was $8 million, authorized for the agent finance office at Milne Bay, New Guinea.[19]

Services given by class A agents were much more limited than those of class B. Class A agents were detailed by orders to make specific payments. Usually they were officers, commissioned or warrant, appointed from a company or battery to present the payroll, collect money from the finance office, and return to the company and pay troops. Their accounts had to be closed and returned to the finance office within twenty-four hours after completion of payment.[20]

From the standpoint of the finance office, it was most helpful to have all individual finance problems channeled through a class A agent. When each man would come to the office to present a voucher or get his pay or allowances straightened out, too much

[18] Cobbs, "Finance Department," pp. 5–6.

[19] Ltr, Capt R. A. Metzger, Fin Off, Hq Base Sec One, AFWESPAC, to Fin Off, Base Sec Three, AFWESPAC, 8 Mar 44, sub: Application for Authority to Increase Cash on Hand; ltr, Lt Col A. H. Miller, Fin Off, Hq Base Sec Three, USASOS, 16 Mar 44 to CG, Hq USASOS, APO 501, & Inds, sub: Authority for Agent Officer to Keep Cash on Hand; ltr, Maj George F. Biles, Fin Off, Hq Base D, USASOS, to CO, Base F, USASOS, 24 Dec 43, sub: Authorization to Keep Cash on Hand, BDF 120; ltr, Capt Quenton Pulliam, Fin Off, Hq Base A, USASOS, to CG, USASOS, APO 501, 3 Mar 44, sub: Authority to Keep Cash on Hand, & Inds. RG 338.

[20] "War Department Conference on Theater Administrative Fiscal Organization," 4 Feb 44, File 310.1. RG 338.

of the office's time would be spent taking care of traffic at the counter. After organizations learned of the decided savings in time, both to the finance office and to themselves, made possible by using agents, they willingly employed them.[21]

One of the great advantages of using class B agents was the ease with which they could be moved to locations where needed. When they finished operations at one station, the procedure was not so involved as when an accountable disbursing officer had to close his account. In the Middle East this mobility was important, for construction projects at the Suez Canal and Benghazi required finance service. When class B agents were used, they could be moved to another location when construction was completed.[22] If an accountable disbursing officer needed to close his books, as was the case with the officer at Khorramshahr in the Persian Gulf Service Command (PGSC), his class B agents could be transferred to another office to facilitate his closeout. This type of transfer could be made without interrupting the finance service where the class B agent was located. In any period of decreasing military activity, an accountable disbursing office could be reduced to a class B agency to continue the necessary service before final inactivation.[23]

The nature of the war in the Pacific made use of agent officers especially desirable, because of their mobility. Many island operations required only the services of a class B agent officer or those of a traveling agent. The use of agents instead of accountable disbursing officers saved a command the extensive paperwork involved in establishing a disbursing account with the Treasury. As a rule, an accountable disbursing officer had a larger operation and staff than an agent. He was also usually senior in rank to any agent officer. In at least one instance, however, this general rule did not prevail.[24]

[21] T/4 Milton Glazer, "Unit History."

[22] Col R. E. Odell, Fis Dir, Hq USAFIME, Memo for USAFIME, 22 Dec 44. RG 338.

[23] Col R. E. Odell, Memo for AMET, "Bi-Monthly Report of Operations for Months of November and December 1945," 30 Jan 46; Lt Col B. L. Ghent, Fis Dir, Memo for AMET, "Bi-Monthly Report of Operations for Months of January and February 1946, and the period 1–10 March 1946," 11 Mar 46. RG 338.

[24] 1st Ind, Capt James N. Stevenson, class B agent Fin Off, to 1st Lt

When the number of men on an island was too small to warrant an agent office, traveling agents made payments. In February 1945, the 175th FDS, located on Biak Island, New Guinea, dispatched an agent officer along with two sergeants to pay the force at Noemfoor, New Guinea. In the temporary office set up in a mess hall, they transacted the usual business connected with a payday. The three-man team spent five days at Noemfoor.[25]

The Persian Gulf Command (PGC, successor to the PGSC) also designated an agent as a traveling paymaster, who went from one station to another paying natives in the employ of the U.S. army. Although a class A agent usually handled this type of payment, the PGC used a class B because the distances and time involved would have made accountability too difficult for a class A agent.[26]

In certain situations, such as in the Philippine Islands and China-Burma-India theater (CBI), agents proved particularly valuable. Before the Philippines fell, the army employed agent officers extensively. As the Japanese capture of Manila became certain, Filipinos furnishing the army goods and services insisted on immediate payment. They realized that the Japanese would probably confiscate their property without any payment. A class B agent had to be attached to every working party that went out from Manila, to make payments on the spot. By the time the Manila finance office closed on 1 January 1942, it was using more than 100 class B agents.[27]

Because of the tactical situation on Luzon at the end of December 1941, no class A agents made payments. Had this customary method of paying troops been used, it would have meant pulling officers out of the line. So that there would be enough finance officers available to act as class B agents, one warrant officer and two

R. P. Williams, Fin Off, Hq USAF, APO 913 (Fiji Islands), 12 Mar 45; "History of Fiscal Mid Pac," pp. 11–12; Public Relations Plan for V-E and Post V-E Day, USAFPOA, Fiscal Section Summary, 20 Mar 45. RG 338.

25 Ltr, 1st Lt J. C. Shapton, Jr., 175th FDS, USASOS, to CO, Hq Base H, USASOS, APO 920, 1 Mar 45, sub: Military History. RG 338.

26 Ltr, Col John B. Stetson, Jr., Fis Dir, PGC, to Col K. E. Webber, OFD, Washington, 27 Mar 44. RG 338.

27 Col R. G. Jenks, Dept Fin Off, Philippine Dept, "Report of Operations, Philippine Department Finance Officer," 30 Apr 42. CMH.

master sergeants were commissioned as first lieutenants on 17 December.[28]

Organizations with special functions used agent officers to great advantage. Geodetic control parties operating in the CBI found it much more feasible to have agents handle their financial affairs than to be saddled with accountable disbursing officers. These parties, which operated out of Bolling Field in Washington, D.C., drew maps and charts in the CBI. Since their work required great mobility, their finance officer had to move right along with them. Members of geodetic control parties were appointed class B agents so that they could handle emergency expenditures in the field. Agents received either $5,000 or $10,000 in government checks, depending on anticipated need. They cashed the checks, denominated in $250 and $500, as needed. Characteristic expenditures included hiring native bearers, guides, interpreters, pack animals, and boats. Washington requested that the CBI give these agents full cooperation in settling their accounts so they could leave the theater quickly, and local accountable disbursing officers to whom these agents were detailed did extend full cooperation in clearing agents' accounts speedily.[29]

Agent officers were held fully as responsible for funds entrusted to them as were accountable disbursing officers, as the following cases document. When funds were lost through no fault of the officer to whom they had been entrusted, relief was understandably granted, but when evidence indicated negligence in handling public funds, the agent was liable. In one instance a class B agent had been forced to jettison $225 worth of stamps and envelopes from an airplane to prevent a crash. The finance officer for whom this man was an agent had himself lost $112,370.80 in stamps and envelopes when a ship sank in enemy action. The Secretary of War in both cases determined that the loss was sustained in the line of duty and without fault or negligence.[30]

[28] Col J. R. Vance, "Report of Operations, Finance Officer, USFIP, Dec 8, 1941–May 6, 1942," 30 Sep 44, p. 3. RG 338.

[29] Ltr, Lt Col Frank N. Graves, CO, Hq First Photo Group, Charting, Buckley Field, Denver, Colo., to CG, CBI, Attn: Theater Finance Officer (thru: CO, 311th Photo Wing, Mapping and Charting, Bolling Field, D.C.), 3 Aug 44, sub: Geodetic Control Class B Agents, 211 Fin. RG 338.

[30] Ltrs, Henry L. Stimson, Secretary of War, to the Comptroller General

When agents were unable to account for funds given them, investigation boards surveyed the circumstances and made recommendations. The exhaustive procedures the army used to establish agents' accountability, as evidenced in these selected cases, indicates the serious responsibility it attached to the custody of public funds. On 28 October 1942 an ordnance second lieutenant acting as a class A agent at Portsmouth, England, received sixty-seven pounds, eleven shillings, and ninepence ($272.70) to pay his organization. When this agent had not made proper returns to the finance office at Cheltenham by 4 May 1943, an investigation ensued. The agent testified that he had paid his men on 29 October, but before he could return the paid vouchers to the finance office, some 120 miles away, his unit was ordered to move. From a ship he mailed vouchers and payrolls back to the finance office, but the Cheltenham office never received them. It held only his receipt for $272.70. A board of officers found that the agent had made no attempt to obtain an acknowledgment for the vouchers nor to determine whether he was clear with the finance office. The board held the officer fully accountable for $272.70 because of his "indifference and negligence" in settling his accounts. He had to repay the money, and his commanding general reprimanded him for carelessness in handling public funds.[31]

The Tenth Air Force, located in the CBI, employed agent finance officers regularly. Since agents had continuing accountability, they were supposed to be ground personnel, rather than officers flying over hostile territory. The Tenth Air Force recommended that S-2's (intelligence staff officers) serve as agents, since they briefed crews before and after missions. One of their most important tasks was supplying and accounting for funds used in aviators' money belts. Carelessness on the part of both agents

[31] Ltrs, Capt W. J. Fabritius, Office of the Disbursing Fin Off, Hq SOS, APO 871, to 878th Ordnance Heavy Maintenance Co., APO 700, U.S. Army (thru: Chief Fin Off, Hq ETOUSA), 1 Jun 43; Col M. E. Rovin, Fin Off, Hq Mediterranean Base Sec, to Chief Fin Off, NATOUSA, 2 Jun 43; Sworn Statement of 2d Lt Robert A. Rummel, Ord., 6 Aug 43; and Findings and Recommendations of Board of Officers, Approved by Brig Gen Arthur R. Wilson, 6 Aug 43. RG 338.

and flyers resulted in shortages. Fliers had to turn in and account for money belts after each mission, and agents reported on the status of money belt funds to their accountable disbursing officer by the twenty-fifth of each month. The only funds for which agents were not accountable were those belonging to fliers downed over enemy territory. When funds were lost under such circumstances, agents secured relief by submitting a form in tripilicate to the accountable disbursing officer. The form listed the names of the men and their units along with the lost money.

Funds for money belts used in operations over Burma consisted of ninety-six rupees in coin. This sum was composed of seventy-two silver one-rupee pieces and forty-eight eight-anna pieces. None of the coins was dated later than 1941. Consequently, Burmese found with the coins by the Japanese were not suspect. Any flier who either lost his money belt through neglect or misappropriated the funds was subject to disciplinary action. He also had to refund the metallic value of the belt, which was greater than the wartime rupee value, since the 1941 rupees had a higher silver content than those used later in the war. Refunds could be made either in cash or through payroll deductions.[32]

Although agent officers were not accountable to the Treasury for public funds entrusted to them, they were responsible to their accountable disbursing officers. Likewise, accountable disbursing officers had to monitor the activities of their agents. When either party shirked his responsibility and a discrepancy appeared in the agent's account, both were in trouble. In Chakulia, India, on the night of 21 December 1943, 2d Lt. Ellsworth Valentine, class B agent of Capt. James S. Peeples, had $39,998.38 stolen from a field safe located in the finance office, which was guarded by two natives. The thieves who stole the money were caught, but without the money. The Inspector General (IG) investigation found four officers equally guilty. Maj. Percy W. Newton, Lieutenant Valentine's accountable disbursing officer until 11 December 1943, had failed to supervise Valentine's account closely enough. His books did not

---

[32] Ltr, Maj Charles Gordon, Fin Off, Tenth Air Force, to CG, Tenth Air Force, 27 May 43, sub: Funds Used in Money Belts, 123; Memo 145-4, Hq Tenth Air Force, U.S. Army, 16 Jul 43. RG 338.

show the amount of cash advanced to Valentine, nor had he issued a detailed letter of instructions to the agent. He required no monthly report of operations; he did not limit cash in Valentine's possession to disbursement needs; he did not require Valentine to turn over receipts; and he did not obtain authority for Valentine to keep cash in his possession at his own risk. Had he secured this authority, it would have required the approval of the commanding officer of the agent's post, which would have brought to the commandant's attention the need for adequate safeguarding of the funds.

The second officer held liable was Captain Peeples, the accountable disbursing officer at the time of the theft. The deficit existed in his account, although he had had the account only ten days when the theft occurred. Lieutenant Valentine was liable because the money was stolen from him. He had been negligent in not requesting adequate guards for his office and in exercising poor judgment by keeping too much cash on hand. Capt. Edison C. Weatherly, the post commander, was liable for failing to insure that funds on his post were properly guarded and accounted for in accordance with army regulations.

The commanding general of the CBI Air Service Command concurred in the liability of the four officers and recommended that they repay the money. He suggested further that any part of the money recovered be deducted from the officers' liability and that no action be taken for a year, since such sums were often recovered in that time. The commanding general of the Army Air Force, India-Burma Sector, CBI, approved these recommendations.[33]

When an agent officer to whom funds had been given was reported either missing or killed in action, a full report had to be made to the disbursing officer to whom he was accountable. If the funds were located among his effects, they could be returned to the finance office to clear the agent's account. If a complete return had not been made, a board of officers was appointed to account for the missing funds. When available, the summary court's list of effects was included in the findings reported by the board to the

[33] Ltr, Brig Gen Robert C. Oliver, CG, Hq CBI Air Service Command, New Delhi, India, to TAG, Washington, D.C., Attn: Chief of Finance, Maj Gen George E. Stratemeyer. RG 338.

Office of the Fiscal Director. If no funds or evidence of payments was located, the accountable disbursing officer would make a notation to that effect in his books.[34]

Personnel Requirements

The effectiveness of the entire finance organization, from theater fiscal offices to the disbursing office and agent in the field, depended on qualified personnel. The army's finance school at Fort Benjamin Harrison (with units located briefly at Duke University and Wake Forest College in North Carolina) trained both officers and enlisted men for finance duty, but under wartime conditions the flow of manpower frequently did not allow the intended channels from school to operating units. Consequently, finance organizations overseas commonly lacked men with the necessary training, and intended services could not be delivered. In both the Far East and Europe, moreover, finance units at all levels of command were usually shorthanded. Just as other service forces did, the Finance Department had a quota of men to train in the United States for overseas assignments. This quota compared with personnel requirements of other service forces, such as transportation, signal corps, and the medical service corps. As it turned out, the exceedingly low casualty rate among those in Finance made a replacement system virtually unnecessary; but ironically there were usually not enough trained finance men to do the work required in the field. Because of a lack of administrative coordination, however, a surplus of finance men occurred in some instances. Such imbalances throughout the entire army during the war reflected the problems of assigning and moving vast numbers of men around the world under trying conditions.

Since requirements for finance personnel were never totally satisfied in the Pacific and Asia, finance officers had to improvise to compensate for the shortages. If trained men were unavailable, anyone at hand had to be trained. In several cases native civilians and WAC's worked successfully in finance offices. While individual offices had training problems, theater headquarters had to deal with scheduling finance units for various operations. Higher echelons

[34] Ltr, Maj E. M. Simmons, Hq ASF, OFD, to CO, Eighth Air Force, APO 633, 4 Mar 44. RG 338.

had to fit finance personnel requirements in with those of other branches. Finance needed men who were more than just technically adept, they also had to be qualified soldiers.

In addition to the obvious reasons that finance offices were shorthanded, certain circumstances caused particular units to be understaffed. The finance offices in the CBI Services of Supply (SOS, the rear echelon) never had above 50 percent of the strength called for in T/O&E 14-500, presumably because they were in India, a noncombat area.[35] In the PGSC and on tropical islands in the Pacific, heat and infections sapped unit strength. The summer of 1942 saw one-quarter of the finance men in the PGSC hospitalized at one time, some for as long as six weeks.[36] When the GALVANIC Operation was launched in the Gilbert Islands, an accountable disbursing officer had to be established on Makin Island because the nearest finance office on Canton Island was over 1,000 miles away. There being no Finance Department reserve in the Central Pacific, requisitions had to be made on established offices. These requisitioned offices, understaffed themselves, were further strained, but the essential new office was created and the strain shared proportionately. The Makin Island finance detachment initially consisted of one officer and five enlisted men.[37]

In view of the general shortage of finance personnel in the Pacific Ocean areas, Col. Bickford E. Sawyer urged finance offices to give service on a geographic, rather than an organizational, basis. By so doing, they would achieve the fullest use of the available men. An example of the effectiveness of area service is a comparison between two finance offices near Fort Shafter, Hawaii. A class B agent office, manned by two officers and twenty-one enlisted men, paid about 25,000 troops within its area. Another office, paying on a strictly organizational basis, paid only 10,000. The staff of the latter was eight officers and sixty enlisted men. The chief deterrent to area finance service came from commanding officers who

[35] "History of the Services of Supply, CBI, Appendix 13, Fiscal and Finance Operations, 28 Feb 42–24 Oct 44," p. 16. CMH.

[36] Ltr, Col O. W. DeGruchy, Chief Fis Br, Hq PGSC, to CG PGSC, 25 Aug 43, sub: History of the Finance and Fiscal Office of the PGSC, F.O. 314.7. RG 338.

[37] Participation of U.S. Army Forces in the Central Pacific Area in GALVANIC Operation, p. 57; "History of Fiscal Mid Pac," p. 2.

thought that they should not authorize the submission of vouchers to finance officers outside their command.[38]

The end of the war hit finance units especially hard. Their duties increased as they prepared men for shipment home. At the same time, the units lost men over thirty-five years of age who could muster out on the point system. Finance units, because of of the nature of the work, had a high percentage of enlisted men over thirty-five.[39]

Finance officers realized early in the war that the problem of personnel shortages would probably continue, so they developed several compensatory procedures. Shortages in the field often dictated that finance offices recruit as best they could and offer on-the-job training. One method of securing men for finance duty was to canvass hospitals for those who were unable to return to combat units for line duty but who could perform finance duties. By this means Capt. Ralph A. Metzger obtained men when he was setting up the Melbourne FOUSA (Finance Office, U.S. Army) in 1942.[40]

In the absence of men who had had formal training at the finance school, disbursing officers undertook to train men on their jobs. Capt. A. H. Miller, finance officer at Headquarters, Base Section Three, in Brisbane, found a good way to cope with the rapid turnover of personnel in Australia. When preparing a new unit for duty in a forward area, he put officers and principal clerks from his own office in key positions. In that way, the most experienced people ran the new station. Then he filled the vacant positions in his office with people who had been understudying those jobs. This arrangement required that he continually train the personnel in his own office, but he thought it better to conduct training in Brisbane than on an island in the forward area.[41]

As the war in the Pacific shifted closer to the Japanese home islands, it became possible to phase out some operations in areas

[38] Col B. E. Sawyer, Fis Off, Hq USAFPOA, to G-4, Inter-Staff Routing Slip, 16 Nov 44, sub: Policy for Utilization of FD Personnel. RG 338.

[39] "History of India-Burma Theater, Appendix 8, Fiscal & Finance Operations, 21 May 45–25 May 46," pp. 1–2. CMH.

[40] Interview with Lt Col Ralph A. Metzger, OCF, 26 Jul 55. Notes of this interview and all subsequent ones cited are in the author's files.

[41] Interview with Col A. H. Miller, OCF, 26 Jul 55.

far from Japan. These phaseouts, which involved closing finance offices, released finance personnel for service elsewhere. When the western portion of the India-Burma theater (IBT) closed down, finance officers and men in the Bombay and Karachi offices were available to the China theater.[42] Not all headquarters handled personnel from roll-up operations as intelligently as the IBT. Headquarters, APO (Army Post Office) 264 in the Palau Islands, for example, decided to dispose of its finance section without consulting higher authority. The finance service it planned for troops remaining in the Palaus was entirely inadequate, and the personnel who were not needed for the new office were assigned harum-scarum. The disbursing officer became the assistant adjutant. This situation was resolved by general orders from the Western Pacific Base Command (WPBC) that activated three new FDS's.[43]

Some Pacific invasions involved specially selected finance personnel. Plans for the FORAGER Operation, the invasion of Saipan, enabled the finance officer, Capt. David S. Price, to choose his men individually. The nature of the mission demanded men not only with technical skill but also with well-adjusted personalities and excellent physical condition. Captain Price made his selection by a careful study of personnel records of men in the Central Pacific area. Because of the urgency of the mission, these men flew to the assembly point on Oahu from scattered islands in the Central Pacific.[44]

With several administrative headquarters operating in one vicinity in the Leyte invasion, finance service was not always as evenly distributed as it should have been, and this sometimes resulted in an excess of finance personnel. Col. Paul A. Mayo, finance officer for the Sixth Army, noted in April 1944 that there were three offices in the same area: the finance sections of the Sixth Army, the Fifth Air Force, and the United States Army Forces in the Far East Services of Supply (USAFFE SOS). Since all three of

[42] "History of Services of Supply, IBT, Appendix 15, Fiscal Section, 25 Oct 44–20 May 45." CMH.

[43] Ltr, Maj William D. Sutton, Special Fiscal Services, CPBC, APO 956, to "Wallie," 12 Jun 45. RG 338.

[44] Ltr, Capt David S. Price, Fin Off, Hq Army Garrison Force, APO 244, to CG, APO 244, 10 Aug 44, sub: FORAGER Operation. RG 338.

these organizations came under the administrative jurisdiction of USAFFE, they agreed to coordinate their future locations through the USAFFE chief finance officer. Through such coordination, duplication of effort could be reduced.[45] This objective was not completely achieved. Colonel Mayo reported that in the Leyte campaign ten disbursing offices and three administrative finance offices arrived in the beachhead area by D (invasion day) plus 20. One administrative office and no more than three disbursing offices with temporary class B agents could have handled the finance load satisfactorily, he thought.[46]

Finance arrangements for the Okinawa campaign, the last major operation of the Pacific war, centered on the Tenth Army's finance section. Yet these included no planning for unified administrative control of the air, ground, and service forces disbursing officers. Many finance officers landed without knowing which units they were to pay.[47] The 230th FDS reported that it arrived on the island on the afternoon of 19 May 1945 in the midst of "turmoil and confusion." After the unit landed, it did not know where to go and no one could furnish any information. Those in charge of the beach distributed cold C rations to the finance unit and told them that if they were not out of the area by 1800 hours to dig in, since a nearby flying strip was the target of frequent air raids. At 1730 trucks from the Tenth Army picked up the unit.

After spending a week in temporary tent quarters, the unit found some equipment on the beach and began "to think about setting up an office." A week later they found they belonged to the Island Command, Army Garrison Forces, but that it had made no provisions for their operation as a disbursing section. So the 230th lent its men to the 229th FDS. At the end of the 230th's first month ashore on Okinawa, it still had not been given a disbursing assignment.[48]

[45] Memo, Col Paul A. Mayo, to cofs, Sixth Army, 3 Apr 44. RG 338.

[46] Ltr, Col Mayo to CG, Sixth Army, 24 Jan 45, sub: Operation Report, K-370.2. RG 338.

[47] "Participation in the Okinawa Operation by USAFPOA, April-June 1945," p. 87; Tenth Army Action Report, Report of Operations in the Ryukyus Campaign, chap. 11, Staff Section Report, Section 19—Finance; Okinawa Participation Report, 1 Sep 45. RG 338.

[48] WOJG Alan O. Williams, "Unit History."

The Tenth Army finance section could service only 20,000 of the 80,000 troops in the operation. But rather than employing one of those idle sections immediately at hand, such as the 230th, the Tenth Army Section requisitioned four additional finance disbursing sections from the United States. These four disbursing officers acted as class B agents to the accountable disbursing officer of the Tenth Army.[49]

In addition to the problems of obtaining an adequate number of properly trained men for duty in the field, another personnel problem of real concern to Finance was that of promotions. The chief value of promotions was as acknowledgment and recognition of jobs well done. A subsidiary benefit was enhancing morale and thus insuring good performance in the future. Finance units were usually handicapped by not being able to promote deserving men. Most units went overseas with full T/O&E's, which meant that a vacancy would have to occur before a man could be promoted. Because of the nature of their missions, finance units had few vacancies. Officers assigned to numbered disbursing sections had similar promotion difficulties. If the T/O&E called for a first lieutenant and no captain, the first lieutenant had no chance of promotion so long as he stayed in that unit. Transferring officers between units to promote them was not common.

While the promotion situation remained fairly static in most finance units throughout the war, it improved toward the end of the war when high-point enlisted men began receiving their discharges. Finance officers could then promote younger men to fill the vacancies. Capt. J. E. Williams, Jr., finance officer of the 195th FDS, wrote to Maj. E. E. Harris, finance officer for the Southern Islands Area Command, that he had two technicians fifth class (T/5's) who had been "victims" of T/O trouble ever since they had been in his section. Captain Williams would promote them when some of his high-point men were discharged, but he was willing to transfer them to Major Harris' section if Harris could promote them faster.[50]

---

[49] Okinawa Participation Report, 1 Sep 45.
[50] Ltr, Capt J. E. Williams, Jr., Fin Off, 195th FDS, to Maj E. E. Harris, Fin Off, Southern Islands Area Command, 19 Oct 45. RG 338.

Sometimes finance officers employed involved machinations to promote deserving men. The 368th FDS had a technical sergeant who was an accountant. He could go no higher in the 368th because there was no vacancy in its T/O&E. The 198th FDS needed an accountant. The commander of the 198th, 1st Lt. A. B. Wrench, learned that the 159th FDS was going to be deactivtated and that the remaining personnel would be transferred to his section. He arranged for the 368th to transfer this accountant to the 159th, which had an opening for a master sergeant. The accountant was promoted on the 159th's vacancy before the deactivation order and then transferred to the 198th.[51] Just as men were promoted as recognition of good performance of duty, men were demoted when they were unable to carry out duties of their grades.[52]

Among the requirements for finance personnel was that, if necessary, they be ready to fight. Since it was not routine for finance units to operate in the front lines or for finance men to participate in attacks or on the main line of resistance, combat soldiers usually regarded the life of finance men as soft. "Fighting Finance" was a familiar sarcastic epithet.

On several occasions in the Pacific, however, finance men did join the fray. Finance sections of the Sixth Army frequently operated in the New Guinea forward areas under hazardous conditions. Aerial bombardments often interrupted their routine. Since the task forces were in constant contact with the enemy, finance units established and manned their own defensive perimeters. Night work was usually impossible since positions could not be exposed. "In several instances finance men were actually on the firing line and in one case were forced to use hand grenades. . . . Needless to say, such action is conducive to [their] good morale"[53]—as if facing the Japanese proved their worth to the army!

[51] Ltr, 1st Lt A. B. Wrench, Fin Off, 198th FDS (Mindanao), to Maj E. E. Harris, Fin Off, Southern Islands Area Command APO 932, 17 Oct 45. RG 338.

[52] Ltr, Capt J. E. Williams, Jr., CO, 198th FDS, to CG, Eighth Army Area Command, 3 Mar 45, sub: Recommendation for Reduction for Inefficiency, 201-Egan, Vincent H. RG 338.

[53] Operational Report, Fin Sec, Hq Sixth Army, 25 Jan 43 to 24 Jan 46. RG 338.

Forty-five minutes after the first troops of the Sixth Army struck Leyte on 20 October 1944, Col. D. M. Forney, finance officer for the Twenty-fourth Infantry Division, landed. The 159th FDS arrived on D plus 2 and established an office in Tacloban, still under enemy fire. Aerial and artillery bombardment during the early stages of the Leyte invasion resulted in the deaths of two finance enlisted men and a considerable loss of funds.[54] Three men from the 171st FDS, operating on Leyte, were casualties of a bombing raid on the night of 25 November 1944. The commander of the 171st, Maj. J. M. Mano, declared, "The activities and events of this finance section for the past month should be recorded as a reminder to those who classify the personnel as 'pen pushers.' It has been proved that they possess the same qualities that are required of the men at the front line."[55] The major did not comment on the impact of the casualties on the morale of the survivors.

While the tactical prowess of finance men might not have been conceded in all quarters, outstanding performance of duty was recognized and awarded. In February 1944 the class B agent at Arawe, New Britain, Lt. Julian Shook, was evacuated to Australia with a jungle fungus infection. Until his replacement was dispatched to Arawe on 2 March, two enlisted men, T/4 Robert F. Stewart and T/4 Dewitt C. Cox, ran the finance office. WOJG J. T. Randall made the actual payments, but all administrative affairs of the office were supervised by Stewart and Cox. Both received the Bronze Star "for meritorious achievement in connection with military operations against the enemy."[56] In May 1944 operations began on the "bird's shoulder" of New Guinea. The 156th FDS, commanded by Lt. J. C. Saladino, went to the Toem-Sarmi area to pay troops that had no organic finance service. With only thirteen men, Lieutenant Saladino paid 25,000 to 30,000 men in the field under adverse combat conditions. The achievement gained him the Bronze Star.[57]

[54] Ibid.

[55] Ltr, Maj. J. M. Mano, DO, 171st FDS, to CG, Base K, APO 72, 17 Dec 44, sub: Unit History, KFIN 314.7. RG 338.

[56] Operational Report, Fin Sec, Hq Sixth Army, G.O. 141, H2, Sixth Army, 2 Sep 44. RG 338.

[57] Ibid.

Office Facilities and Equipment

For finance organizations to operate effectively, they had to have not only appropriate personnel, but also adequate facilities and equipment. Often in overseas locales, especially in what later became known as underdeveloped countries, finance units had to function in inadequate space and with inferior equipment, just as they had to operate with too few or insufficiently trained personnel. To accomplish their highly technical mission, they needed certain unique facilities. To the extent that these were lacking, finance service suffered.

During the war, finance units complained about the lack of various kinds of facilities and equipment. Vital to disbursing operations were means of safeguarding funds. When a unit could use a bank building with a satisfactory vault, it had few problems, but when such facilities were unavailable, other office space had to be located or devised. Finance units often got engineers to construct concrete vaults that proved much more satisfactory than field safes. If concrete was not available, engineers sometimes fabricated vaults from sheet metal.[58] Field safes proved too heavy to be practical, since their weight precluded any quick movement. Usually safes assigned to finance sections were from obsolete quartermaster stock. In many instances, signal officers had better safes for cryptographic equipment than finance officers had for public funds.[59]

Examples from Italy and Leyte illustrate the problems of handling large amounts of currency with inadequate equipment. Once, after a finance unit in Italy had made all preparations for paying a division, the division was ordered into the line to prevent a breakthrough. When the division pulled out, the finance unit was left exposed, with over $1 million in its field safes. Such a situation illustrates the need of finance units for light safes and their own transportation.[60] When no safes or vaults were available, funds

---

[58] Ltr, 2d Lt J. C. Shapton, Jr., 175th FDS, USASOS, to Fin Off, Hq USASOS, 2 Dec 44, sub: Military History, 314.7; 2d Lt R. J. Gragier, "Unit History," 184th FDS, USAFUSAPAC, APO 75, 2 Sep 45, 314.7. RG 338.

[59] Interviews with Col George R. Gretser and Lt Col T. W. Archer; "History of Fiscal Mid Pac," p. 19.

[60] Lt Col Regis W. Luke, Technical Intelligence Report #671, ASF, OCG, Washington, D.C., 28 Apr 45. RG 338.

simply had to be stored in a building. In December 1944 the 171st
FDS was disbursing on Leyte when it received a shipment of 3,634
boxes containing 5,213,000 Filipino pesos (1 peso equaled $.50).
Since the finance office had no facilities to store the equivalent of
over $2.6 million, the commanding general designated the base
chapel as the most secure building and the provost marshal provided guards.[61]

Other important kinds of equipment for finance offices were
typewriters and adding machines. Those issued were not sturdy
enough to withstand either the constant packing and unpacking required when a unit moved or the rust and corrosion induced by
tropical jungles. Nor were they substantial enough to withstand
the battering of movement over beaches and rough roads. Most
sections therefore constructed carrying cases to protect fragile
office machines while in transit. Replacement of scarce equipment,
after it wore out, was also a serious and chronic problem.[62]

The shortage and delicate condition of office machines caused
critical problems early in the Pacific war. Lack of equipment was
caused sometimes by poor liaison. When the Americal Division was
organized for duty on Guadalcanal, there was no finance section,
so it requisitioned one from Fort Benjamin Harrison. The unit
activated there was informed that they need take nothing with
them to the South Pacific, since they would find complete office
equipment there. So the unit arrived on Guadalcanal without even
a pencil. Rather than finding a fully equipped office, they found
nothing. All the other finance offices in the South Pacific Area
contributed various pieces of equipment to the Americal Division
finance section so it could begin operations, although it was still
inadequately supplied.[63]

As essential to a finance office as its hardware were blank
forms. Few transactions were possible without some kind of paper
instrument—vouchers, payrolls, and various accounting ledgers.
Any time a finance office was without these supplies, it was in

[61] Ltr, Maj J. M. Mano, CO, 171st FDS, to CG, Base K, APO 72, 30 Dec 44,
sub: Unit History, KFIN. RG 338.
[62] Ltr, Maj J. J. Madigan, Jr., Fin Off, 232d FDS, to Fin Off, AFWESPAC,
8 Jul 45, sub: Historical Report, Jun 45.
[63] Interview with Col B. J. Tullington, 2 Aug 55.

trouble and had to take measures to get the necessary forms or devise some workable substitute. The chief difficulty in obtaining blank forms came in the early days of the war in most theaters. When supplies were unavailable through normal channels, finance officers used several field expedients—having forms printed locally, mimeographing them, or borrowing from a better-supplied neighbor.[64]

Unit personnel offices originated many of the forms used in finance offices. Finance officers had no actual responsibility for supplying personnel officers with finance forms, yet the Sixth Army finance officer felt a "moral responsibility" to supply personnel officers with proper forms. By doing so, he facilitated fiscal service for all parties, since personnel sections often reported to the Sixth Army without blank forms. Colonel Mayo advised them to requisition blank forms through normal channels, but supplied them sufficiently until their requests were filled.[65] Likewise, he ascertained that subordinate finance offices had adequate supplies. Each time a finance unit of the Sixth Army moved into forward areas in New Guinea and New Britain, it took a six-month supply of blank forms. No finance forms were available in forward areas, so the initial supply had to last until the unit could get in touch with Sixth Army headquarters again.[66]

As frustrating to finance operations as the inadequacies of equipment was the lack of proper office space. Finance units could not be choosy about adequate working space and lighting—they had to take what they could get. Sometimes tents, Nissen huts, railroad cars, or dugouts constituted the best space units could find for offices. Such facilities usually lacked such amenities as proper lighting and desk space. For lighting, finance units used candles,

[64] Historical Record of Headquarters Service Command, APO 502; Ltr, Col O. W. DeGruchy, Chief Fis Br, Hq PGSC, to CG, PGSC, 25 Aug 43, sub: History of the Finance and Fiscal Office of the PGSC, F.O. 314.7. RG 338; interview with Lt Col Metzger, 26 Jul 55; ltr, Capt W. H. Fischer, Fin Off, 159th FDS, to CO, 198th FDS, 5 Sep 45. RG 338.

[65] Memo, Col Paul A. Mayo, Fin Off, Sixth Army to cofs, 3 Apr 44. RG 338.

[66] Operational Report, Fin Sec, Hq Sixth Army, 25 Jan 43–24 Jan 46. RG 338.

Coleman lanterns, and natural light—all at times undependable.[67] Finance offices in Europe never had proper lighting until they could use captured German generators.[68] During 1942 and 1943, when the Second Corps headquarters finance section was in North Africa, the shortage of working space was so acute that clerks actually had to compute payrolls on each others' backs.[69]

Closely allied with the Finance Department's need for suitable office equipment and supplies was the need for reliable transportation. Not only was the equipment furnished a finance unit not adapted to being packed and unpacked frequently, but a great deal of time was consumed in setting up and dismantling the office. Had the proper type of transportation had been available, these difficulties would have been obviated. Finance officers in the field recommended that a new type of vehicle be adapted for mobile disbursing units. Lt. Col. Regis W. Luke, commanding the Forty-ninth FDS in Italy, suggested a truck that would permanently house safes and office machines. The rear end could be designed as a cashier's cage, so that all operations could be performed within the vehicle.[70] Elaborating on this idea, Col. George R. Gretser, finance officer for the Eighth Armored Division, suggested a trailer truck such as the quartermaster laundry van. The justification for having the finance equipment in a trailer was that if the prime mover were knocked out, finance operations could continue. To change locations, the van would need only a new prime mover.[71]

Besides needing a vehicle for unit mobility, finance sections also had to have transportation to secure funds. The most recurring complaint of FDS's was that they lacked organic transportation. The Ninetieth FDS, while disbursing in England, had to make trips to

[67] "Historical Report," Detachment Fin Sec, Alaska Department; CWO Elve T. Westgaard, "Unit History"; CWO Murray J. Chilton, "Unit History"; Capt W. H. Lord, "Unit History"; 1st Ind, Maj H. E. Pettersen, Fin Off, Hq Army Garrison Force, APO 86, to Fis Off, POA, 12 Apr 45; Chilton, "Unit History"; Lt Col Ivy J. Schuman, "Unit History"; Maj Alfred A. Abbott, "The Army as Banker," *Army Information Digest*, Aug 1947, p. 41.

[68] Interview with Col Gretser, 30 Mar 54.

[69] Interview with Lt Col Archer, 3 Mar 54.

[70] Luke, Technical Intelligence Report #671, ASF, Office of the Commanding General, Washington, D.C., 28 Apr 45. RG 338.

[71] Interview with Col Gretser, 30 Mar 54.

banks ten to thirty miles away to obtain funds. Because the motor pool was always low, "service . . . was irregular and inconsistent when the need of a vehicle was urgent."[72]

In one particular invasion, that of southern France on 30 August 1944, no one had arranged to move a finance unit off the beach. When the Seventy-ninth FDS landed on the shore, it could not reach its destination without transportation. Only after it had hitched a ride to its location could it commence operations.[73]

The War Department, in prescribing administrative structures and practices for finance organizations at various levels, naturally based wartime formulas on its peacetime experiences. It provided one basic organizational system for the various theaters, irrespective of the differences in their missions and geography. Theater fiscal offices made necessary adjustments in procedures during the war, as conditions warranted. The burgeoning of finance bureaucracy in the rear echelons, with concomitant administrative duplication, merely reflected problems with mass mobilization and the inherent tendency of any bureaucracy, especially the military, to husband personnel jealously—even when the work load did not justify it. Many of the problems of administrative structure would have been mitigated had the Office of the Chief of Finance planned sufficiently before the war.

One of the glaring deficiencies in planning was the lack of provision for finance units for troops not attached to combat organizations. Until finance disbursing sections became operational, existing finance offices filled the gap, but with resulting strains to the offices and poor service to the troops. Despite inequities of work load created by different T/O&E's for finance offices organic to divisions and those for separate finance disbursing sections, the basic finance organizational structure worked reasonably well overseas—once the finance disbursing sections were created.

Flexibility achieved through use of agents enabled the army to meet its fiscal obligations in the field without a large finance bureaucracy. This flexibility enabled Finance, representing around two-tenths of 1 percent of the army's strength, to serve the largest

[72] Westgaard, "Unit History."
[73] Maj J. A. Stewart, "Unit History."

organization of men in the country's history. The system of accountable disbursing officers and agents was one that extended successfully from peacetime to wartime fiscal operations.

The administrative structures planned in Washington for finance operations overseas worked well only to the extent that qualified men filled the T/O&E's. Under wartime duress, the models prescribed by planners frequently could not be realized. Had personnel requirements been satisfied "by the book," wartime finance officers and men would have been trained at the finance school, located at pleasant Fort Benjamin Harrison, a few miles northeast of Indianapolis. But the exigencies of overseas operations often prevented the complete staffing of finance offices with properly trained personnel. In many areas WAC's and native civilians could be employed successfully. In others, soldiers untrained in finance had to be pressed into service and given on-the-job instruction. The combat zones, where only soldiers could handle financial operations, demonstrated frequently that finance men had to be prepared as both technicians and fighters. Those finance men who operated under enemy fire in island invasions learned what combat soldiers knew only too well: confusion reigned. Orderly battle plans somehow had a way of getting disrupted by uncooperative enemies, and finance units discovered that they had to fend for themselves —just as everyone else did.

In matters of office facilities and equipment, the finance organization also had to improvise. Rarely did a unit at any level find optimal facilities and working conditions. Far more common was the experience of working without proper equipment, forms, buildings, or transportation. Such inconveniences, while preventing ideal financial service, only reflected the plight of the entire army while functioning on foreign shores. The following comment from early in the war typified Finance's overseas experience.

The first finance unit to cross the Atlantic after the war began landed at Belfast, Northern Ireland, on 26 January 1942. "Had no office equipment—just one typewriter and one portable adding machine, which was lost somewhere in shipment, no idea what happened to it," lamented an officer of the unit. Since there were no army regulations or pay tables in Ulster, the first two months' payrolls had to be computed from memory. "Apart from the above, had very easy time. Personnel, including officers, not trained!!!"[74] This complaint echoed around the world throughout the war.

Prewar planning could have eased some of Finance's administrative problems, especially in the realm of organizational structures. Sufficient forethought would have indicated that geographical differences would dictate differences in organization, from theater fiscal offices to finance disbursing sections. Operations in Europe and the Pacific demanded different kinds of units and facilities to render fiscal services, but under wartime pressures, Washington initially issued uniform T/O&E's for worldwide use. Fortunately, those working overseas made the requisite adjustments and adaptations, but the process involved considerable duplication, loss of time, and inefficiency. Similarly, all personnel and equipment problems could not be foreseen and field expedients had to be employed. Had the right number of men, all sufficiently trained, been available where needed and with the proper office facilities, the situation would have reflected the artificiality of the army's classic "textbook solution" rather than the actuality of overseas theaters during World War II.

[74] Personal ltr, from Capt Clarence Neely, identified by Col Louis A. Hawkins. RG 338.

CHAPTER 2

Fiscal Diplomacy: Coordination and Liaison

To FULFILL its mission in World War II, the Finance Department not only had to fit its duties into the broad strategy of the American army, but it also had to cooperate with Allied governments and armies. In dealing with foreign governments, the Finance Department rarely established fiscal policy. Such matters were handled on higher levels—by theater commanders (usually with the advice of fiscal officers), ambassadors, cabinet officers, or occasionally by the president himself. From time to time, however, with an immediate decision mandatory, fiscal officers took actions that resulted in operating policy. Irrespective of who set fiscal policies involving relations between the army and foreign governments, the Finance Department had to implement them. The skill with which Finance handled these encounters influenced the quality of relations between governments.

High-level policy issues involving Finance during the war included negotiating with France on the franc exchange rate, establishing occupation costs in Italy, providing currency for Chiang Kai-shek in China, and serving as the fiscal office for the new Philippine government. Payment of foreign troops and commercial accounts constituted a lower level of diplomatic involvement, as did the negotiation of taxes on foreign purchases. Yet foreign governments and vendors had to be satisfied with the way Finance handled such matters if the requisite cooperation were to exist. Sometimes, of course, they were not, with resultant difficulties and friction. Within the U.S. government, as well as the army, the Finance Department needed to coordinate activities to insure efficient functioning. This coordination included payments to persons from other government agencies and furnishing services for such outfits as Army Post Offices (APO's). The examples that follow represent various levels of fiscal coordination, showing how different theaters and different nations demanded a wide range of fiscal diplomacy.

With the French

Fiscal negotiations involving the French franc proved particularly sensitive, since the United States could deal only with the provisional French government, reeling from the German defeat of France in 1940 and nominally allied with Pierre Laval's puppet regime in Vichy. The most consequential matters worked out with the French involved exchange rates and tax payments. In September 1942 planning for the invasion of North Africa made it imperative that the United States come to a decision over the official rate of exchange for the French franc. European theater commander Gen. Dwight D. Eisenhower, directing planning from London, stated that since the policy was to "sweeten" the French as much as possible to promote a friendly reception for the invading forces, he advocated an exchange rate close to that which existed prior to the war. After consulting with the British Foreign Ministry, Eisenhower "strongly" recommended an exchange rate of forty-five francs to the dollar, which no doubt would have sweetened the French because of its appreciating effect on French money.

Later in the month Chief of Staff Gen. George C. Marshall cabled Eisenhower that the exchange rate had been fixed at seventy-five francs to a dollar. Political and propaganda considerations were not strong enough to justify a rate more beneficial to France, particularly since costs of living and currency in commercial circulation had multiplied 2.5 times. More important than pleasing France was GI morale and purchasing power. Even the 75-to-1 rate was much more favorable to France than the rate of exchange that prevailed on the open or free market. When the State, War, and Treasury departments, in collaboration with the British, set the exchange rate, they stipulated that adjustments could be made depending on local conditions. At the Casablanca conference in

January 1943, Roosevelt, Churchill, and the French provisional government agreed upon the official rate of 50-to-1, which was maintained until several months after the war ended. When, after the invasion of the French mainland, the disparity between the official rate of exchange and the actual value of the currency became too great, American authorities announced to the French that they planned a new rate that would depreciate the franc. Rather than have the franc suffer the loss of value in commercial transactions, however, the French government made a deal with the United States to prevent the adoption of a new rate. The French began paying the American army the monthly differences between the existing and the proposed rate for the total amount of troop pay drawn in francs.[1]

With the Italians

The economy of Italy had been so disrupted by her activities as an Axis power that she was unable or unwilling to assume any appreciable portion of her financial obligations after she joined the Allied cause on 13 October 1943.[2] This failure meant that the U.S. government had in effect to carry Italy's portion of the load. At the same time, the United States received no payment for the subsistence items it poured into Italy's domestic economy. The only contribution the Italian government made toward financing the Allied effort was in furnishing the Allied Financial Agency with the lire it in turn gave to the armies to disburse. Had this system continued, it would have meant that the cost of the occupying troops would have been borne by the Italian government, since it bore responsibility for its lire. Throughout history such a practice had generally been followed by conquering armies. In all cases the Wehrmacht transferred its terrific occupation costs to defeated nations. For example, after the Nazis totally occupied France in

---

[1] Cables, Eisenhower, to AGWAR, Washington, D.C., no. 2417, 19 Sep 42; Marshall Fis Div, Hq sos, to CG, USFOR, London, 29 Sep 42; Marshall cofs, U.S. Army, to CG, ETOUSA (USFOR), 7 Nov 42, RG 338; Arthur L. Funk, *Charles de Gaulle*, p. 78.

[2] For background information, see Vladimir Petrov, *Money and Conquest*, pp. 80–88.

November 1942, they assessed the Vichy regime 25 million marks per day for occupation costs.[3]

Since the U.S. government fought to oppose aggression, it reasoned that to require Italy to bear the financial burden of American troops on Italian soil would belie its democratic principles. The Italian government, moreover, could not have stood the enormous expense. Consequently, the U.S. government decided on 10 October 1944 to reimburse the Italian government in dollar credits for the equivalent amount of money American troops had injected into the Italian economy. The motive behind this decision was that the Italian government would immediately use these dollar credits to pay for subsistence items the American government had been furnishing gratis. The American government thought it better for the Italians to pay the United States for goods received than to be on a dole. American justification for giving Italy money to return was that the United States would bear the cost of its occupying forces rather than transferring it to the occupied country. The British and the allies vigorously decried this unilateral action of the United States. They did not object to the principle involved, but to the timing and lack of coordination. Naturally, this gesture made the Italians look with more favor upon the United States than they did upon other Allied nations that were unable to be similarly generous.[4]

These equivalent sums given the Italian government by the United States were called "net troop pay." Since a sizable portion of military pay was being transmitted back to the United States in the form of war bonds and allotments, net troop pay was not nearly equal to the total amount that could be drawn. When a disbursing officer received lire from the Allied Financial Agency, his treasury account was charged with the dollar value of the Italian money. The Treasury credited this dollar value to a special lire reserve account. When the Finance Department had computed net troop pay for a given period, it informed the Treasury Depart-

---

[3] Thomas Reveille, *The Spoil of Europe*, pp. 89–297; Gordon Wright, *The Ordeal of Total War, 1939–1945*, pp. 119–120; Robert O. Paxton, *Vichy France*, p. 362.

[4] "History of the Fiscal Services, 1940–1945," p. 502. CMH; Frank A. Southard, Jr., *The Finances of European Liberation*, pp. 30–31.

ment of the amount due the Italian government. Then the Treasury would make a settlement with Italy from the special lire reserve account.

In computing the net troop pay figure that would be certified to the Treasury, the Finance Department used a complex formula. The starting point was the total lire drawn from the Allied Financial Agency for the period. From this amount would be deducted the remainder in the possession of finance officers at the end of the month. This subtraction would yield the net amount of lire put into circulation by the army. Then from this figure, lire used in local procurement would be subtracted. The result would be the maximum amount used to pay troops. Whatever portion of pay had not reached the Italian economy, but had been retained by servicemen or spent in post exchanges and army post offices, was subtracted from the maximum amount used to pay troops; this determined the final figure of net troop pay for the Treasury.

Put another way, the Finance Department performed the following operations to arrive at the reimbursement figure:

a. Total lire drawn from the Allied Financial
   Agency during the month   _____
b. Subtract the remainder in possession of finance
   officers at the end of the month   _____
c. The result is the net amount of lire put into
   circulation by the army   _____
d. From c deduct the lire used for local
   procurement   _____
e. The remainder is the maximum amount used for
   troop pay   _____
f. From e subtract an estimated reserve to cover
   lire in the hands of troops or spent in quasi-official
   organizations. These sums are regarded as potential
   returns to disbursing officers   _____

Under the terms of the armistice signed by Italy and the Allied nations, the Italian government agreed to supply the Allies with certain items from their economy. Their inability to fulfill their commitments resulted in a growing backlog of unpaid bills for goods and services furnished the Allies. To remedy this situation, the Allies agreed with the Italian government that its Ministry of the Treasury would accept responsibility for settling unpaid accounts. The Italian government never stated that it would pay the bills, but did say it would "take action." After the Italians had made this much of an acknowledgment, the Allies forwarded all bills to them. After they had receipted the bills, the Italians sent copies of the receipts back to the agencies that had procured the materials for which the bills were sent. These receipts never mentioned any amounts of money due individual vendors. Throughout the war, payment policy in Italy was determined by local procuring boards rather than any centralized agency.[5]

With the Chinese

Several considerations shaped America's policy toward China: its remoteness, its long battle against Japan, President Roosevelt's conviction that China was an essential ally against a common enemy, and Roosevelt's personal interest in the Chinese scene. This interest proved sufficient for him to negotiate directly with China on fiscal matters, with some assistance from Henry Morgenthau, Jr., Secretary of the Treasury. Roosevelt based his Far Eastern military policy on the premise of mandatory cooperation with Chiang Kai-shek. This cooperation extended to vast amounts of monetary aid for the Chinese government. As early as 9 January 1942, Roosevelt sent the following memorandum to the Secretary of the Treasury: "In regard to the Chinese loan, I realize that there is little security which China can give you at the present time, yet I am anxious to help Chiang Kai-shek and his currency. I hope you can invent some way of doing this. Possibly we could buy a certain amount of this currency, even if it means a partial loss later on."[6] The following month the president guided a joint resolution through Congress that provided China with a $500-million loan ". . . upon such terms and conditions as the Secretary of the Treasury with the approval of the President shall deem in the interest of the United States."[7] As the wording indicated, the terms allowed considerable latitude. Actually,

[5] *Logistical History of* NATOUSA-MTOUSA, pp. 401–402.
[6] Quoted in Arthur N. Young, *China and the Helping Hand*, p. 219.
[7] Ibid., p. 224.

no strings were attached to this loan, which, at the fall of the Kuomintang, became a gift.

The president pledged the American government, moreover, to reimburse the Chinese for any wartime expenditures on behalf of the army. These included furnishing quarters, food, materiel, and the construction of bases and airfields. On 20 January 1944 Roosevelt said the "United States would pay in dollars the equivalent of Chinese currency made available to cover the cost of all American military expenses in China."[8] Fortunately, the later reimbursement of $210 million was not at the disastrous 20-to-1 rate the Chinese government insisted represented the official value of its Chinese National Currency (CNC) dollars (yuan). (The previous month the free market exchange rate had been 84-to-1.)[9] By the end of hostilities the United States had spent $392 million for Chinese National Currency dollars, which covered the Chinese government's direct costs in supporting the American military in China during the war.[10]

Despite the president's intentions toward the Chinese, the mechanics of reimbursement proved trying to all parties. A misunderstanding arose between the Chinese and American governments over the method of payment for the subsistence and quartering of American troops in China. According to Gen. Ho Ying-chin, Chief of the Chinese General Staff, President Roosevelt had "indicated time and again" that the U.S. government would pay for the food and accommodation expenses of the American army in China. Because no exchange rate had been set between CNC and U.S. dollars, up to May 1944 no settlement had been made and the high prices made it harder for the Chinese to continue supporting the ever-increasing number of American troops. The issue of American obligation in "no-rate funds" was settled by the Memorandum of Agreement of 25 November 1944 between the War Department

---

[8] Ibid., p. 286.

[9] For a discussion of wartime Chinese currency inflation, see Walter Rundell, Jr., *Black Market Money*, pp. 16–18, 66–68, and Barbara W. Tuchman, *Stilwell and the American Experience in China, 1911–45*, pp. 525–530.

[10] Young, pp. 292, 400.

and the government of China.[11] The agreement provided that money spent for the board and lodging of American armed forces in China would be credited to the National Government of China as reciprocal aid under Article VI of the Mutual Aid Agreement of 2 June 1942. The National Government of China had requested these terms.

This Memorandum of Agreement left some issues undecided. The cost of the Chengtu airfields was not included in the $210-million settlement. The Chinese government contended that this cost also should be treated as reciprocal aid, but at the time the memorandum was signed, no definite decision had been made. Henry Morgenthau stated that the $210-million settlement was without prejudice to the Chinese contention.[12]

With the Philippines

Dealings between the Finance Department and the Philippine government after the liberation of the islands differed from those with other foreign governments. One reason for the difference was the Philippines' status as a Commonwealth of the United States. The Tydings-McDuffie Act of 1934 had provided full independence for the islands after a ten-year period. Of course, the war made independence in 1944 impossible, but the islands established the republic on 4 July 1946, the earliest feasible date. Because of this close relationship between the two countries, the army took a benevolently protective attitude toward the Filipinos. The army also cooperated with the civil units of the Philippine government and helped reestablish the finance service of the Philippine army. In these activities finance officers played a much larger role than in dealings with the governments of France, Italy, and China.

After the army reestablished itself in the Philippines in 1944,

---

[11] See p. 98 for further discussion of "no-rate funds."

[12] Ltr, Ho Ying-chin, Chief of the General Staff, Chungking, to Lt Gen Joseph W. Stilwell, CG, CBI, 20 May 44; 1st Ind, Lt Col Paul L. Morrison, Actg Theater Fis Dir, to Actg cofs, CT, 28 Apr 45; Memorandum of Agreement, 25 Nov 44; ltr, Henry Morgenthau, Jr., Sec of the Treasury, to Dr. H. H. Kung, Minister of Finance, National Government of China, 25 Nov 44. RG 338.

it assumed responsibility for the financial activities of the Commonwealth government. In the Southwest Pacific Area (SWPA) the Allied command fiscal officer was the custodian of all Filipino funds used in the islands and also the representative of the Commonwealth Treasury. Army finance officers disbursed funds chargeable to Filipino civil affairs appropriations. Initially the Filipino finance officers for Philippine Civil Affairs (PCAU) were class B agents of a U.S. Army accountable disbursing officer.[13]

To help prepare the Philippine army for independent operation, the fiscal director, U.S. Army in the Pacific (USARPAC), supervised organization of the Finance Service of the Philippine army. This Finance Service paid all military bills of the Commonwealth government. By 30 August 1945, the USARPAC fiscal director had trained enough Filipinos and established sufficient offices so that the Finance Service no longer needed American assistance.[14]

Instrumental in the organization of the Philippine army Finance Service was Col. Paul A. Mayo. The Philippine army on 22 August 1945 awarded him the Distinguished Service Star Medal for "eminently meritorious and valuable service" for helping to establish and operate the Finance Service between 1 September 1944 and 1 February 1945. Colonel Mayo did this work with the Philippine army in addition to his regular duties with the Sixth Army.[15]

When the Commonwealth government became fully operative in 1946, several changes occurred in financial procedures. Filipino finance officers began disbursing independently, and the Commonwealth government assumed responsibility for its own funds and expenditures. Any U.S. army finance officers paying vouchers for the Army of the Philippines did not debit them in their accounts. They transferred the vouchers to the 172d FDS, which secured reimbursement from the Philippine government. Payment of the Philippine army and guerrillas became strictly the concern of the

---

[13] Instructional Notes on Philippine Civil Affairs, GHQ, SWPA, 22 Nov 44. RG 338.

[14] Administrative History, OFD, GHQ, USARPAC, 6 Apr 45–31 Dec 46. CMH.

[15] Operational Report, Fin Sec, Hq Sixth Army, 25 Jan 43–24 Jan 46. RG 338.

Commonwealth government. No American funds could be used for either purpose.[16]

Payment of Foreign Troops

On various occasions during the war, finance officers found it expedient or necessary to pay foreign soldiers. Such payments represented a kind of fiscal diplomacy less heady than that resulting from high-level policy negotiations, but they reflected the army's desire to maintain friendly relations with allies on the personal level. Most of these payments were routine. After finance units paid British, Canadian, or even surrendered German troops, standard procedures governed reimbursements. Two such instances of liaison with foreign governments were sufficiently involved to illustrate difficulties that could arise from paying foreign troops.

A major problem of coordination in the CBI theater was the payment of Chinese troops training in the Assam region of India. The Finance Department began paying these troops in March 1943, acting only as an intermediary service agency. The principal parties were the British and Chinese governments. The British lent money used for troop payments to the Chinese government, but American finance officers handled actual payments and bookkeeping. No strength data were required by the British before they turned money over to the finance office at headquarters, sos. All they wanted was the assurance of the commanding general of the CBI sos, with the concurrence of Gen. Joseph W. Stilwell, CBI commander, that payments would be rigidly supervised. The British did require a postpayment report, but specified no time limit.

The payment procedure was initiated when Chinese commanders figured the number of men to be paid. Then Chinese finance officers computed the pay and certified their figures to the American finance agency. Before the Finance Department paid these claims, the American chief of staff or G-1 (the staff officer for personnel), who maintained the latest strength figures and tables of organization of the Chinese army in India, checked them. With

---

[16] 2d Ind, Col C. W. Stonefield, Deputy Fis Dir, USAFFE, to Fin Off, 186th FDS, 30 Apr 45, FETF 120.1. RG 338.

verified figures, the finance officer in the field radioed sos headquarters for necessary funds. Headquarters would immediately
transmit the amount to the station finance officer. The only report
required of individual finance officers after payments was an improvised account current supported by a summary report of strength
and pay data, based on information received from the Chinese
army.[17]

Coordination between the Finance Department and the Netherlands government was exemplary. Just as army finance officers had
paid Chinese and British Commonwealth troops, they also made
disbursements in forward areas of New Guinea to Dutch soldiers
without paymasters. These 1944 disbursements were partial payments, with noncommissioned officers receiving one Australian
pound a day, and other enlisted men, ten shillings. Receipted
vouchers went to the finance office in Brisbane, Australia, which
presented them to the representative of the Dutch government for
reimbursement.[18]

Only one minor difficulty arose between the Dutch and American governments. swPA had to purchase Netherlands East Indies
guilders for disbursements. The Dutch naturally desired payment
in American dollars, but the Office of the Fiscal Director (OFD) in
Washington specified that payment be in Australian currency.
Although Dr. R. E. Smits, the Netherlands Indies commissioner,
insisted on payment in dollars, swPA could not comply. swPA settled
the guilder debt for between 5 and 6 million Australian pounds.
Soon after this settlement, OFD authorized swPA to purchase guilders
for dollars. Thereupon, Dr. Smits immediately requested a conversion into dollars of the Australian pounds already given him. Col.
Louis W. Maddox, the swPA chief finance officer, said that the
Dutch representative was "well within his rights," but Maddox
realized that if the dollars were exchanged for pounds, the excess

[17] "History of Fiscal and Finance Operations, sos CBI, from Activation
thru 31 Dec 1944," 15 Jan 45. CMH.
[18] 2d Lt J. M. Taylor, "Unit History," Hq Base Sec Three, USASOS Office
of the Fin Off, 30 Jun 44, 314.7; radio, CG USAFFE sgd MacArthur to CG, Sixth
Army, 25 Apr 44, W-21745. RG 338.

Australian money in the accounts of Lt. Col. James B. Rothnie, the funding officer, would present a serious problem. The exchange would have brought the funding account up to some $40 million in pounds—much more than the army needed, since Australian operations were waning.

The situation was further complicated by the reluctance of the governor of the Commonwealth Bank, Hugh T. Armitage, to repurchase any large amount of pounds from the army. Armitage wanted the pounds left in Lieutenant Colonel Rothnie's account to be dissipated by current expenditures. Colonel Maddox doubted that the $40 million could be liquidated before operations ceased in Australia, but Armitage agreed to repurchase any pounds remaining in the account when the army was ready to close out. Colonel Maddox was "particularly anxious" to comply with Armitage's request, since Armitage had saved SWPA "many embarrassing moments" through his wholehearted cooperation.[19]

When OFD in Washington learned the particulars of the case, it authorized a solution that pleased everyone. The account of the Netherlands Indies was credited with $43,515,295.34. The Dutch commission then transferred the Australian pounds back to Lieutenant Colonel Rothnie's account, and the Commonwealth Bank repurchased pounds remaining in the account after the phase out.[20]

By no means was fiscal diplomacy a one-way street. American soldiers benefited from payments made by British paymasters quite as much as vice versa. By 1943 the British paid American troops who were separated from their units, patients in British hospitals, or on British vessels. Usually when men were temporarily within a British paymaster's jurisdiction and had to have funds, they could get partial payments, which would be deducted from their regular monthly salaries. While with the British, American troops received rations and quarters, so the need for money for other purposes was

[19] Ltr, Col L. W. Maddox, Chief Fin Off, SWPA, to Office of the Chief of Foreign Fiscal Affairs, ASF, OFD, 17 Aug 44, sub: Report of Fiscal Operations in the SWPA, FEF 123.7. RG 338.

[20] Ltr, Lt Col J. B. Rothnie, Office of Theater Fiscal Off, to Dr. R. E. Smits, Netherlands Indies Commissioner for Australia and New Zealand, Melbourne, 24 Aug 44. RG 338.

slight. Consequently, these partial payments were for urgent expenses and held to an absolute minimum, such as ten dollars per month. The nearest American finance officer reimbursed British expenses incurred while providing for American troops. Each American receiving a partial payment from the British had to see that the amount was no greater than his accrued pay and allowances and that it was deducted from his next pay voucher.[21]

Payment of Commercial Accounts

As important as paying foreign troops was, an even more significant aspect of fiscal diplomacy concerned paying commercial bills. Since Finance did not pay a great number of foreign soldiers, any breakdown in this service went largely unnoticed—and the army was extending a courtesy in the first place. Commercial contracts were a different matter. The army depended on securing many supplies from the countries where it operated overseas, and it had to contract for the construction of many facilities, since it would have been manifestly impossible for all supplies and facilities to have been shipped over from the United States. Under wartime conditions, the army experienced difficulties in securing needed items overseas, but these difficulties could be minimized or magnified, depending on how finance officers paid those who had contracted for goods or services.

Such payments were as complicated as any Finance had to make in World War II, since it had no control over contracting officers. These officers wanted to get a job done or goods secured expeditiously and were often unconcerned about the niceties of what payments from public funds the GAO would sanction. When finance offices received contracts that violated GAO prescriptions, they had to withhold payment, thereby taking the heat for mistakes over which they had no control. Unpaid contracts left many parties unhappy: contracting officers, foreign vendors, and finance officers—and they sometimes impeded the war effort. Since the Chief of Finance had not anticipated this problem with any prewar

[21] Ltr, 1st Lt H. A. Parker, Agent Fin Off, Hq Southeast Asia Command, APO 432, to CG, IBT, 7 Nov 44, sub: Payment of American Troops Assigned to Duty with the British Army. RG 338.

planning and the Office of the Fiscal Director did nothing to solve it once OFD became operative, finance officers in the field had to improvise. Understandably, the GAO could not approve any kind of contract made overseas, and it was obviously difficult for that office to gear procedures to wartime exigencies. Given this situation, disbursing officers had to rely on their own judgment about contract payments. Some were willing to risk a GAO disallowance and to take the consequences, while others were not. The following instances demonstrate the types of problems Finance faced with commercial accounts and typical responses to them.

The American construction firm of Johnson, Drake, and Piper, Inc., signed a contract with the army for some work in the Middle East. Terms of the contract stated that the firm would be reimbursed for all proper expenditures. This wording implied that money would have to be spent before an application for reimbursement could be made. At the time the contract was signed, however, both parties agreed that the builder should not have to use his own funds to finance the project. This mutual agreement, while contradictory to the original language, was later incorporated in a supplement to the contract. In February 1942 the contractor began operations and needed funds for payrolls and local purchases. When the North African District Engineer requested the finance officer of the Eritrea Service Command to advance funds to Johnson, Drake, and Piper, Inc., he refused to do so because of the original wording of the contract. The finance officer contended that any payment would have to be made as a reimbursement. Failing to get the cooperation he needed on the local level, the district engineer appealed to the North Atlantic Division for a payment of $100,000 on the fixed fee so that the contractor could have a working fund. The division refused this request, since government policy was to make a minimum of expenditures at the work site. The contractor consequently had two alternatives—either to suspend operations or to borrow funds. Choosing the latter, the firm began to borrow from Barclay's Bank. Over a period of fourteen months interest on the loans amounted to $14,323.94. The North African District Engineer filed a voucher to cover this amount, since the work had to be completed. Headquarters, USAFIME, upon the advice of the staff judge advocate, interpreted the contract and current War Department publications so that the contractor could be reimbursed for the interest paid to Barclay's Bank, and the USAFIME disbursing officer made the final settlement.[22]

When the army dealt with American contractors, problems of payment could be solved according to mutually understood principles. With foreign parties, however, less common ground could be assumed, even when language was not a barrier. The only serious problem between the army and a member of the British Commonwealth developed in Australia early in the war. Because the army depended on the Australian economy for a large part of its sustenance, it was subject to caprices of that economy. When Australian workers realized they held the upper hand in bargaining, they pressed forward with demands for more pay and better working conditions. First they wanted rest breaks with pay, and then they demanded that the American government provide their lunch money.

When workers' demands exceeded authorization for payments, the disbursing officer at the Melbourne FOUSA, Capt. Ralph A. Metzger, who was responsible for paying all commercial bills in Australia, stopped payments. Gen. Douglas MacArthur, upon learning of the difficulty with commercial payments, called Captain Metzger in to discuss the matter. The general pointed out that, in comparison with the Australians, the American people enjoyed a high standard of living and made few sacrifices. As long as American money could keep the war away from American shores, General MacArthur thought there should be no hesitancy in meeting the Australian demands. Even with these concessions, Australian workers would not earn as much as comparable American laborers, MacArthur pointed out. Captain Metzger stated he was aware of these facts, but as a disbursing officer, he was obliged to follow army regulations and was accountable to the GAO. He felt that he could not

[22] Ltr, Maj J. A. MacLarney, District Engineer, North African Engineer District, Cairo, Egypt, to ASF USAFIME, Cairo, Egypt, 24 May 43, and 1st Ind, Capt H. Kunzler, Asst Adj Gen to Disbursing Fin Off, ASF, USAFIME, Cairo, Egypt, 25 May 43. RG 338.

be personally liable for making payments he knew to be questionable. General MacArthur then told Captain Metzger that he would give him written permission to make the payments.

In 1944 the GAO began auditing the commercial payments Captain Metzger made earlier in Australia. It took exception in the amount of $3,368,000 and carried this amount against him until it accepted as basis for the payments the written directive of MacArthur and copies of the contracts signed by competent army authorities. The GAO periodically decreased Metzger's accountability for the $3,368,000, and final relief came through congressional legislation.[23]

Australia, with its developed economy and shared English traditions, presented far fewer contractual problems for finance officers than the Philippine Islands. While the army was consolidating its position in the Philippines, it was also laying the foundation for an all-out offensive against Japan. This preparation required a great deal of construction, especially of airstrips. Since military necessity and suitable topography dictated the location of airstrips, the army frequently had to displace Filipinos from homes and farms. In such cases, purchasing and contracting officers made purchase or rental agreements with the Filipino property owners. Many factors made it difficult for finance offices to make payment on these purchase agreements. Usually the uneducated Filipinos did not know exactly in whose name the property was registered or the extent of their holdings. Under the Japanese occupation, property frequently changed hands and many civil records were destroyed. Some Filipino claims were hence tenuous at best. But the most difficulty arose from the inexperience of many of the purchasing and contracting officers, who had been told to accomplish their mission regardless of method. Consequently, they often drew up contracts that did not conform to specifications, which therefore could not be paid by finance officers. The 186th FDS, commanded by Capt. W. A. Edgar, received daily requests for payments on these contracts, which it had to refuse on technicalities. When denied payment on what they took to be just obligations, the "poor, illiterate Filipinos seemed to lose faith in the U.S. Government." Many class A agents were not so cautious in making

[23] Interview with Lt Col Ralph A. Metzger, 17 Aug 55.

payments as the 186th FDS. These agents, who possibly were not aware of the statutory restriction on paying contracts, justified their advance payments by saying that the people were poverty-stricken and had to have the money immediately to build new homes after they had been dispossessed by the army.

To offset the ill will created by such slipshod contracts, the army tried to be liberal in contracting for property damaged by the Japanese. The army might have been able to use such property without paying for it, but to preclude any possible claims, it acted in good faith and made outright purchases.[24]

By far the most intricate and risky fiscal diplomacy that Finance had to arrange involved the Chinese. While high-level agreements between the American and Chinese governments manifested a certain amount of concord, individual finance officers were wise to handle all monetary dealings with the Chinese with great caution. The finance office for Headquarters, Base Section Two, CBI, was located in Calcutta, but the commanding officer was in Kunming, China. This separation complicated problems of finance coordination with the Chinese and British. A prompt payment of commercial contracts was essential to supply American forces in the CBI with the goods they needed. Nonetheless, finance officers had to watch the Chinese closely so they would not work some sly deal. A general Chinese practice was to leave blank on purchase orders the space for the payee. Consequently, neither the purchasing officer nor the finance officer was protected. In one instance, a finance officer refused payment because of gross irregularities in the case. A different kind of irregularity involved a Chinese colonel, Sammy Yuan, representing the Cathay Syndicate, who demanded payment of purchase orders in rupees. Payment in this currency would have violated Indian laws. Colonel Yuan wanted to buy goods in India and smuggle them into China or to smuggle rupees into China. Because of his freebooting, Yuan was ousted from India and requested not to return. By virtue of his position in the Chinese army, however, he was able to work his way back into Calcutta. Frequently the British comptroller of foreign currency requested American finance officers not to make payments to the Chinese. But until they

[24] Ltr, Capt W. A. Edgar, Fin Off, 186th FDS, to Fis Dir, USAFFE, 24 Mar 45, sub: Payments. RG 338.

received orders to the contrary, the finance officers had to continue to pay Chinese purchase orders, regardless of their being suspect.[25]

American finance officers attached to the Chinese sos, which was activated 9 February 1945, were in a more precarious position than those who simply paid Chinese firms on purchase orders. Officers with the Chinese sos were torn between two desires. Primarily, they were assigned to aid the Chinese in administrative matters. To get things done, they would cooperate with the Chinese. On the other hand, they felt compelled to exercise caution in the disbursement of public funds, whether the funds were Chinese or American. Since American finance officers countersigned checks authorizing expenditures, they could control payments. The ordinary caution exercised by these finance officers frustrated the Chinese, who were loath to let regulations come between them and a desired objective. In one instance the sos finance bureau at supreme headquarters of the Chinese army refused to make payments for the Chinese quartermaster because there was no authority for the payments in regulations or instructions from the Ministry of War. Thereupon, headquarters ordered the finance bureau to advance the quartermaster CNC $200 million. Presumably, this money was used by the quartermaster to make payments that had been refused by the finance bureau. Chinese commanders repeatedly criticized American officers in the finance bureau for refusing to advance funds, even though no money had been earmarked for the requested purposes.

While conditions were bad for American officers in the Chinese sos headquarters, they were even more trying for those in branch offices. The branch offices had no American assistants, so the finance officers had to rely entirely on the Chinese to keep records, prepare vouchers, and make audits. Since all the books were kept in Chinese and vouchers and checks were written in Chinese, Americans had no protection against possible fraud. Yet they were accountable for the Chinese funds entrusted to them. The injustice of their having to answer for the gross inefficiencies

[25] Ltr, Maj D. F. Boichot, Fin Off, Hq Base Sec Two, to Col. Lewis P. Jordan, CO, APO 627, 27 May 44. RG 338.

and intrigues of the Chinese prompted the chief of the finance bureau, Maj. D. U. Emmert, to request that they be relieved from the responsibility of approving payments and countersigning checks. In response to Major Emmert's request, the China theater published a memorandum stating that all U.S. military and civilian personnel assigned to the Chinese SOS were subject exclusively to U.S. control and military law. The Chinese government had to assume full responsibility for all losses and shortages in connection with the disbursement of Chinese funds by Americans.[26]

Among the challenges the end of the war produced for finance offices was that of clearing commercial accounts. Depending on the circumstances, Finance could sometimes bend rules to tidy up ledgers; but sometimes it could not. Payment of commercial accounts in Czechoslovakia presented a problem after hostilities had ceased. On 7 October 1945 the finance officer for the Eighth Armored Division received notice that all commercial funds had been withdrawn as of 1 October. Obligations already incurred had to be fulfilled, so the commanding general authorized the disbursing officer to ignore the directive and pay Czech firms that had supplied the American army with goods. The decision to continue payment was based on the assumption that it would be a serious blunder to treat liberated Czechoslovakia like conquered Germany, where occupation expenditures could be charged to reparations.[27]

Incomplete information about old bills, some dating back to 1942, complicated settling commercial accounts with Middle Eastern firms. Sometimes the claims could not be paid for lack of such essential items as copies of contracts, supporting purchase orders and receiving reports, or certificates of receipt of services. A typical example of an unpaid claim was that of the Anglo-Iranian Oil Company for $14,790 for the construction of gasoline facilities in Iran.

[26] Ltr and 1st Ind, Maj D. U. Emmert, Chief Finance Bureau, Hq SOS Supreme Hq Chinese Army, to COFS (thru Director of QM Depot), 4 Jun 45, sub: Retention of Finance Officers as Liaison Personnel Chinese SOS: Memo 84, Hq CT, 4 Jun 45. RG 338. On 24 October 1944 the CBI split into the China theater and the India-Burma theater.
[27] Interview with Col George R. Gretser, 30 Mar 54.

Since no record was available of either the performance or the acceptance of this service, no action could be taken on the claim.[28]

Payment of Foreign Taxes

From the time American soldiers set foot on foreign soil, the army faced the troublesome problem of taxation. Not only did the army want to protect its members from having to pay taxes on purchases, but it also wanted to avoid liability for such taxes on local procurements. The army's negotiation of tax agreements with the governments of Great Britain, France, Italy, and Egypt constituted another aspect of fiscal diplomacy.

An early American objective in England was to get the levy on bank drafts canceled. This rate of taxation was one-eighth of 1 percent of the amount of the check. With some reluctance, the British canceled the tax in July 1942.[29] The British made no alteration in the commercial tax system for the benefit of American army buyers, but they agreed to rebate the purchase taxes paid by the U.S. Army. Through European theater headquarters, disbursing officers made quarterly claims on the British treasury for purchase taxes paid during the period. Claims derived from consolidated figures furnished by purchasing and contracting officers.[30]

One of the first actions taken by the American high command after the invasion of North Africa was to agree with the French provisional government on paying taxes on purchases from the local economy. The Clark-Darlan Agreement, drawn up on 22 November 1942, exempted Allied forces, both collectively and individually, from any form of taxation.[31] Yet the agreement did nothing to exempt vendors selling goods to the U.S. Army from paying regular taxes to the French government. Naturally, vendors added the amount of taxes they were obliged to pay to the cost of goods. The French government, after receiving protests from the American army, announced publicly that Allied forces would pay no

---

[28] Lt Col E. L. Dlugensky, Asst Chief, Rec and Disb Div, OCF, "Report on the Finance Activities of the Finance Office, US Army, Cairo, Egypt," 310.1, 9 Nov 46. RG 338.

[29] Interview with Brig Gen William P. Campbell (Ret), 27 Apr 54.

[30] Cir No. 9, ETO, 14 Aug 42. RG 338.

[31] For the political background of the Clark-Darlan Agreement, see Funk, *Charles de Gaulle*, pp. 37–42.

taxes and reimbursed those already paid. The Tron-Davis Agreement, transacted between M. Ludovic Tron, director of the Commissariat du Finance, and Brig. Gen. T. J. Davis, adjutant general of Allied Forces Headquarters, confirmed this policy. The agreement provided that reimbursement could be made for taxes paid under protest in cases where vendors stubbornly refused to grant a tax exemption. The only exception to this reimbursement rule was in the case of alcoholic beverages. To enable the American Treasury Department to make final settlements, disbursing officers kept a monthly record of taxes paid under protest and transmitted a consolidation of these monthly reports to the Treasury.[32]

When supplying the Allies with goods, Italian civil authorities agreed to make no attempt to impose taxes, imposts, or duties of any nature upon the transactions. Purchasing and contracting officers, as well as disbursing officers, were therefore to make no payment of any Italian tax that a vendor might attempt to add to prices. A buyer could never expect a refund even if he paid a tax under protest. With the exemption agreement established, no provisions existed for recouping involuntary payments.[33]

This system of tax exemption for local procurement by the U.S. Army was adopted by the Egyptian government as early as 1942. In addition, those items imported into Egypt for exclusive use of the American army were also free from customs duties. As a matter of fact, the Egyptian government went so far as to grant a sizable rebate to the American army for duties paid on imported items before the exemption agreement was made. The Cairo finance office set up a section to compute the refund entitlement and to execute the necessary Egyptian forms. By August 1944, rebates totaled 15,179.25 Egyptian pounds, or $62,818.92.[34]

While the following example of fiscal coordination with the Indian government does not relate to sales taxes, it demonstrates the cooperation of an Allied nation in eliminating procedural difficulties. India's willingness to share the financial burden of the war indicated her recognition of the threat posed by Japan. Among the

[32] *Logistical History* of NATOUSA-MTOUSA, pp. 397–398.
[33] Adm Memo No. 28, Allied Force Hq, APO 512, 3 Jul 44. RG 338.
[34] Memo for U.S. Army Forces in the Middle East, from Hq USAFIME, OFD, Cairo, Egypt, 27 Sep 44, sub: Report of Operation, File 319.1. RG 338.

first operations undertaken by the American army in the CBI was establishing supply bases in India. The army made special financial arrangements with the Indian government to use ports through which goods would be funneled to supply bases. Originally, finance officers paid expenses of U.S. Army Transport Service vessels in Indian ports. These expenses included charges for coal bunkering, stevedoring, and wharfage maintenance and repairs. After the government of India agreed to reimburse the army, finance officers submitted paid vouchers as the basis for reimbursement. This arrangement proved unsatisfactory because reimbursement took too long and required needless paperwork.

On 1 July 1943 the government of India agreed to a different procedure. It began advancing disbursing officers at ports 20 million rupees (worth $605,254 in U.S. currency) to use as a working fund in a special deposits account. When disbursing officers exhausted their working funds, the Indian government would reimburse them. If the reimbursement was late, finance officers had to make payments from their available U.S. funds. Then when the reimbursement came through, they would deposit the money to their regular account. Such transactions were complicated and demanded a great deal of extra bookkeeping. After the Indian government was apprised of this difficulty, it agreed to double the rupee working fund.[35]

Coordination within the Government

When conducting fiscal liaison with foreign governments on a wide range of issues, Finance did not lose sight of the need to coordinate its activities with those of other agencies of the U.S. government. Negotiation with foreign governments, in fact, probably sensitized army fiscal officers to the need for full intragovernment cooperation, which could not be assumed as the norm in either peace or war. Among the government agencies operating overseas, the army dealt extensively with the navy and to a lesser extent with the War Shipping Administration and several quasi-official organizations.

Within the government, the army had the most financial deal-

[35] "History of Fiscal and Finance Operations, sos CBI, from Activation thru 31 Dec 1944," 15 Jan 45. CMH.

ings with the Navy Department. If naval supply officers in the Mediterranean needed North African funds, they could go to army disbursing officers at Oran, Algiers, or Tunis and get a check for local currency in exchange for a Treasury check. The navy, in fact, was encouraged to deal with the army, rather than to maintain accounts with various local banks. Behind this encouragement was Treasury Department reasoning that it was desirable to keep foreign depositary bank balances to a minimum and to restrict local currency holdings in areas where military activity was waning. In highly exceptional cases where a naval supply officer could not purchase funds with a Treasury check, the Africa–Middle East Theater (AMET) made provisions for him to receive funds on an invoice of funds transferred. When money was transferred thus, forms and explanatory letters went to the OFD in Washington, which secured reimbursement from the Navy Department.[36]

Individual sailors and marines could be paid by an army finance officer in any place that had no naval supply officer.[37] Usually with transfers of funds or disbursements to another service, the army finance officer would submit a voucher for reimbursement. In SWPA, though, the finance officer at Melbourne paid the expenses of the First Marine Division directly from army appropriations.[38]

The army was not always on the giving end of financial relations with other services. The marine paymaster in the Samoan Defense Force, Lt. Col. Harry C. Grafton, Jr., furnished funds to the Fifty-third FDS. This disbursing section, commanded by Capt. Louis Koretz, was just beginning operations on Samoa in December 1943 when the marine paymaster made his offer.[39]

In addition to providing finance service for the navy and marines, the army made disbursements to other government agen-

---

[36] Fin Cir Ltr No. 30, Hq SOS, ETO, OCF, 6 Jan 42. RG 338.

[37] Col John R. Vance, "Report of Operations, Finance Officer, USFIP, Dec 8, 1941–May 6, 1942," 30 Sep 44, p. 13. RG 338.

[38] Ltr, Col L. S. Ostrander, AG, Hq USASOS, to CO, Base Sec Four, APO 924, 14 Jan 43, sub: Expenditures on Behalf of First Marine Division, GSDF 120.1. RG 338.

[39] Ltr, Lt Col Harry C. Grafton, Jr., USMCR, Force Paymaster, Defence Forces, Samoan Group, to Capt Louis Koretz, DO, Fifty-third FDS, 5 Dec 43; ltr, Koretz to Grafton, 9 Dec 43. RG 338.

cies such as the War Shipping Administration. When vessels of this agency could not obtain funds from regular sources, they could get them from an army disbursing officer. If due to emergency conditions, the authority for the transfer could not be obtained from a vessel's master, the army finance officer could advance no more than $10,000.[40]

Throughout the war a few quasi-official American organizations, such as the Red Cross and the USO (United Service Organization), received the privilege of using army finance facilities. Field directors for the American National Red Cross got their funds in forward areas by cashing checks at finance offices. In the South Pacific Red Cross checks had to be drawn in dollars, but they were paid in the currency being regularly disbursed.[41] Funds for paying such civilians as USO entertainers and war correspondents came from the Chief of Finance, intermediary for the employer organizations that sent money for him to transmit to disbursing officers overseas.[42] Technical representatives of aircraft companies working in the South Pacific also obtained money through finance offices. Companies deposited funds with the Treasury to the credit of the disbursing officer nearest their representative.[43]

Soon after the liberation of the Philippines began, Finance, in cooperation with the State Department, initiated aid to liberated citizens of the United States and other Allied nations. A needy person, identifiable as a U.S. citizen, could be paid a maximum of seventy dollars per month if he signed a statement promising repayment to the government. In case the citizen needed less, he would be paid accordingly.[44] Disbursing officers sent vouchers for these relief payments to Col. Carl Witcher at the Washington

[40] Gen G. C. Marshall, Memo 55–44, "Transactions Between the War Department and the War Shipping Administration," 29 Sep 44. RG 338.

[41] Ltr, Lt Col B. J. Tullington, Theater Fis Off, Hq SOS, APO 502, to Fin Off, Service Command, APO 292, 27 Mar 44, sub: Cashing Red Cross Checks, 122. RG 338.

[42] Fin Cir Ltr No. 7, Hq AMET, Cairo, Egypt, OFD, 4 Jun 45. RG 338.

[43] Radio, Comgen, SOS SPA, to Comgens, APO 25, 37, 40, 43, 93, Americal Division, Fourteenth Corps, et al., 28 Mar 44, 311.23. RG 338.

[44] Radio, Marshall, Washington, to Det GHQ SWPA (MacArthur) 21 Feb 45, W 22518. RG 338.

FOUSA, who forwarded them to the State Department, which then reimbursed the War Department.[45]

The Finance Department was an agency through which various groups in the United States could support citizens in the Philippines. Business firms, newspapers, churches, or individuals remitted money to the State Department. The State Department placed this money in a special deposit account in the Washington FOUSA, which notified U.S. Army Forces in the Far East (USAFFE) of the deposit. The theater then instructed the disbursing officer nearest the payee to make the payment.[46] Finance officers were forbidden to use the Commonwealth funds in their accounts for any direct relief to Filipinos. Such relief had to come from the Commonwealth government directly.[47]

Coordination within the Army

The problems of coordinating army finance activities with foreign governments and other branches of the U.S. government were often complex. While the Finance Department was attending to these problems, it also had the job of coordinating its activities with other parts of the army. Usually relationships were smooth, but sometimes poor cooperation between various elements of command caused ill will and inferior service.

Frequently a lack of coordination on financial matters created misunderstandings between independent army commands, as in the Middle East. The wing commander of the Central African Division of the Air Transport Command from the early days of operation had appointed purchasing and contracting officers, who received allotments directly from the War Department Budget Division. For a while they made payments without being questioned. But when USAFIME headquarters processed some vouchers for local procurement, the fiscal director, Col. R. E. Odell, disallowed

[45] Ltr, Col C. W. Stonefield, Deputy Fis Dir, Hq USAFFE, to Fin Off, Hq USAFFE, APO 501, 15 Mar 45, sub: Transmission of Funds to Refugees and Repatriates in the Philippine Islands, FETF 132(P). RG 338.

[46] Memo, Col L. W. Maddox, Chief Fin Off, USAFFE, to Lt Col A. H. Miller, 172d FDS, 9 May 45; ltr, Miller, to American Consul, Manila, 12 Apr 45, sub: EFT #1, PBF 122.1. RG 338.

[47] Stonefield to Fin Off, Hq USAFFE.

payment on the grounds that the wing commander had no authority to appoint purchasing and contracting officers without theater
approval. While the authorities tried to straighten out the situation,
unpaid vouchers began to accumulate and vendors began to complain. The vouchers represented legitimate expenditures, but did
not get paid promptly because of violation of prescribed procedures.[48]

In the North African and Mediterranean theaters,[49] local purchasing was facilitated through the close cooperation between G-4
(the staff officer for supplies and equipment) and the finance staff.
G-4 directed the procurement of all local supplies and labor, but
the chief finance officer had to approve all purchases on the basis
of availability of funds. The two staffs established a system whereby
all purchase requests would be reviewed by the chief finance
officer in light of previous expenditures and approved or disapproved. He would then send the request back to G-4. To keep the
expenditures of major commands within given limits, the finance
staff set up a master account to reflect major allotments and expenditures for each command. Major commands submitted monthly
reports of expenditures to the chief finance officer, who posted
them to the master account. In this manner a current check could
be kept on the expenditures; if more money were needed to complete necessary projects, it could be requested.[50]

In planning the financial aspects of Pacific island operations,
the ground forces cooperated closely with the air forces. Preparations for the Western Carolines operation were made by the
USAFPOA fiscal office in collaboration with the Army Air Forces
Pacific Ocean Area (AAFPOA) fiscal office. The two offices working
together decided to use air forces finance units to pay both air and
ground forces during the first stage of the occupation of Angaur
and Peleliu. In September 1944 the Thirteenth Air Services Group
established the first office on Angaur. Later the Eighty-first Division
finance section established an office on Peleliu and, with the help

[48] Ltr, Brig Gen Bob E. Nowland, Hq ATC, AAF, Washington, D.C., to
Maj Gen B. F. Giles, Hq USAFIME, APO 787, 20 Jul 44. RG 338.
[49] NATOUSA was redesignated MTO on 1 Nov 44. USAFIME was redesignated
AMET on 1 Mar 45.
[50] Logistical History of NATOUSA-MTOUSA, p. 393.

of the Angaur office, paid all the troops in the Western Carolines. While finance service got under way in the main group of the Palau Islands, a class A agent flew in from Guam to pay troops on Ulithi, an outlying island.[51]

In the CBI close cooperation existed between finance officers and APO's. Finance offices furnished APO's with official rates of exchange, which the APO's used when selling soldiers money orders. At the close of every day's business, finance offices would give APO's Treasury checks in exchange for their cash.[52] In Shanghai immediately after the war, good coordination also existed between the finance office and the purchasing and contracting office. The latter had no blank forms, so the finance office improvised purchase order forms to prevent delay in securing needed equipment.[53]

Friction sometimes occurred between finance officers and other staff members because of the natural conservatism of those to whom public funds were entrusted. By "following the book right down the line, finance officers left themselves no latitude in their operations," declared Brig. Gen. William P. Campbell (Ret.), wartime fiscal director for the Eighth Air Force. In England Campbell's commanding general wanted to buy some linen for the officers' mess, but the fiscal director thought it an improper expenditure and refused to grant the necessary funds unless the general provided a written directive stating that it was in the best interests of the government to buy the linen. "I got my statement," said General Campbell, "but I also made enemies of the commanding general and the G-1. Had I been wiser, I would have gone ahead and bought the linen and somehow fixed it up later. While it is in the best interests of a disbursing officer in the field to follow the book religiously, the finance officer on higher echelons must allow himself some leeway."[54]

Lack of confidence in the judgment of finance staff officers could cause commanding generals undue trouble. When Campbell

---

[51] "History of Fiscal Mid Pac," pp. 36–37. CMH.
[52] CBI Finance Memo 13, 18 Aug 43. RG 338.
[53] "Historical Report of Shanghai Base Command," 1 Feb 46. RG 338.
[54] Interview with Gen Campbell, 27 Apr 54.

was assistant military attaché at the American embassy in London, American enlisted men stationed at the embassy, which was owned by the British government, drew an allowance for quarters. Campbell, a major, advised the commandant that such a payment for quarters was erroneous and should cease. Rather than take the finance officer's advice, the general wired the War Department to ask for a decision. The Washington reply upheld the payments. When the general received this, he called Campbell in, informed him of the contents of the reply, and asked if he wanted to change his mind. Campbell refused to change his advice since he was convinced of its soundness. He told his commander that the Comptroller General often declared payments sanctioned by the War Department illegal. When the general heard this, he told Campbell to wire the War Department again in his own name and state his case. If Washington continued to uphold the payments, the general would relieve Campbell for inefficiency, but if the War Department changed its mind and upheld Campbell, the general said he would give him a letter of commendation. Staking his military career on this one decision, Campbell wired Washington. The reply came back that, upon reconsideration, payments of quarters allowance should cease.[55]

One example of the latitude a high-echelon finance officer needed to leave himself concerned disbursing appropriated funds to aliens not employed by the U.S. government. Lt. Col. E. R. Melton, finance officer for the First and Twelfth Army groups in 1944, claimed chief responsibility for the resumption of production of the Hadir steel mills in Luxembourg. When the First Army Group arrived in Luxembourg, the mills were not producing steel useful to the American army because of no money to pay employees. "As soon as my office provided the money, production began, and we got our steel," said Colonel Melton.[56]

The sudden surrender of Japan presented what might have proved Finance's biggest job of coordination in the Pacific war. Elaborate plans had been made for the invasion of Japan, with sixty FDS's moving from Europe to the Pacific. While seasoned units were being staged for the invasion, new ones were equipped and staffed.

[55] Ibid.
[56] Interview with Lt Col E. R. Melton, 19 May 53.

When the surrender came, redeployment from Europe was halted. Those units that had been trained and staffed went to various components of USAFFE. Three sections went to the Sixth Army, four to the Eighth Army, and one to the Twenty-fourth Corps. The mission then changed from conquest to occupation.[57]

With the end of the war, the closing of theaters demanded extensive coordination among finance offices—from individual disbursing officers, through the OFD in Washington, to the Treasury. Although the phasing out of the China theater presented some unique situations, the process was largely the same as when finance offices closed in other theaters.

The following procedures obtained in the China theater after V-J Day. The disbursing officer first notified the Treasury to revoke deputyships. Then he applied to the OFD to cancel surety bonds of enlisted men. (Officers maintained their bonds until they arrived back in the United States.) Next, the disbursing officer transferred Treasury credits to the China theater's central officer through the National City Bank of New York, Calcutta Branch. He transferred balances in the Central Bank of China and other depositaries to the central funding officer by telegram. He sent any U.S. or Chinese National currency to either the Shanghai or the Kunming finance officer, and he forwarded special deposit funds to the central funding office with pertinent identification. The central funding officer also received Treasury checks from disbursing officers who were closing out. When these checks went to the central funding officer, reports also went to the Treasury and OFD. The disbursing officer forwarded the final account current to the audit and accounts branch of the central funding office and prepared a monthly report of operation. Finally, he settled all accounts with vendors. Any unpaid military accounts reverted to individuals, who had to submit them to another disbursing officer.[58]

As General Campbell indicated, finance officers were not intellectually or emotionally conditioned to act as diplomats. Their training stressed circumspection and careful following of the rules. By disbursing within guidelines prescribed by army regulations and

[57] Semi-Annual Report, AFWESPAC, 1 Jun thru 31 Dec 45. RG 338.
[58] Disbursing Information 28, China Theater, 28 Sep 45. RG 338.

special regulations, they could usually fulfill their military obligations expertly, without fearing notices of exception from the GAO. But such disbursing was of the sort described in textbooks. Once finance officers came in contact with representatives of foreign governments in wartime, they often had to adjust their thinking and sometimes their procedures to serve the best interests of their country. Occasionally, military regulations allowed needed latitude in fiscal dealings with other governments, but most often finance officers, in conjunction with other staff officers, had to work out new arrangements to accommodate situations not covered by previous planning.

One of the difficulties with planning for the fiscal coordination and liaison necessary in wartime was that each foreign country presented different challenges. Any policy that would cover operations in all theaters would have been so general as to be inconsonant with military regulations. Similarly, a policy that tried to cover all eventualities would have been hopelessly detailed and complicated. As a consequence, the army chose the practical path of working out solutions to problems as they arose. Finance officers recognized that they had little influence on such matters as the rate of exchange between the dollar and the French franc, the assessment of occupation costs for Italy, or the size of "loans" to the Kuomintang government. They also recognized that in the Philippine Islands they could take concrete steps to fashion the fiscal policies and procedures of the new government, and they did that.

Because of their training and work habits, finance officers took satisfaction in paying troops and commercial bills properly. This care extended to giving finance service to foreign troops, when practical, and to paying accounts owed to foreign vendors. Since finance officers liked to expedite such routine tasks, they served the needs of fiscal diplomacy well. Similarly, if through disbursements they could smooth relations with other U.S. government agencies or other elements of the army, they gladly did so. Being task oriented, they took satisfaction in getting things done, whether they were paying British troops, Czech vendors, or USO performers, or coordinating payments with the navy or purchases with G-4.

Fiscal diplomacy, because of the different tasks involved and because of the uniqueness of many of its aspects, became more interesting than routine finance work. It offered varied and some-times exotic experiences that, for many finance officers, frequently lent new dimensions to their careers. As they performed the work of fiscal coordination and liaison, these men contributed to the army's success overseas.

CHAPTER *3*

Budgeting and Accounting

BEFORE World War II the Chief of Finance, doubling as the War Department budget officer, formulated and administered the army's budget. He received estimates from each army agency with specified funds, consolidated these estimates, and forwarded them to the War Department general staff, which then took them to Congress via the Bureau of the Budget. The administration of whatever monies Congress approved for the army's annual budget became Finance's responsibility. As the budget specialist for the War Department, the Chief of Finance supervised the expenditure of funds, according to strict budgetary classifications.

Once America entered the war, the army made significant changes in the budgeting process. Realizing that the Chief of Finance was not an aggressive policymaker or foresighted planner, the War Department on 9 March 1942 made the new Fiscal Director, Maj. Gen. Arthur H. Carter, its budget officer to administer this important function. Then on 1 July 1943 it returned the budget responsibility to the general staff, naming neither the Chief of Finance nor the Fiscal Director as budget officer.[1] Congress, understanding that the army could not fight with a peacetime budget, in effect gave the army budgetary carte blanche to spend what it needed to achieve victory. For the preparation of annual budgets, however, theater fiscal officers did have to project types of expenditures. They were the only ones overseas with an important role in the budgetary process, since the War Department handled the other aspects of budgeting.

A cardinal principle of sound business management is that the businessman must know how much money he takes in and how much he spends. He achieves this knowledge through accounting.

[1] "History of Fiscal Services, 1940–1945," pp. 60, 80, 253. CMH.

While a close comparison could not be drawn between civilian enterprise and the wartime financial management of the army, the two did share some common accounting principles. For the army to know whence its money came was plainly easier than for a private business. During the war the army was not bothered by limitations on appropriations that were in effect in peacetime. But, in return, Congress expected from the army a proper accounting for the approximately $176 billion it spent.[2] In this respect—of knowing how money was spent—private enterprise and the army faced similar responsibilities, but with differing objectives. Business needed to know where its money went as a matter of profit analysis. The army was not concerned with profits. All it has to do was give an honest accounting for its stewardship of public funds. The ultimate object of army accounting was to inform Congress of how much money was spent and for what purposes.

The Finance Department, as the army's disbursing agent, had various types of accounting missions. Most important was accounting for funds spent from congressional appropriations. The Finance Department used no new methods for this type of accounting, since the wartime system extended those methods used in peacetime. The only differences consisted of more appropriations to cope with and larger sums to handle. Auditing, an aspect of accounting, entailed checking the accounts of disbursing officers to determine if they were correctly posted and balanced. While appropriation accounting held center stage, the army devised new phases of accounting to meet wartime needs, which included accounting for lend-lease, reciprocal aid, and captured funds.

Budgeting

Congress, realizing that the army's primary mission was to achieve victory, streamlined budgeting and accounting procedures. It gave the budget officer of the War Department a comparatively free hand to formulate procedures by which agencies outside the United States could be furnished funds needed to prosecute the war successfully. The system devised was called the Finance De-

[2] *History and Organization of the Finance Corps*, St14-160, 25 Sep 51.

partment General Allotments (FDGA). Theaters and commands outside the United States received lump sums with no designation as
to appropriations, subappropriations, or projects. The budget division of the War Department general staff established reserves
against all categories of appropriations available for expenditure in
overseas commands, except for those activities in the "open allotment" category. This open allotment was the carte blanche for the
War Department, an act of good faith from Congress. Although
theaters given funds under the FDGA received no specific amounts
in each appropriation, they had to report expenditures chargeable
to the appropriations included in the FDGA. Theaters were not
limited in the amount they could spend from FDGA funds, but they
did have to report what they spent because the budget division in
Washington maintained reserves behind the FDGA by appropriation
number. If overseas theaters did not inform the budget division of
how much money was chargeable to a certain appropriation, the
budget division would have no idea when its reserves had been
exhausted. Conversely, by receiving reports from overseas, the
budget division could replenish its reserves when they ran low.
No charges were listed against those project account activities in
the open allotment category. Such activities included pay and travel
of the army, court-martial expenses, subsistence, transportation, ap-
prehension of deserters, and property and death damage claims.

FDGA funds were coded by theater and country symbols. In Fiscal Year (FY) 1945, the European theater was designated by "60,"
the first part of the serial number. The latter part consisted of three
digits representing a country. For example, obligations for purchases
made in the United Kingdom were charged to 60-136; those in
France, to 60-114; and those in Belgium to 60-105. A complete
FDGA serial number for an expenditure made in Belgium, for instance, would be 60-105, followed by the applicable appropriation,
project, and object code numbers. Even if expenditures made in
different countries were identical, they could not be handled on
the same voucher. The determining factor for the country code
was the place where money was actually spent, rather than obligated. If collections were made to FDGA funds, they were coded
according to the country where cash was received or where a check

was drawn. The chief occasions for collections were when FDGA money was refunded.

After the close of each fiscal year, the unobligated balances of FDGA funds reverted to the Treasury. Had these unobligated balances been left open from year to year, the bookkeeping in Washington would have been unduly complicated. Each fiscal year provided sufficient FDGA funds to cover necessary expenditures, so there would have been no need to spend from lapsed allotments.

When overseas commands performed work for an agency of the government other than the War Department, they could charge FDGA funds, but not those listed in the War Department fiscal code. The appropriations charged were those applicable to the agency for whom the work was done. Only a theater commander could authorize charging FDGA funds with non–War Department appropriations.[3]

As a result of the free hand given overseas theaters in obligating funds during combat, few budgetary problems arose. Ordinarily, the army operated on a budget based on the fiscal code. It requested funds according to their accounting classification; then when an agency received allotments for expenditure, it obligated and spent by accounting classifications. The wartime use of FDGA funds minimized the work of planning a budget.

When the North African invasion—the first major land operation against hostile territory—was being planned in 1942, logisticians anticipated that many needs of American forces could be supplied from the North African economy. If the invading forces could make local procurements, it would save valuable shipping space. The planners therefore assumed as much and devised a scheme that logically required elaborate knowledge on the part of fiscal officers of the North African economy. Unfortunately, no one knew quite what to expect. The only fiscal information available at the time of the invasion was the rate of exchange and the fact that yellow seal dollars would be the invasion currency. This

[3] Ltr, Lt Col Richard P. Fisk, Asst, Hq ETO, to CG, U.S. Strategic Air Forces in Europe, sub: Instructions Regarding Finance Department General Allotments for FY 1945, AG 121 opFD, 27 Jul 1944; Fin Cir Ltr 65, Hq ETOUSA, OFD, 22 May 44; Fin Cir Ltr 22, Hq NATOUSA, OFD, 8 Sep 44. RG 338.

money was distinguished by having the Treasury Department seal printed in yellow rather than blue. Little, if anything, was known about the effect dollars would have on the local economy, the normal standard of living, wage scales for labor, standard prices, and goods available for military purposes. All this intelligence was necessary for a fiscal planner to make correct estimates for the budgetary needs of units operating in foreign areas. Lacking this information, those planning the fiscal aspects of the North African campaign had to make arbitrary guesses. They estimated the needs of a division, taking 15,000 as average strength. Then for each additional 15,000, the same amount of funds was allowed. Had fiscal officers not been allowed to work with lump sums, rather than specific appropriations, such planning would have been impossible. The budget officer in Washington, recognizing the difficulties in the North African operation, assured fiscal officers there that any funds needed would be provided. He promptly approved the first request for $20 million.[4]

In the European theater fiscal procedures were closely controlled until the intensive buildup for the invasion began in February 1944. Before that time, the War Department had allotted the theater commander specific amounts, and he, in turn, made definite suballotments to lower levels.[5] The fiscal officer for an army had to account for and suballot appropriated funds. He consolidated the monthly reports from units into the army's monthly fiscal report.[6] After February no echelon was limited in its procurement. The War Department gave blanket authority to the European theater to obligate funds.[7]

On tactical levels, funds were allotted in specific amounts for two items only: intelligence and entertainment. The principal fiscal accounting required of finance offices in army groups, air forces, armies, and corps concerned these two funds. Army groups made open suballotments to its armies, but canceled the allotments when the subordinate command transferred to another headquarters.

[4] *Logistical History of* NATOUSA-MTOUSA, pp. 391–392.
[5] Brig Gen N. H. Cobbs (Ret), "Finance Department, European Theater of Operations," Jan 46, pp. 12–13. RG 338.
[6] Col L. A. Hawkins, Jr., "Unit History."
[7] Cobbs, "Finance Department," p. 13.

Sometimes as many as three such transfers were made each month. Correspondence connected with these cancellations proved far more work than making the allotments originally. Armies receiving definite suballotments for intelligence and entertainment made further specific suballotments to corps and divisions. As with the army groups, the armies withdrew unobligated balances when corps and divisions transferred to another command. The fiscal office of the First Army received monthly reports of obligations based on the fiscal code from corps and division finance offices. Lower echelons also made monthly reports on the status of the two specific allotments. The army fiscal office consolidated reports and forwarded the information to European theater headquarters.[8]

The end of hostilities in Europe did not bring an immediate change in budget and fiscal procedures. So long as fighting continued in the Pacific, the War Department made no attempt to begin curtailment of expenditures in other theaters. Shortly after V-J Day, however, the government slashed the army's budget by 60 percent. This drastic cut necessitated the army's abandoning FDGA and giving strict allocations of all funds. Beginning with the second quarter of FY 1946 (1 October 1945), fiscal officers had to make requests for funds and reports of expenditures by full fiscal code accounting classifications.[9]

Phasing out operations in AMET made estimating budget requirements difficult. For instance, the War Department approved the fiscal director's estimate for the funds necessary for the third quarter of FY 1946; but in making his estimate, the fiscal director assumed the continuation of reciprocal aid for local purchases. When the aid was suddenly withdrawn, the theater had to request an additional $500,000. In one respect the theater was fortunate, for it could obligate the funds remaining in the account of the Persian Gulf Command after it was deactivated. These PGC funds countered the deficit caused by cancellation of reciprocal aid.[10]

[8] Hawkins, "Unit History"; "Report of Operations," Twelfth Army Group, p. 38. CMH.

[9] Ltr, Hq AMET, OFD, sub: Bi-Monthly Report of Operations for Months of September and October, FD 319.1 (General), 23 Nov 45. RG 338.

[10] Memo, Col R. E. Odell, Fis Hq AMET, to CG, sub: Bi-Monthly Report of Operations for Months of November and December 1945, FD 314.7, 30 Jan 46. RG 338.

Because of the steady decrease in the activities of AMET, the War Department permitted some latitude in its fiscal operations. The fiscal director could transfer funds between individual projects within the same major project account classification. For example, within the major project account of "operating," he could transfer funds from transportation of troops to transportation of equipment; but without prior approval of the War Department, he could not move funds from the "operating" to the "construction" series. He listed approved transfers in the monthly report of obligations and expenditures.[11]

Budget and fiscal problems of the European theater in the immediate postwar period were similar to those of AMET, only intensified because of the larger sums involved. Another complication in Europe was that combat had strained all administrative operations. Confusion concerning the refinements of budgetary procedures was more natural in combat areas than in noncombat theaters like AMET. The postwar situation in Europe resulted in a lack of experienced men to calculate and report budget requirements. As military duties grew less stringent, some of these problems began to be solved. Appropriations were adjusted, proper reports of obligations were rendered, and staffs were trained in estimating budget requirements.

Appropriated Dollars

While keeping tabs on lend-lease, reciprocal aid, and captured funds were segments of the Finance Department's accounting mission, the primary emphasis was on accounting for routine disbursements and collections of appropriated dollars. Finance officers around the world, regardless of the currencies they disbursed or received, kept their books in American dollars. They figured payrolls in dollars and then converted to foreign currencies. All vouchers, or certificates of payment and collection, were stated in dollars as well as alien terms. Rates of exchange for computations also showed on vouchers.

[11] Memo, Lt Col B. L. Ghent, Fis Dir, Hq AMET, for CG, AMET, sub: Bi-Monthly Report of Operations for Months January and February 1946 and the Period 1-10 March 1946, FD 314.7, 11 Mar 46. RG 338.

The mechanics of accounting for public funds were the same in all theaters, with possibly a few variations because of local conditions. Accounting procedures used by a finance office in the United Kingdom could be considered fairly typical. This flow of accounting documents through a disbursing office in England shows how the office kept books. Vouchers and certificates of deposits were numbered serially beginning with each fiscal year or the opening of a new disbursing account. The check writer, who numbered vouchers, routed them to the accounting branch, which abstracted them on a schedule of disbursements. Methods for paying vouchers appeared in the appropriate column on the schedule—"paid by check," "paid by cash," and "total amount paid." After the accounting branch abstracted and checked each day's vouchers, it totaled the schedule of disbursements and then gave the following results, along with the vouchers, to a clerk to post in the cash book, a ledger in which *all* transactions affecting the disbursing officer's account were listed:

Disbursed by check	$———
Disbursed by cash	$———
Voucher collections	$———
Total disbursed	$———

A daily inspection verified the total for check payments as shown on vouchers and the checks themselves against the total listed on the schedule of disbursements. Similarly, a daily inspection verified with the cashier and finance officer the total for vouchers paid by cash as reflected on the schedule of disbursements.

The clerk responsible for the cash book and accounting papers entered vouchers paid by cash in the cash blotter, a ledger listing only cash transactions. He entered vouchers paid by check in the check register, a ledger for check transactions only. The clerk also abstracted voucher collections on a schedule of collections. He entered deductions made from civilian payrolls on a schedule of retirement and disability fund credits. Collections and class A pay reservations for the purchase of war bonds appeared on a schedule of voucher deductions. After going through all these steps, the clerk had completed abstracting daily disbursements. He proved his figures by adding the following:

Check	$————	(using figures furnished by check writers)
Cash	$————	(using figures posted in the cash blotter)
Voucher collections	$————	(using figures from schedule of collections)
Retirement deductions	$————	(using figures from schedule of retirement deductions)
Class A pay reservations	$————	(using figures from schedule of voucher deductions)

The total of these figures should equal the total on the schedule of disbursements.

A finance office entered every cash collection in the cash blotter and listed it on an appropriate form. The most common types of cash collections included soldier's deposits (originated in peacetime, these enlisted men's savings accounts paid 4 percent annual interest), receipts from scrap property sales, general fund receipts, and special deposit funds. This last category included cash derived from performance bonds, telephone and gasoline taxes, and bids on sales of scrap and salvage.

At the close of a business day, after all cash transactions had been entered in the cash blotter, the accounting section computed the cash balance reflected on the blotter and notified the finance officer. He checked the blotter figure with the actual cash in the safe and against his personal record. After he ascertained this sum, the accounting section posted daily receipts and disbursements in the cash book. It listed money coming into and leaving a disbursing officer's account by check in the check register. It transferred the balance shown there to the cash book also.

Finance officers had to post more than the total debit and credit columns in the cash book. They had to break down entries into various categories to satisfy requirements of the account current, the monthly report a disbursing officer rendered on the complete status of his account. On the reverse of the account current was a section, Analysis of Balance Due the United States, that required a division of the cash figure into various currencies on hand and rates at which they were converted.

At the end of each month the cash book was totaled. The cash balance plus the Treasury account balance were supposed to equal the difference between the credit and debit columns. Comprising the cash balance was the cash in the office safe, cash in the hands of agent officers, and money in the local depositary. The figures derived from these computations carried forward to the cash book for the new accounting period.[12]

Accounting for expenditures bearing a security classification demanded a different procedure. Such expenditures came from one appropriation only, contingencies of the army, established for cases when ordinary accounting steps could not be followed. The Secretary of War had to approve any expenditures from this appropriation. A special voucher devised for classified expenditures was filed in quadruplicate, and the finance officer making payment retained the triplicate. He sent the original and duplicate, bearing all supporting papers to substantiate the disbursement, directly to the War Department. These documents were accompanied by four copies of the schedule of disbursements. The War Department receipted one of the copies and returned it to the disbursing officer, who then picked up the amount of the disbursement in his account.[13]

Finance officers in the Mediterranean theater authorized to disburse British military authority notes were usually funded directly by British paymasters. The British notes entered a disbursing officer's accounts as a credit in the cash blotter. Any time an American officer received British notes, he reduced in his cash

---

[12] Fin Cir Ltr 21, Hq SOS, ETO, 12 Oct 42; Fin Cir Ltr 22, Hq NATOUSA, OFD, 8 Sep 44. RG 338.

[13] Ltr, Col N. H. Cobbs, Fis Dir, Hq ETOUSA, WD, TAGO Washington 25, D.C., to: CinC, Southwest Pacific Area; CG, Theaters of Operation, et al., sub: Accounting Procedure for Confidential Overseas Expenditures from the Appropriation "Contingencies of the Army," AG 130-OB-S-B-M, 30 Mar 44. RG 338.

book the balance on deposit with the U.S. Treasury by the amount of British currency drawn, just as if he had issued a Treasury check for it. Disbursing officers cabled the theater fiscal director each time they received British currency.[14]

When disbursing officers received Allied military lire from the Allied Financial Agency, accounting procedures were similar. For the Allied military lire received, the War Department charged equivalent dollar amounts to the applicable appropriations. The Treasury held these dollars in special account. Disbursing officers receiving lire reduced the dollar balance on deposit with the Treasury by the amount of lire drawn.[15]

A new accounting procedure for overseas areas was approved by the Treasury and GAO early in 1944. It particularly benefited the Mediterranean theater, where disbursing officers collected lire from the sale of surplus property. Before the new method was developed, the Treasury had recognized only U.S. currency in its accounting operations and insisted that before an accountable disbursing officer could have a balanced ledger, only American money could be credited to his account. The new system allowed a disbursing officer to have a general depositary account with foreign banks so that foreign currencies in his account could be deposited to the credit of the Treasury. This system also served in accounting for the unexpended balances of disbursing funds in foreign currencies.[16]

Accounting in the field was but one, albeit the most important, phase of the army's overseas accounting mission. At the theater level, fiscal offices checked accounts from disbursing officers for errors, summarized accounting data, and prepared monthly reports of the results for the War Department. The accounting branch in the theater fiscal director's office supervised all accounting connected with foreign activities. It handled accounting for civilian supplies furnished to liberated and occupied territories and former enemy nations. This branch coordinated accounting for funds

14 Ltr, Brig Gen L. H. Sims, Fis Dir, Hq MTOUSA, to All Concerned, sub: Accounting for BMA Currency Used in Greece, Albania, and Yugoslavia, 30 Nov 44. RG 338.
15 "History of Fiscal Services," p. 582; see the preceding discussion of settlements with the Italian government, pp. 41–44.
16 "History of Fiscal Services," pp. 443–444.

derived from the sale of surplus property and from foreign currencies advanced to disbursing officers by Allied governments or agencies. Also, it supervised the account of Allied military governments.[17]

Auditing

The accounting work of theater fiscal offices was of a dual nature. The first part was supervisory; the second consisted of the intensive examination of accounts known as auditing. In July 1943 the War Department authorized for each major overseas command a central fiscal office similar to the stateside regional accounting offices. This office carried out administrative examinations and analyses of disbursing officers' accounts, using sixteen finance disbursing sections to conduct audits. These sections analyzed accounts of all finance officers in the theater, including ground forces, air forces, air transport command, and communications zone (the rear-echelon supply area of a theater). By checking reports from these sections, fiscal directors could get a complete picture of the operations of each finance officer and determine who needed assistance. It was a boon to individual disbursing officers to have a section compile reports on foreign currencies, procurements obtainable under reciprocal aid, and cumulative monthly expenditures. The section gave disbursing officers a current audit of their accounts and initiated notices of exception.[18]

Not all theaters considered the central fiscal office an unmixed blessing. The North African theater contended that it was accomplishing its own audit assignment satisfactorily and needed no new program. The disadvantages of transportation shortage, lack of adequate office space and equipment, and lack of facilities for the additional officers and men required to staff a new office seemed to outweigh any advantages a central fiscal office could offer. When the theater protested the new program in August 1943, the War Department temporarily suspended the requirement in North Africa. Under pressure, the theater agreed to establish a central fiscal office on 3 March 1944—provided that Washington furnish

[17] Ibid.
[18] War Department Conference on Theater Administrative Fiscal Organization, 310.1, 9 Feb 44. RG 338.

the necessary personnel and equipment. It also insisted on having an officer assigned to organize the office and instruct the staff on their duties. The theater's central fiscal office was operating by 1 June 1944.[19]

Theater fiscal offices sometimes had to audit accounts other than those of disbursing officers. In AMET the fiscal office was responsible for auditing property accounts for the theater as well as for the Persian Gulf Service Command. When that command was deactivated, the AMET fiscal office also performed the final audit on its unit accounts and nonappropriated funds.[20]

Many disbursing offices in the field had elaborate procedures for auditing the vouchers that they processed. An air forces finance office at Brampton Grange, England, began auditing disbursement vouchers for pay of military personnel by recomputing the pay account. It then checked nonquantitative elements such as proper wording, authorization, complete names, spelling, correct serial numbers, and accurate citation of appropriation data. Travel vouchers received the same type of meticulous audit.[21]

Lend-Lease and Reciprocal Aid

In March 1941, in response to President Roosevelt's intense desire to aid Great Britain, Congress passed the Lend-Lease Act, authorizing the transfer of American facilities, defense articles, information, or services to Allied governments.[22] After Germany attacked the Soviet Union the following June, Roosevelt also extended lend-lease to the Russians. Great Britain and the Soviet

[19] *Logistical History of* NATOUSA-MTOUSA, p. 406.

[20] Memo, Col R. E. Odell, Fis Dir, Hq AMET, for CG, AMET, sub: Bi-Monthly Report of Operations for Months of November and December 1945, FD 314.7, 30 Jan 46. RG 338.

[21] Ltr, Maj R. K. Andrews, Fin Off, AAF Station No. 111, APO 557, U.S. Army, to Fis Off, Hq First Bomb Div, APO 557, sub: Auditing Disbursement and Collection Vouchers, 132.2, 18 Jun 44. RG 338.

[22] See Warren F. Kimball, *The Most Unsordid Act*, for the diplomatic background of this important legislation. For information on the operation of lend-lease, see Richard M. Leighton and Robert W. Coakley, *Global Logistics and Strategy, 1940–1943,* and Coakley and Leighton, *Global Logistics and Strategy, 1943–1945.* The most troublesome accounting problems involved lend-lease to the French, which was ordinarily shipped to the American theater commander for transfer in the theater. See James J. Dougherty, *The Politics of Wartime Aid,* chap. 10.

Union became its greatest beneficiaries, although thirty-nine countries received such aid.[23]

Lend-lease policymaking and accounting centered in Washington, with a civilian agency, the Foreign Economic Administration, and the Undersecretary of War sharing responsibilities. This arrangement meant that most accounting for transfers to foreign governments occurred in Washington before the United States turned goods over to other countries. Lend-lease decisions usually involved only the highest levels of government, as emphasized by the fact that overseas theaters never received blanket authority to issue lend-lease. The War Department general staff gave specific orders only to individual theaters to engage in lend-lease. When it did, theater fiscal officers had the responsibility of assessing the value of transferred goods.[24] With reciprocal aid, fiscal officers played a larger accounting role, because they had to evaluate the cost of goods and services received within the theater from Allied governments and to report these figures to the Office of the Chief of Finance.[25] Both of these accounting functions remained at the theater level, with disbursing officers in the field rarely involved.[26]

As soon as the American army began operations in England, the theater fiscal director became responsible for lend-lease accounting, principally with the supply of air forces equipment and services from American stocks to the Royal Air Force and the British army. The most important influence of the Finance Department on lend-lease in England was that the theater fiscal director prepared the initial directive on lend-lease administration. So only at the highest level—that of the fiscal director—in both the North African and the European theaters did Finance have much hand in lend-lease accounting.[27] Reports on lend-lease transactions orig-

---

[23] International Division, Army Service Forces, "Lend Lease as of September 30, 1945," vol. 1, pp. xlii–lii. CMH.

[24] Ibid., pp. 670, 702.

[25] International Division, Army Service Forces, "History of Reciprocal Aid, 9 May 1941–31 December 1945," p. 59. CMH.

[26] International Division, Army Service Forces "Lend Lease as of September 30, 1945," vol. 1, pp. 758–759.

[27] Col William P. Campbell, "Summary Report of Reciprocal Aid and Lend Lease Administration, U.S. Strategic Air Forces in Europe, From Inception in 1942 to 30 June 1944," pp. 13–14. RG 338.

inating in Europe and North Africa were forwarded to the respective chief finance officers (later fiscal directors), who consolidated these reports and made their own accounting to headquarters, Army Service Forces (ASF) in Washington.[28]

The North African theater used shipping tickets to transfer items from American custody to that of the other Allies. It prescribed an exact formula for filling out these shipping tickets, since they yielded data for subsequent accounting. When a unit supplying lend-lease goods to Allies sent in shipping tickets every two months, it also had to prepare a summary report of transactions. The chief finance officer checked both sources of information in devising his own account for the ASF.[29] Despite such efforts, lend-lease accounting in the theaters lacked precision, because few fiscal officers were conversant with supply problems. Supply officers similarly provided little aid for accounting purposes. Since theater commanders put low priority on this accounting, their fiscal officers usually followed suit.[30]

When American forces began operating overseas, it became apparent that it was easier to obtain many supplies and services directly from Allied governments than to bring them from the United States. Hence, a new system of reverse lend-lease, or reciprocal aid, came about. Reciprocal aid credits of foreign governments were applied to their lend-lease debits. The official definition of reciprocal aid, as could be expected, was just the reverse of that for lend-lease: the method by which Allied governments gave facilities, services, defense articles, and information of all types to U.S. forces under the provision of the Allied Master Agreements. Reciprocal aid included any service or article made available to the army under terms of the agreement, except pay and allowances of military personnel. When the army received reciprocal aid property, it was not accountable to the Allied government, but rather accounted for reciprocal aid material through army channels. The chief areas where the army received reciprocal aid were England

[28] Southern Line of Communication, ETOUSA, AG Sec Lend-Lease Files, Nov 1944 to Feb 1945, Cir Hq ETOUSA, Jan 1945; Report of Operations, Eastern Base Sec, NATOUSA, Sep 1943. RG 338.

[29] Report of Operations, Eastern Base Sec, NATOUSA, Sep 1943. RG 338.

[30] International Division, Army Service Forces, "Lend Lease as of September 30, 1945," vol. 1, pp. 758–759.

and North Africa. Governments supplying that aid were Great Britain and the French Committee of National Liberation in North and West Africa.[31]

During buildup operations in the United Kingdom, the reciprocal aid program developed fully. The British government, in addition to furnishing expected items such as military equipment, ammunition, and construction material, extended its reciprocal aid to civilian labor, strategic materials, revolving funds, airfields, housing, sea transport, freight, air and motor transport, mail service, and public utilities. As with lend-lease, the Finance Department entered the reciprocal aid program on a high level. The European theater delegated the responsibility for the administration of the program to the chief finance officer. The Finance Department's reciprocal aid section at headquarters, Services of Supply, European theater, was the agency that consolidated all reciprocal aid data for the theater and reported to Washington. In the U.S. Strategic Air Forces in Europe, the fiscal officer found that his staff was spending an undue amount of time in connection with reciprocal aid reporting, essentially a supply activity. He recommended that this accounting be transferred to the parties most directly concerned, the chiefs of various supply services.[32] This recommendation was not followed, however.

The chief finance officer of the European theater was instrumental in developing accounting procedures for American obligations to the British as well as the administrative system for reporting. As with lend-lease, much of the reciprocal aid in the United Kingdom was for the air forces. Every member who flew a sortie over the Continent received an escape kit consisting of a map, compass, and purse containing the appropriate foreign currency. These articles, worth about $50, would facilitate escape if fliers were shot down over occupied or enemy territory. Because of the secrecy necessarily attached to assembling these items, ordinary accounting methods could not be used. The chief finance officer devised an effective accounting system, which in no way interfered

---

[31] Cir 36, Hq ETOUSA, 1 Apr 44; Administrative Memo 18, "Reciprocal Aid," Hq NATOUSA, 4 Nov 43. RG 338.

[32] Campbell, "Summary Report," pp. 1–2, 9; Cir 32, Hq ETOUSA, 24 Aug 42. RG 338.

with air forces operations. Total value of the escape kits obtained from the British as reciprocal aid was $6,663,041.26.[33]

The use of airdromes occupied jointly by British and American air forces early in the war was limited. As air operations increased in number and intensity, such joint use of facilities became common. The chief finance officer helped devise a procedure for determining the proportionate shares of operating costs. The senior American and British air officers at each jointly occupied air base would determine the percentage of use, based on the number of landings per month and the relative personnel strength. Depending upon who used the field most, operating expense adjustments were handled as either lend-lease or reciprocal aid.[34]

Initially, the reports that came into the reciprocal aid section showed dollar values of items, estimated by receiving officers. This procedure resulted in varying evaluations on similar articles. Despite the unreliability of the first reports because of varying evaluations, they still had great worth since they contained item and dollar totals and could therefore be readjusted subsequently. After October 1942 the requirement for reporting dollar values was abolished, except when the Allied government furnished official values or unless a joint agreement existed between governments whereby values could be agreed upon. Later governments furnishing reciprocal aid published catalogs and price lists of items given to the army. When dollar reporting was reinstated in June 1945, these publications solved the problem of uniform values.[35]

Administrative conditions for reciprocal aid in North Africa differed from those in England. From the beginning of operations in the United Kingdom, American forces dealt with a friendly power, but when they invaded North Africa they opposed the government of Vichy France. For a while after the French in Africa capitulated, the army could deal with no official body. Yet

---

[33] Cobbs, "Finance Department," p. 12.

[34] Ibid., p. 19.

[35] Col Ralph A. Koch, Lt Col Harold W. Uhrbrock, and Lt Col Maynard N. Levenick, "The Activities of the Finance Department in the European Theater of Operations," Study 75, Report of the General Board, USFET, File R 013/1, 46, pp. 9–11. RG 338.

many sympathetic natives were willing to furnish goods and services to Americans. The army recognized that as part of bringing about the creation of a friendly government, it had to make immediate payments to small vendors who provided supplies. But the army deferred payments for large items such as utilities, communications, and port facilities, since it could expect some services free under the surrender terms and since reciprocal aid negotiations were under way with the government being formed, the French Committee of National Liberation.

On 25 September 1943 the U.S. government and the French Committee signed a modus vivendi that activated reciprocal aid in North Africa. The French Committee could not have been expected to furnish actual materiel to the army, so instead it set up a fund, called the franc account, in the Banque de l'Algerie and Banque d'Etat du Maroc, for purchases on the local economy.

Use of the franc account in North Africa was not uniform. Under one system, based on the method used before the modus vivendi, purchasing officers bought goods with appropriated money, but when finance offices made out vouchers for these local purchases, they inserted "Franc Account" instead of citing an appropriate allotment number. Periodically the theater submitted these franc account vouchers to the French for reimbursement.[36] The Eastern Base Section of the North African theater employed the franc account only for emergency purchases when the normal requisition process was too lengthy.[37]

Signing the modus vivendi on 25 September 1943 indicated the willingness of the French Committee of National Liberation to cooperate with the American forces in their fight against the Axis. But it did not put the reciprocal aid program into effect immediately, for the machinery was lacking. The new system caused "considerable confusion" in many finance offices. Each case seemed to present a different problem. The Twenty-fifth FDS had particular trouble paying a commercial bill for auto parts, since payment was handled under the reciprocal aid agreement. After

[36] *Logistical History of* NATOUSA-MTOUSA, p. 396; Frank A. Southard, Jr., *The Finances of European Liberation*, p. 19.
[37] Report of Operations, Eastern Base Sec, NATOUSA, Sep 43. RG 338.

the program had been operating for a few months, it ran smoothly.[38]

French devaluation of the franc in December 1945 created as much extra work for those maintaining reciprocal aid accounts as it did for cashiers exchanging currency in disbursing offices. In March 1946 all French reciprocal aid after 26 December 1945 was audited and evaluated at the new rate of exchange, 119.1066 francs to the dollar. Prior to devaluation, reciprocal aid had been evaluated at the rate of 50 francs to the dollar.[39]

Reciprocal aid agreements with the British in North Africa were much simpler to make than with the French, since they were part of the large lend-lease–reciprocal aid program between the American and British governments. Nothing such as the modus vivendi with the French was necessary for the army to obtain reciprocal aid from the British. The system established in the United Kingdom was approximated in North Africa. One variation was the use of task funds. The British gave the American army imprests known as task funds with which to pay obligations usually fulfilled by the British. These task funds were used to pay expenses incurred by the American army while performing tasks for the British. After July 1942, when task funds were first given the army, adaptations were made in their use. When it was convenient, the Finance Department disbursed task funds when the benefit was as much American as British. For instance, in Eritrea, it paid native civilian laborers from a task fund. In such cases, it made subsequent adjustments. Gradually reciprocal aid replaced the use of task funds in North Africa.[40]

Often in Africa and the Middle East, military duties put servicemen nearer British than American units. In those cases, Americans were quartered and fed by the British, who charged the individuals nothing, but reported the cost as reciprocal aid. Meals

[38] Ibid.; Capt R. A. Alexander, "Unit History"; T/4 Milton Glazer, "Unit History."

[39] Memo, Lt Col B. L. Ghent, Fis Dir, Hq AMET, for CG AMET, sub: Bi-Monthly Report of Operations for Months of January and February 1946, and the period 1–10 March 1946, FD 314.7, 11 Mar 46. RG 338. For a discussion of exchange problems resulting from the new franc rate, see p. 219.

[40] Memo, Col R. E. Odell, Fis Dir, Hq USAFIME, for CG, USAFIME, sub: Report of Operations, 15 Aug 44. RG 338.

were reported at the same rates officers would pay for American field rations—twenty-five cents per meal.[41]

Captured Currency

The Finance Department, as fiscal agent of the army, was required by law to account for captured enemy funds. Directives required that all enemy money falling into the hands of American soldiers be turned in to a finance office promptly, along with a report on its capture. Finance offices did not commingle captured money with appropriated funds, but carried it in special deposit accounts and treated it as a trust fund. Accounting reports did not convert these funds into dollar values, but listed their original denominations. Finance officers could disburse these funds, subject to the decision of a commanding general, for the support of occupation troops or military government. Captured currency did not fund ordinary combat operations.[42]

Frequently during the course of battle soldiers captured large sums of enemy funds at one location. In such cases the money was accounted for as a unit. But when currency was taken from the body of an enemy soldier and submitted to a finance office, it had to be recorded separately and credited to the estate of the deceased.[43] Similarly, when American soldiers were killed, disbursing officers who last paid the deceased constructed their pay accounts up to the time of death. Expedient handling of these accounts enabled quick settlement of estates. When American officers were killed in the European theater and the Office of the Fiscal Director could not locate the disbursing officer who had last paid them, it sent urgent letters of inquiry to all disbursing officers and class B agents.[44]

[41] Cir 69, Hq USAFIME, 248.7, 28 Sep 44; Cir 9, Hq USAFIME, 26 Jan 45. RG 338.

[42] Basic Field Manual 27-5, Change 1, par. 13.5, 22 Dec 42; Col N. H. Cobbs, Fis Dir, Hq ETO, Fin Cir Ltr 59, 30 Dec 43; SOP No. 11, Fiscal Procedures, 20 Apr 44. RG 338.

[43] Memo for the Record, sub: Disposition of Currency found on Deceased Bodies of the Enemy, 30 Sep 44, FFA-16xPOW sub 27, Sec 2, POW Allied Personnel. RG 338.

[44] Ltr, Lt Col M. F. Moriarty, Deputy Hq ComZ, ETO, OFD, to all Fin Offs, Ltr of Inquiry, 240B, 15 Aug 44. RG 338.

Although no question existed about the disposition of captured funds, actual practices sometimes did not follow established procedures. At times, such large amounts of enemy money were captured that it would have been impossible even to begin counting the funds, as when a disbursing office once received five tons of currency. Although policy specified that all funds taken from dead soldiers had to be accounted for, it was not always followed. Many finance offices burned blood-soaked currency. The finance section of the Twelfth Army Group strongly advocated immediate burning of any currency threatening health. "It is very foolish to expect a man in combat to risk his health in order to account for a few pieces of paper otherwise known as money."[45]

This strong conviction was based on the experiences of the Fifty-ninth and Fiftieth FDS's. For a full month after the Fifty-ninth hit the Normandy beach on D plus 12, it did nothing but handle effects of soldiers killed in action. The graves registration section of the Quartermaster Corps removed money from bodies and turned it over to finance units for counting. "We took tons of money from dead American soldiers. It smelled awful!" declared Maj. Raymond E. Graham, the Fifty-ninth's commandant. The unit sent checks for money it could identify and count to the quartermaster effects agency, which made final disposition of personal property. If the money could be used, the Fifty-ninth kept it; otherwise, it was destroyed.[46] The Fiftieth, commanded by Maj. Ocie A. Goleman, reported that while it served ranger and paratroop battalions operating at the Anzio beachhead, its job was overwhelming. It processed great numbers of final statements of those killed in battle. Even more unpleasant was the task of checking blood-soaked currency. Some of this money had been on corpses for several weeks. The stench made it impossible for finance clerks to stay in the room with the money except for short periods, but the job had to be done, since before the currency could be destroyed, serial numbers had to be recorded.[47]

Most reports of the capture of large sums of enemy money came toward the end of hostilities. Germans, as defeat drew near,

---

[45] Report of Operations, Twelfth Army Group, p. 11.
[46] Interview with Lt Col Graham, 8 Feb 54.
[47] Maj Ocie A. Goleman, "Unit History."

understandably became more concerned with saving themselves than their money. In Italy, the Fifth Army finance officer, Col. H. F. Chrisman, reported that from 14 May through 30 June 1945, captured German funds swamped his office. On 26 May, funds in the office occupied 2,000 cubic feet. The Fifth Army finance section handled this money in three phases: storing and securing, establishing accounting procedures, and finally, transmitting the funds to the Allied Financial Agency. Most of the bills captured from the Germans in Italy were lire, but they had money from nearly every European nation. By 30 June the Fifth Army had turned over the last of its millions in captured currency to the Allied Financial Agency.[48]

In Austria, as well as Italy, May featured more reports of captured currency than any other month during the war. For instance, the finance office of the Sixth Corps handled approximately $2.5 million in captured funds, consisting of Reichsmarks, lire, rubles, and Romanian lei. The Reichsmarks and lire went to the property control officer of military government, who placed them in a blocked account at the Reichsbank in Innsbruck to be used to defray occupation costs. The rubles and lei went to military government, Seventh Army. In the area of Garmisch, Bavaria, the Counterintelligence Corps (CIC) located a gold bullion cache valued at $1.5 million, which it turned over to the military government property control officer, pending determination of ownership. This cache brought the total funds captured by the Sixth Corps in Austria to approximately $4 million, exclusive of any funds captured by the corps' divisions.[49]

With great volumes of currency being transferred from one nation to another, some confusion in policy was inevitable. The finance office of the Forty-fifth Division received some Banque de France 500-franc notes in July 1943. The French Committee of National Liberation had declared these particular bills nonlegal tender, so they no longer had to be accounted for. Men in the finance office passed them out as souvenirs. Then in September

[48] Reports of the Fifth Army Commander's Weekly Conference, 14 May–30 June 1945. RG 338.

[49] Col H. L. Leighton, "VI Corps History," Hq Sixth Corps, Office of the Fin Off, 11–31 May 45. RG 338.

1944, after the invasion of southern France, the French government changed its policy and declared the Banque de France 500-franc notes legal tender once more. Men who had held onto theirs thereby found that they had an unexpected windfall.[50]

Since most people dream of finding large quantities of money, special excitement attached to capturing money—even if it was foreign currency. The account of how Pvt. Louis G. Rey came to possess 23,000 francs was quite exciting and unusual. Private Rey was liberated from a German prison camp by the Russians on 30 January 1945. When the Russians asked him about shoes, Rey led them to a warehouse full of them. In return, his liberators presented him with 23,000 francs they found in a German safe. Rey turned the money over to a disbursing officer in Naples and got a receipt for it. But owing to the peculiar circumstances by which Rey got the money, it was picked up in the finance officer's accounts as a miscellaneous receipt. As such, it had to be deposited in the Treasury general fund and was not available for disbursement until appropriated by Congress. Consequently, Rey could never convert his receipt into dollars.[51]

In the areas of budgeting and accounting, Congress and the War Department exercised sound judgment. From the outset of the war, there was no pretense that peacetime procedures could be extended into the emergency. Prosecution of the war took precedence over orderly business methods, for it was manifestly more important to win the war than to maintain a tidy set of books. Since the Chief of Finance appeared best equipped for the latter, the War Department removed him as its budget officer in March 1942, supplanting his authority in this area with that of the new Fiscal Director. Loss of estate in this key function illustrated the fact that the War Department did not think the Office of the Chief

---

[50] Interview with Col Ross H. Routh, Property and Disbursing Officer, Oklahoma National Guard, 24 Jun 54.

[51] Testimony of Pvt Louis G. Rey, 38010014, taken at Army Ground and Service Forces Redistribution Station, Santa Barbara, Calif., on 28 Jun 45 by Maj Alfred H. Young, MI, Chief Security and Intelligence Branch; 5th Ind, Col E. J. Bean, Deputy Dir, Hq ASF, OFD, SPFDF Confiscated Currency, to CO, Army Ground and Service Forces, Redistribution Station, Santa Barbara, Calif., 23 Aug 45. RG 338.

of Finance had the capacity for the innovative fiscal planning needed during wartime. After the War Department activated the Office of the Fiscal Director, the Office of the Chief of Finance clearly played a secondary role in fiscal planning and management for the remainder of the war.

Had the realistic judgment evidenced in the areas of budgeting and accounting been applied to other aspects of the army's fiscal management, the entire monetary operation would have been more efficient. In these activities, common sense dictated loosening controls for efficiency. Perhaps accounting for lend-lease and reciprocal aid was too imprecise, but these programs exemplified President Roosevelt's desire not to put a dollar sign on the price of victory. This accounting was probably as accurate as could have been expected, given the nature of the transactions. Accounting for captured currency, including that among the effects of dead soldiers— both American and enemy—brought finance units as close to the fighting and the carnage of combat as most ever came.

If the kinds of approximations the army used in budgeting and accounting had been applied to soldiers' pay, that enormously important responsibility would have been simplified. But in this area the Finance Department adhered to the minute computations and regular payments of peacetime, thereby remaining encumbered with an unwieldy system ill-suited for overseas theaters. Bound by its traditions and afraid to risk shattering soldiers' morale, Finance did not choose to achieve administrative efficiency and simplicity.

CHAPTER 4

Funding

FUNDING, as used in World War II military parlance, was a special term with several meanings. None of these meanings coincided with dictionary definitions that have to do with (1) providing money to pay the interest or principal of a debt or (2) converting general outstanding debts into more or less permanent debts or loans represented by interest-bearing bonds.

Among military finance men, the most common meaning of funding involved the logistics of getting currency from supply centers to disbursing officers. The foremost logistical task in funding was getting the right types and amounts of currency to disbursing officers, who ultimately used the money to pay the army's bills—whether monthly payrolls or commercial accounts. Additionally, the term had several connotations supplementary to the purely logistical one. It could mean the transfer of credits from the books of one echelon to those of another. Such a transfer was purely a paper transaction involving no physical handling of currency. Congress "funded" the War Department by appropriating money for the army's operation. The War Department "funded" overseas theater headquarters by allocating money for their use. From theater headquarters down through various tactical commands, such as army group, air force, army, corps, and division, the delegation of the authority to spend money through allotments and suballotments was known as funding.

Funding usually denoted the process of furnishing disbursing officers with currency, but the term described other physical transactions also. Part of the funding process was the collection from finance officers of currencies they no longer needed, as well as the intentional destruction of currency. So in the physical sense, funding meant regulating the amount of currency in a disbursing officer's possession so that he had sufficient funds to meet his needs without having any unwarranted surplus. Such regulation was accomplished through supplying and collecting currencies as needed. Another, less frequent, usage of *funding* was as a synonym for *pay*. For instance, when troops participating in an invasion were funded with an invasion currency, they were paid in this particular invasion money. The army vested the Finance Department with the responsibility for funding—in all its various meanings.

Methods of Funding

The Finance Department used seven main methods during World War II to obtain currencies for funding in foreign countries. The primary way was to make an outright purchase of the needed currencies from the U.S. Treasury, which had acquired them as the government fiscal agent. When using this method, the Finance Department would make a monthly consolidation of requests for the entire theater simplified the Treasury's work and Most theaters handled these monthly requests through central funding officers. Having one central agency making telegraphic requests for the entire theater simplified the Treasury's work and enabled the theater to maintain close control. After the Office of the Chief of Finance in Washington received the requests, it would inquire if the Treasury held the needed currencies in its foreign depositaries. If the Treasury did, the OCF would send the Treasury a check for the amount of foreign currencies needed, drawing each checks on funds appropriated to the War Department by Congress. The Treasury would then notify its foreign depositaries to credit disbursing officers with the amount requested and purchased.[1]

A second way a finance officer could obtain foreign currencies was to buy them with American dollars, an involved process. The OCF would send a check to the Treasury for the amount in dollars that a disbursing officer needed. The Treasury would credit the dollars to a bank in this country that doubled as a foreign depositary for the overseas bank with which the disbursing officer transacted business. Next, the American bank (the foreign bank's *own* foreign depositary) would instruct the foreign bank to credit the

[1] "Funding Arrangements in Overseas Theaters," OFD ASF, 19 Jun 43. RG 338.

disbursing officer with the specified dollars. After the bank established dollar credits in the disbursing officer's account, he could use them to purchase any foreign currency he needed.

The central funding officer in the United Kingdom used this system to supply his disbursing officers. The Guaranty Trust Company of New York had a London branch. The Treasury would credit dollars to the New York office, and that office would transfer these dollar credits to the London branch. In London they became sterling credits, and as such could be placed at the disposal of disbursing officers. After April 1943, when the Treasury designated the London branch of the Guaranty Trust Company a general depositary, the process of collecting excess currencies was greatly simplified. As a general depositary, the London branch could accept deposits for the Treasury, which meant that currency transactions across the Atlantic could be drastically reduced. The only step a disbursing officer had to take to get sterling credited to his account was to exchange a dollar check at Guaranty Trust for the equivalent amount in sterling. The ease of this operation made funding service in the United Kingdom equal to that available in the United States. Also, it saved a great amount of interest on funds in transit.[2]

An overseas shortcut in the process of exchanging U.S. dollars for foreign currency was selling Treasury checks or actual dollars for local money. Still a simpler way was possible when a disbursing officer's request did not have to be cleared through Washington. When the theater central funding officer had accumulated a sizable amount of foreign currency, he could easily credit his disbursing officers with these local currencies rather than with American dollars.[3] The chief finance officer in swpa[4] used this third, shortcut method to procure guilders from the Netherlands Indies government, as described in chapter 2.

A fourth way to secure foreign currencies was to get advances from governments in liberated and occupied countries. The G-5

[2] Col Ralph A. Koch, Lt Col Harold W. Uhrbrock, and Lt Col Maynard N. Levenick, "The Activities of the Finance Department in the European Theater of Operations," p. 17. RG 338.

[3] "Funding Arrangements in Overseas Theater," OFD ASF, 19 Jun 43. RG 338.

[4] Gen Douglas MacArthur commanded SWPA, as well as USAFFE, the American part of this Allied command.

(the staff section for civil affairs and military government) currency section handled these transactions, securing the money from the foreign government and turning it over to disbursing officers. The amount given the disbursing officer was charged against War Department appropriations. Charges were based on reports made by the individual disbursing officer and G-5. Congress made these appropriations with the assumption that the Finance Department would draw on them when it needed funds. Since the funds had been secured from an Allied government, the equivalent amount of appropriated money would not be used. Hence the Treasury set up a special deposit account to receive charges against the original appropriations. From this special deposit account, the Allied government would be reimbursed for the currency it advanced through G-5 to disbursing officers. These reimbursements came as net troop pay.[5]

The fifth funding method, used in India, resembled that which G-5 employed in liberated and occupied countries. The difference was that in India the army dealt with sovereign governments rather than reconstituted ones. Since American troops in China drew pay in dollars, the only reason the army needed Chinese currency was to make purchases on the local economy. But in India and Burma, the army needed local currencies to pay troops, to spend on the economies, and to make disbursements for Allied governments. The Chinese government maintained a large training center in Ramgarh, India. The army provided officers to train Chinese soldiers in American tactical methods. Also, the Finance Department paid the Chinese with funds advanced by the Indian government on behalf of the British Empire. When the Chinese government furnished the Indian government with monthly estimates of money needed to cover the pay and allowances of its trainees, the latter advanced the necessary rupees to the American army disbursing officer at New Delhi. He, in turn, transferred the funds to disbursing officers actually paying trainees. Initially the advance per month was 450,000 rupees, equivalent to $136,182.15 (one rupee equaled $.302627). By the time the training center reached its peak strength of 80,000 in May 1944, the monthly advance was 2.8 million

[5] See p. 42, for a definition of net troop pay.

rupees ($847,355.60). In the fall of 1944 the British government assumed responsibility for advancing funds for the Chinese. Instead of making monthly advances through the disbursing officers, the British funded disbursing officers' banking accounts directly.[6]

The unique method by which the U.S. Army obtained currency from the Chinese government constituted the sixth type of funding. Before February 1944, the army had bought Chinese National currency dollars at the established rate of 5.125 American dollars to 100 CNC dollars, commonly known as the 20-to-1 rate. The army used this Chinese currency to make purchases on the local economy. By early 1944 extreme inflation had made this rate such an excessive overvaluation of the Chinese money that the American government insisted on some adjustment in the exchange rate. Consequently, the Chinese agreed to furnish the American army with CNC dollars through the Central Bank of China. The bank would supply the army with any amount it needed and would obtain a written receipt for all advances. At some future date negotiations between the two governments would settle the amount due the Chinese. Since no exchange rate was placed upon these funds advanced by the Chinese, they were known as "no-rate funds." The need for a change from the 20-to-1 rate was strikingly demonstrated by fluctuations of the value of the American dollar on the free market in 1944. At various periods the dollar would command from 80 to 600 CNC dollars. In November 1944, the War Department made a settlement with the Chinese government on all obligations in "no-rate funds" incurred before that date. The amount of the settlement was $210 million[7] with an approximate exchange rate of 300-to-1.

Despite the fact that the army, acting as the fiscal agent of the U.S. government, had negotiated the agreement with the Chinese government for "no-rate funds" in February 1944, other American government agencies persisted in spending American money on the free market to buy CNC dollars. The navy, State

---

[6] "History of the Services of Supply (SOS), CBI, Appendix 13, Fiscal and Finance Operations, 28 Feb 42–24 Oct 44," pp. 18, 20. CMH.

[7] Ibid., pp. 22–23; Memorandum of Agreement, Robert P. Patterson, Actg Sec of War, and H. H. Kung, Minister of Finance for the Government of the Republic of China, 25 Nov 44. RG 338.

Department, Office of War Information, Foreign Economic Administration, and Office of Strategic Services spent half a million dollars a month and more for Chinese currency for local purchases. The finance officer in Kunming protested to Washington that it was "unsound" for other agencies to make their own funding arrangements on the black market when "no-rate funds" were available.[8]

The seventh and final funding means resembled obtaining advances from governments in liberated and occupied countries. This method, a requisition from the combined headquarters of the Allied military commander of the area, involved military currency only. The commander-in-chief of the Allied armies, acting as head of the military government, could proclaim military currency legal tender under provisions of international law. No Allied government was responsible for its redemption—that was relegated to the occupied country's government. When a military currency was proclaimed legal tender, it became equivalent to regular local currency. A disbursing officer needing military currency received his supply from the G-5 currency section. The process of reporting and charging War Department appropriations was the same as when funds came from an Allied government. Although the U.S. government bore no responsibility for redeeming military currencies, the army charged expenditures of any military currency overseas against War Department appropriations at the official rate of exchange to determine the amount spent.[9]

The method used for funding in Italy was an adaptation of this basic procedure. The Allied Military Financial Agency, the name of which was later shortened to the Allied Financial Agency, was the central agency through which all Allied military lire flowed. Credit for initiating Allied military lire in February 1943 goes to Harry Dexter White, Assistant Secretary of the Treasury,[10] better remembered for his role in providing the Soviet Union with printing plates for Allied military marks.[11] When the Forty-seventh

8 Radio, Kunming to Chungking and Washington, 14 Dec 44, csf4834. rg 338.

9 "History of the Fiscal Services, 1940–1945," pp. 587–590. cmh.

10 Vladimir Petrov, *Money and Conquest*, p. 77.

11 Walter Rundell, Jr., *Black Market Money*, pp. 42–43.

FDS, attached to the North African theater's Peninsular Base Section, arrived in Naples, it was designated the funding office for all the finance sections of the PBS, as well as the Fifth Army finance units. The Forty-seventh received all its Allied military lire directly from the Allied Financial Agency, rather than from the Allied military commander.[12]

The Pacific

In Pacific operations the several commands faced similar funding problems. After two years, they found it impractical to have individual disbursing officers receive funds directly from the Treasury, so they consolidated funding on a theater basis. From the beginning, both the climate and the folkways of the area hampered funding arrangements. Because of limited opportunities for spending on Pacific islands, much more currency returned to finance channels than had been planned; hence the collection of excess money tempered requests for new funds. Most aspects of funding in the Pacific, as elsewhere, were compounded by shipping uncertainties. Precise calculations counted for little when transportation was unavailable. All these contingencies altered the usual funding formulas, while the liberation of the Philippines and the preparation for the Japanese invasion presented new challenges.

Funding operations in the Pacific showed a definite trend toward centralization. From the start of the war through 1943, the Treasury directly funded officers in various Pacific commands. From the beginning of 1944, funding was centralized in theater fiscal offices. The Treasury, rather than funding disbursing officers' accounts directly, funded the theater fiscal officer. He in turn funded individual disbursing officers under his jurisdiction. This change in funding methods was not uniform or simultaneous. It occurred at different times in the several commands. The principle of centralization followed in each command was, however, substantially the same as each command constantly moved toward an orderly consolidation of the funding process.

When the U.S. Army Forces in the Middle Pacific (USAFMID-

[12] "History of the Peninsular Base Section, NATOUSA, 28 Aug 1943 to 31 Jan 1944," vol. 2. RG 338.

PAC) reorganized its fiscal activities on 1 January 1944, it established a fiscal accounts branch, which received funds for the entire command. This branch handled the funding of disbursing officers in USAFMIDPAC, a function formerly performed by the Treasury. Prior to the change, each disbursing officer had made monthly estimates of currency needs and had sent his requests to Washington. To avoid being overdrawn in his accounts, the disbursing officer usually requested excess funds as a cushion. When funding became centralized in the fiscal accounts branch, individual disbursing officers no longer needed to maintain those excesses, since currency was readily available in the theater. To have funds credited to his account, a disbursing officer had only to radio a request to theater headquarters.[13]

In April 1944 the U.S. Army Forces in the South Pacific Area (USAFISPA) fiscal director began centralizing funding similar to that initiated earlier in the year by USAFMIDPAC. Rather than having each of the twenty-one disbursing officers in USAFISPA prepare separate requests for funds and send them to the Treasury, the fiscal director consolidated the requests. When the Treasury received the consolidated request from the theater, it sent a lump sum to the theater fiscal office, which then apportioned the money among the disbursing officers.[14]

Funding was a comparatively minor problem for USAFISPA. American currency, used for troop pay, was always plentiful because "the navy left a trail of dollars all over the Pacific," according to the USAFISPA fiscal director. Despite an abundance of dollars in the area, the life of paper money was short, partly because of the heavy transfer of bills between the disbursing office and troops. With comparatively few opportunities for expenditures on local markets in USAFISPA, soldiers released their money in fiscal channels such as post exchanges and APO's and through turn-ins to the finance office. Such rapid exchange wore bills out quickly, as did the South Pacific humidity.[15] Because of the durability of silver money

---

[13] "History of Fiscal Mid Pac," pp. 29–30. CMH.

[14] "Organizational History, SOS SPA, 1 Apr to 30 Jun 44." RG 338.

[15] Interview with Col. B. J. Tullington, CO, U.S. Army Finance and Accounts Office, Washington, D.C., 2 Aug 55.

in tropical regions, finance officers sometimes used it for payrolls. Between October 1943 and March 1944, they paid 8 percent of USAFISPA payrolls with silver. But silver currency in army channels did not last even as long as paper money, since natives eagerly acquired coins. New Caledonians withdrew from American servicemen at least half the silver they had received. Soldier spending on New Caledonia, probably the most civilized area in USAFISPA, amounted to $100,000 a month. The theater fiscal officer purchased monthly from the Banque de l'Indochine in Noumea, New Caledonia, an amount in American dollars equivalent to soldiers' expenditures on the local economy. These purchases enabled the fiscal office to maintain a proper supply of funds.[16]

The collection of excess currencies from finance officers, while never as great a problem as getting funds into their hands, was yet of some importance. One disbursing officer's surplus might relieve a critical shortage elsewhere, and it was poor management for a finance officer to keep on hand a substantial excess of currency. The South Pacific Base Command (SPBC) instructed all its finance officers not to let cash on hand exceed current monthly disbursements by more than 50 percent. In areas with limited opportunities for troop spending, such as the SPBC, experience proved that a disbursing officer would make collections from post exchanges and APO's virtually equal to his disbursements. He would therefore have no need for more than a 50 percent surplus. SPBC disbursing officers with funds in excess of this 50 percent had to transfer them to the fiscal officer at command headquarters.[17]

The Sixth Army, whose operations ranged from Australia through the Philippines, had difficulty securing funds after it left its base in Australia. The problem was always the lack of shipping space. In October 1944 the finance section at Sixth Army headquarters, the 171st FDS, located at Hollandia, New Guinea, urgently needed pesos to supply assault troops headed for the Philippines. It received 838 cases of Philippine currency, containing 20 million pesos and weighing thirty tons. Finance men unloaded this money

---

[16] "Organizational History, SOS SPA, 1 Oct 43 to 31 Mar 44." RG 338.

[17] Ltr, Maj R. A. Mislock, Asst Fis Off, Hq SPBC, APO 502, to all DO's, SPBC, 27 Sep 44, sub: Surplus Currency. RG 338.

from the boat, case by case.[18] But even this large supply of currency was insufficient for the needs of assault troops.

Shortly after the 171st FDS received this first shipment of Philippine currency, the S.S. *Monterey* docked at Hollandia with approximately thirty-five more tons of pesos consigned to the 171st. Despite the urgent need for the money to fund assault troops that would land on Leyte on 20 October, a sufficiently high priority for unloading the currency could not be secured. During the three days the vessel was at the pier, only priority combat materiel was scheduled for unloading. On the afternoon before the sailing date, the Sixth Army finance officer obtained permission of the ship's master to unload part of the money from a bulkhead near the waterline on the offshore side of the ship. Using a barge borrowed from the navy, finance men worked all night unloading about 10 million pesos in coin. When the *Monterey* sailed early the next morning, it still had the greater portion of the currency shipment aboard. These funds were unloaded at Oro Bay and shipped back to Hollandia two weeks later. But by the time they arrived, the assault troops had left for Leyte without pesos.[19]

When the Sixth Army finally had ample shipping space for needed currency, it found that combat operations presented new funding problems. The disbursing officer who concentrated all his funds in one forward location ran a great risk. In a memorandum to his subordinates, the Sixth Army finance officer illustrated the virtues of "split loading"—or not putting all the eggs in one basket. A class B agent officer loaded part of his money on one LST (landing ship, tank) and part on another. The LST he was on sustained a direct bomb hit and the funds disappeared, but because he had other funds, he still was able to disburse immediately upon debarkation.[20]

Funding the Philippine Commonwealth government and its

18 Ltr, Maj J. M. Mano, 171st FDS CO, to CG, Base K, APO 72, 17 Dec 44, sub: Unit History, KFIN 314.7. RG 338.
19 Report of the Leyte Operation, 20 Oct–25 Dec 44, Sixth Army, p. 276. CMH.
20 Memo, Col Paul A. Mayo, Fin Off, Sixth Army, to G-4, 23 Jul 45, sub: Concentration and Conservation of Funds. RG 338.

army was a tremendous task for the American army after it liberated the islands from the Japanese. Beginning with the invasion of Leyte on 20 October 1944, the army used a new "Victory Series" of Filipino currency that had been prepared by the Bureau of Engraving and Printing in Washington. A new series of Filipino coins was minted in the United States, again at the request of the provisional Commonwealth government as in prewar days. All issues of currency to the Philippine government were backed by Philippine reserves in the U.S. Treasury, so the funds provided to the Filipinos were not gifts from Uncle Sam.[21] To facilitate payments in the Philippines, the Commonwealth government deposited funds in the Treasury accounts of U.S. Army disbursing officers. After liberation of the islands, the Philippine government's need for currency was constant. The Filipinos placed an immediate order with the Treasury for a total of 288 million peso notes and 12 million pesos in coins.[22] This request was typical of those made in 1945.

In the early summer of 1945 the Philippine Islands served as a buildup center for the invasion of Japan. To cover the currency needs of the Philippine garrison and the estimated troop increase, the U.S. Army Forces in the Western Pacific (AFWESPAC) requisitioned 885 million pesos from the United States. With the sudden cessation of hostilities in August came a complete change of funding plans. The order for pesos was canceled, and a request followed immediately for yen to be flown from the United States. Because of the inevitable delay in getting yen, the G-5 section of the General Headquarters of the Supreme Commander Allied Powers (SCAP) decided to use Japanese yen rather than military yen. To handle funding of yen currency, the Office of the Fiscal Director in Washing lent an officer to SCAP G-5 in Tokyo.[23]

European Theater

Before June 1944, funding in the European theater amounted

[21] "Statement of the Treasury Department on Invasion Currency," Press Service No. 45–45, 14 Mar 45. RG 338.

[22] Radio, MacArthur for Hernandes, 1617 Massachusetts Ave., N.W., Washington, D.C., 6 Mar 45, UAD 62731. RG 338.

[23] "Semi-Annual Report, 1 Jun–31 Dec 1945," AFWESPAC, RG 338.

largely to negotiations between American forces and British banks. But with the spread of theater operations to the Continent, funding grew much more complex. Field operations in the European theater resulted in many variations in funding procedures. Demands of particular situations, such as the unexpectedly rapid advance through France and the large return of currencies, caused procedural alterations according to specific needs. After credits were established in overseas theaters for funding, methods of supplying currencies to the field differed from one situation to another. For example, those finance officers with the air forces were usually provided with air transportation to their funding offices, which enabled them to save a great deal of time in comparison with disbursing officers attached to ground force units. No separate funding facilities existed for the air forces either in the United Kingdom or on the Continent. Their disbursing officers received funds from the Services of Supply, Communications Zone, and armies.[24]

According to original plans for Continental operations, the G-5 currency section would fund. In March 1944, G-5 notified the theater fiscal director that it would be unable to do so. Immediately, the fiscal director made the fiscal branch of the Communications Zone's Advance Section the central funding agency for the invasion. (The Communications Zone had base sections to the rear and an Advance Section closer to the front.) Each disbursing officer going to the Continent was to carry a two-month supply of currency. In planning for the operation, the Advance Section funding office, which operated in Bristol, England, in March 1944, procured 3,387,136,000 French francs, with a value in American dollars of $68,335,468.80. This money was crated in 989 footlockers, each of which weighed ninety-five pounds when packed and waterproofed. Officers and military policemen guarded the money in transit across the channel.

Shortly after the fiscal unit of the Advance Section arrived in France on 20 June 1944, it became evident that its funding program had to be enlarged to handle the unexpectedly large receipts of currency from troops. In addition to pay returning as in the

[24] Koch, Uhrbrock, and Levenick, "Activities of Finance Department," p. 35.

Pacific, other instruments such as checks, captured funds, and mutilated bank notes came in. Twice a week the air forces flew two footlockers full of money back to London to reduce currency buildup in the funding office.

The theater fiscal director had anticipated that the Advance Section's funding service could be discontinued when the central disbursing officer arrived on the Continent. But by the time the central disbursing office became operative in Paris, the armies were so far forward that the theater fiscal director decided the Advance Section should continue funding. So its funding office provided service for the First, Third, Ninth, and Fifteenth armies, as well as air forces and Communications Zone units in forward areas. With the Advance Section funding rather than the central disbursing office, finance officers saved thousands of miles of travel as well as saving much in terms of gasoline, tires, and manpower to guard the currency. During the period the Advance Section funding office operated, it handled, without any loss, currency valued at $1,330,762,105.60.[25]

Collecting currencies no longer needed by finance officers was as much the job of the central disbursing officer in Paris as the supplying of funds in the first place. When finance officers had excess negotiable instruments and currency, the European theater fiscal director instructed that they be turned in to the nearest funding officer. In December 1944 there were eight funding officers on the Continent, scattered in Namur, Belgium; Cherbourg, Dijon, Marseilles, Rennes, and Toul, France; and Luxembourg, Luxembourg. In Rennes, both the Forty-third and Ninety-first FDS's acted as funding offices. The former only furnished currency and the latter only collected it. Finance units operating in the field were to handle all their currency transactions through these funding offices. Only if they were closer to Paris than to any funding office could they deal directly with the central disbursing office. Many finance officers nonetheless thought it necessary to make trips to Paris themselves to deliver their monthly report on foreign currency and to turn in their excesses. The theater fiscal director soon

[25] "History of the Fiscal Section," Hq Ad Sec, ComZ, Office of the Fin Off, APO 113, U.S. Army. RG 338.

ended these sight-seeing excursions, to the undoubted disappointment of many.[26]

A difficult funding problem concerned the lack of coordination at high tactical levels. The army fiscal officer had primary responsibility for funding the corps and divisions below him. Although funding was merely a matter of supplying and evacuating currencies, many army fiscal officers, lacking sufficient knowledge of the principles of logistics, apparently did not conceive of their task in these terms. As a result of this lack of understanding, some army fiscal officers did not employ their organic and attached finance units properly as funding agencies.[27]

The report of the First FDS revealed wastage caused by incompetent advice from army and corps fiscal officers. A team from the unit, located in Neurath, Germany, made a trip to Bad Godesburg to obtain funds. Upon arriving there, they learned that the funding office was in Liége, Belgium. When they drove to Liége, they found the funding office had again been moved to Hersfeld, Germany. This last trip consumed three days, wasting gasoline, equipment, and the time of the disbursing officer, deputy, guards, and drivers. The First FDS laid the responsibility for this egregious mismanagement on the doorstep of the army fiscal officer because he never established proper liaison with his funding officers.[28]

Another incident, which occurred in Japan in September 1945, displayed a similar lack of coordination in funding matters. The situation was considerably more sensitive, so consequently more serious, than that in which the First FDS participated. The Eighth Army urgently needed funds for occupation and redeployment purposes, but could get none because AFWESPAC delayed approval of a disbursing officer's bond.[29] Since there was but one disbursing officer to service the Eighth Army headquarters in Yokohama and other nearby units, the delay in his bond approval was

[26] Ltr, Col W. F. Moriarty, Deputy Fis Dir, Hq ETO, OFD, APO 887, to Fin Offs, 7 Dec 44. RG 338.
[27] Koch, Uhrbrock, and Levenick, "Activities of Finance Department," p. 53.
[28] S/Sgt Glynn E. Hall, "Unit History."
[29] In the European theater a finance officer's bond application was considered approved when it was mailed through channels.

"causing an embarrassing curtailment of disbursing functions." The commanding general of the Eighth Army requested AFWESPAC to use every possible means to expedite the bond approval.[30]

The end of fighting in Europe threw funding and other calculations awry. In the Chanor Base Section in northern France, the Fourteenth FDS served as a funding unit for redeploying troops. When its supply of American currency coming directly from the United States ran low, it could obtain supplements from the United Kingdom. But in September 1945 with conversions for redeploying troops only about half completed, the section's supply of coins and bills was almost exhausted. When no more funds could be obtained in England, a member of the unit had to travel to Casablanca to secure five-, ten-, and twenty-dollar bills.[31] Despite the inconvenience, he may not have considered the trip a hardship.

China-Burma-India Theater

Ordinarily, major funding operations emanated from rear or support areas, those least accessible to enemy attack. When the CBI was a unified command, India was a supply base for operations in Burma and China and funding for combat areas came from there. On 24 October 1944 the Chief of Staff relieved Gen. Joseph W. Stilwell of command and split the organization into the China theater and the India-Burma theater (IBT) because of personal differences between General Stilwell and Generalissimo Chiang Kai-shek.[32] For all practical purposes, this division did not alter the logistical operations in the area. The IBT remained the supply base for the China theater.

The finance office of the IBT's Base Section Two in Calcutta funded most American forces in China, flying much of the currency over the Hump. The average monthly allocation was 20 tons of bills, but in October 1944, planes flew 100 tons to Kunming. While the greater portion of currency transported into China

[30] Radio, Eichelberger, CG, Eighth Army, to Fis Off, AFWESPAC, 27 Sep 45, D 85018. RG 338.

[31] "Historical Report of Operations," Chanor Base Sec, Fiscal Station, APO 562, V-E Day to 20 Feb 46, pp. 2–3. RG 338.

[32] Charles F. Romanus and Riley Sunderland, *Stilwell's Command Problems*, pp. 443–471.

was paper, a considerable amount of gold also went across the Hump. The Chinese government made no secret of its intense desire for gold bullion in payment for American army expenses, but any shipment of gold to China disturbed the routine in finance offices. At both transportation terminals extra officers and men were required for loading and unloading the barrels of gold, as well as in making an exacting account of funds involved in the shipment. To supply more gold to the China theater, the finance officer in Calcutta had to request an increased tonnage allotment in flights over the Hump. Before May 1945, the army had flown less than $10 million in gold into China, but between May and December, it shipped $108,137,291.11 in gold. After the fighting ceased, American forces in China were funded primarily through Shanghai.[33]

Funding operations in the CBI were not always limited to currency. The army paid for many services in backward regions with goods. On one occasion the CBI requested the OFD in Washington to procure Siamese ticals, Indo-Chinese piastres, and sewing needles. The Washington office radioed back that it could obtain the needles, but not the ticals or piastres.[34]

Destruction of Currency

A cardinal principle of warfare has long been to deny the enemy any logistical advantage. The Russian removal of grain and cattle before Napoleon's invading Grande Armée in 1812 stretched French supply lines and systematically weakened the troops. Then the burning of Moscow shortly after its fall deprived the French of its value. During the undeclared war between Japan and China in the late 1930's, the Chinese successfully frustrated the invaders with their scorched earth policy. Similarly, army disbursing officers had standing instructions in World War II to destroy currency in their possession if capture became imminent. When currency became no longer fit for use, whether through burning, mutilation, wear and tear, or contamination, it was also destroyed. This destruction of currency reversed the principle of funding, but nonetheless was an aspect of the process since disbursing officers' accounts reflected negative figures as well as positive ones.

[33] "History of Base Section Two, SOS IBT," 21 May 45–31 Dec 45. RG 338.
[34] Radio, Carter to Hq CBI, 24 Oct 44, SPFET WAR 51037. RG 338.

The first instance of currency destruction in World War II came with the fall of the Philippines. When American forces retreated to Corregidor, they carried most of the currency on Luzon with them. As the surrender of the island fortress drew near, finance officers began systematically disposing of funds. On 1 March 1942, the finance officer for the U.S. Forces in the Philippines (USFIP), the finance officer at Fort Mills, and a Philippine army officer burned 20 million pesos. On 27 April 1942 they burned another 30 million. Then the USFIP finance officer supervised destruction of currency in the vaults on Corregidor. Soldiers cut up the money with scissors and burned some. On the night of 5 May, before the next day's surrender, they burned the remaining bills—1 million pesos and $40,000 in American dollars. When the bills ignited, many soldiers gave free rein to their imaginations and speculated on what they could do with the money under happier circumstances. One Tennessee farm boy decided he would be glad to trade the whole lot of it for a chance to be back home. Some with exhibitionist bents, like the naval aide to the high commissioner of the Philippine Islands, could not resist the temptation to light cigarettes with $100 bills. In addition to destroying money, finance officers on Corregidor also burned Treasury checks. They reported details of this currency destruction to the Chief of Finance by radio.[35]

If paper money was easy enough to destroy, coins presented a greater problem. The safest solution was to scatter them in deep water. Sometimes when no body of water was available, coins were buried. The commander on Corregidor decided to preserve for American use, while denying them to the Japanese, the millions of silver pesos on the island. Finance officers devised a plan to dump the coins in the bay. They hauled pesos in their original metal containers to the bay and transferred them to a navy barge. When the barge reached the spot where the funds were to be dumped, azimuth readings were carefully plotted on harbor charts. Then the

[35] Col John R. Vance, "Report of Operations, Finance Officer, USFIP, Dec 8, 1941–May 6, 1942," 30 Sep 44, pp. 5, 10. RG 338; *Sixth Annual Report of the United States High Commissioner to the Philippine Islands to the President and Congress of the United States Covering the Fiscal Year July 1, 1941 to June 30, 1942*, p. 152.

The tent office of the Second Corps finance section, Tebessa, North Africa, 8 February 1943. *U.S. Army photograph.*

Adding machines were indispensable to finance offices preparing enlisted payrolls, as on Kiska Island, Alaska, 9 November 1943. Note the improvised lampshades. *U.S. Army photograph.*

The base finance office at Port Moresby, New Guinea, had more suitable facilities on 19 January 1944 than those offered by tents in the foregoing photographs. *U.S. Army photograph.*

Among the equipment in the Port Moresby office were coin counting and wrapping machines. *U.S. Army photograph.*

Two officers handle a package of new bills in the vault of the Sixth Army finance office, Hollandia, Dutch New Guinea, 26 August 1944. The diamond on the left collar of the man in the center was the Finance Department's insignia. *U.S. Army photograph.*

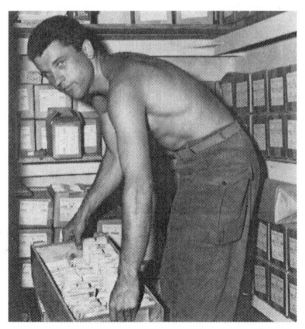

Maj. C. E. Ego stores Type B military yen in a vault on Okinawa on 9 July 1945. At that time the army planned to stage the invasion of Japan from Okinawa and to use the military yen as invasion currency. The vault was an old navy pontoon. *U.S. Army photograph.*

Types of Currency Used by U.S. Army in World War II

(Currency photographs courtesy of C. Frederick Schwan)

Ten dollars, Hawaiian overstamped

Ten pounds, Bank of England

Ten shillings, Australian

One yuan, Central Reserve Bank of China, 1936

Ten yuan, Central Reserve Bank of China, 1940

Five hundred francs, Banque Nationale de Belgique, 1943

Fifty francs, Banque de France, 1939

Ten francs, Banque de France, 1941

Two francs, Free French issue for Oceania, 1942

One lira, Italian

One lira, Allied Military Currency

Fifty lire, Allied Military Currency

Five hundred drachmas, Greek

Twenty Reichsmark, 1939

One Reichsmark, Wehrmacht payment order
(not legal tender)

Ten Reichspfennig, Wehrmacht emergency scrip

One thousand mark, Allied Military Currency (dash before serial number identifies Soviet printing)

One Japanese yen, Type B, Allied Military Currency

One thousand Japanese yen, Type B, Allied Military Currency

One hundred Japanese yen, Type A, Allied Military Currency

Any time that soldiers captured currency from dead enemies, they were to turn it over to their finance office for accounting. After this Japanese soldier died on New Georgia on 1 August 1943, these infantrymen confiscated his money. *U.S. Army photograph.*

When American troops captured a bank in Manila in March 1945, they found themselves waist deep in Japanese bills that Finance had to account for. *U.S. Army photograph.*

This Chinese currency fell to earth when a transport plane exploded in midair near Kunming in 1944. As supplier of the funds, the American army had to guard and account for the money. *U.S. Army photograph.*

Enlisted men kept their SIPR with them always as evidence of payments. It was especially useful when the individual was separated from his unit, for it enabled him to draw a partial payment. *U.S. Army photograph.*

The enlisted pay section of the Tenth Army finance office on Okinawa did not insist on a formal dress code in July 1945—either for its staff or for its customers. *U.S. Army photograph.*

More formality prevailed in this finance office in Bizerte, North Africa in January 1944. At the right end of the counter men could send money home via a personal transfer account (PTA) or put funds into a soldier's deposit, which earned 5 percent interest. *U.S. Army photograph.*

The enlisted pay section of the 127th Finance Disbursing Section (FDS) prepares December 1944 payrolls at its office in Namur, Belgium. The sign on top of the trunk promoted war bonds and insurance as ways of reducing cash in the hands of troops. *U.S. Army photograph.*

Maj. Leonard H. Van Horne and WOJG Ellard L. Johnson of the 127th FDS check payrolls against the forms on which they entrusted money to agents for the December 1944 payday. *U.S. Army photograph.*

S/Sgt Frank J. Leslie, Lt. Col. Arthur B. Dwinnell, and CWO Bert L. Beck of the Fifth Infantry Division finance office ascertain they they have the necessary funds for the May 1944 payday in County Down, Northern Ireland. *U.S. Army photograph.*

Men of the 127th FDS in Namur, Belgium prepare for the December 1944 payday by putting money sufficient to cover each payroll in a separate bag for agents to collect. *U.S. Army photograph.*

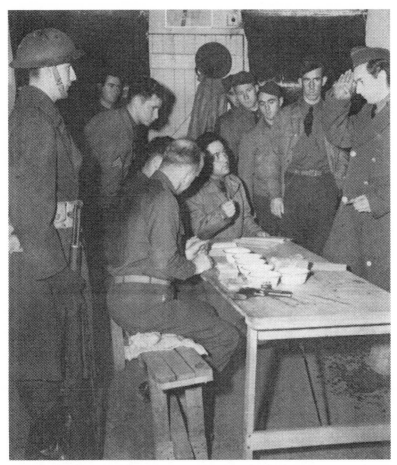

Once finance offices had made their computations, the troops could be paid, as in Northern Ireland in March 1942. In case the guard's M-1 rifle did not offer sufficient protection, the officer kept his .45 pistol handy on the table. *U.S. Army photograph.*

Payday for flyers of the Forty-ninth Squadron of the Fourteenth Fighter Group at Berteaux, North Africa, 11 February 1943. *U.S. Army photograph.*

Lt. Col. Robert L. Phinney, finance officer of the Thirty-sixth Division, gives Cpl. William A. Warrick a partial payment on 6 January 1944 in Italy. Warrick sent the remainder of his pay back home. Texans proudly wore the T-patch of their National Guard division in the campaigns of North Africa and Italy. *U.S. Army photograph.*

These soldiers bound for Normandy draw invasion pay in French francs at a marshaling area in England on 28 May 1944. The finance officer is Capt. Charles R. Williams. *U.S. Army photograph.*

A WAC receives a partial payment at Winchester, England on 13 July 1944 before shipment to France. *U.S. Army photograph.*

Using an upturned footlocker for a table, Lt. Sam T. Jackson on 11 August 1944 issues francs for the invasion of southern France. Italy was the staging area for that invasion. *U.S. Army photograph.*

Payday near the German border on 11 September 1944. A GI blanket over the hood of a jeep improves the work surface. *U.S. Army photograph.*

The crew of an M-54 in an anti-aircraft artillery battery get paid in the field near Saverne, France on 1 February 1945. *U.S. Army photograph.*

On 8 April 1945 the Sixth Army finance office enabled these Filipino troops to get paid for the first time since December 1941. Their delight is obvious. *U.S. Army photograph.*

Even the partial payment of 250 yen ($25) in May 1945 brings a smile to Pfc. Clifford O. Hodge of the 77th Infantry Division on Okinawa. Hodge had fought in the Pacific during the entire war. *U.S. Army photograph.*

"Get 'em Paid!," Finance's unofficial motto, applied to dependents' allotments, as well as to soldiers. Here, in August 1942, the precursor of the Office of Dependency Benefits prepared family allowance checks. *Left to right*: Maj. F. J. Wesley, Col. Harold N. Gilbert, Lt. Col. T. G. McGullock, Col. Thruston Hughes, and Col. John W. Clark. *U.S. Army photograph.*

money went overboard. After the liberation of the Philippines, navy divers recovered this currency and turned it over to the Base X finance officer in Manila. Before he could take the currency into his disbursing account, it had to be thoroughly cleaned of algae and barnacles.[36]

Policies on the destruction of currency varied from theater to theater and from time to time. It would have seemed logical to have established a uniform procedure early in the war, but such was not the case. In the early years of the fighting, the South Pacific Area had transferred currency unfit for circulation to the San Francisco FOUSA. Such transfers involved shipping risks and prevented disbursing officers from clearing their accounts speedily because of the delay in getting receipts for the destroyed currency. On 25 May 1944 the theater established its own currency destruction committee, which received and destroyed all unusable funds from the South Pacific area.[37]

When currency was destroyed for any reason, finance officers had to make full reports of the circumstances. If time permitted, as in the Philippines, before funds were disposed of serial numbers on bills were recorded and reported to the Treasury or the Chief of Finance. Or when money was lost because of a ship's sinking or an airplane crash, a full account of the circumstances was required. Australian Commonwealth banks serving as official depositaries for American funds gave full credit for burned currency if reports were submitted, even though only fragments of the bills remained. On the other hand, when reports were not made, banks would give only partial credit. The Commonwealth Bank in Sydney acted as a clearinghouse for mutilated currency. It deposited in the official account of the finance office at Headquarters, Base Section Three, U.S. Army Services of Supply (USASOS, the USAFFE SOS) in Brisbane whatever credit it gave for the mutilated currency received. The

---

[36] Austin Nisonger, Memorandum for the files, sub: Account of the Treasurer, U.S., with the Treasury of the Philippines, 6 Aug 43. RG 338; interview with Col Royal G. Jenks (Ret), 17 Aug 55; interview with Col A. H. Miller, Asst Chief of Fin for Plans and Programs, 15 Aug 56; interview with Maj D. E. Benson, Office of the Asst Chief of Fin for Plans and Programs, 21 Dec 56.

[37] "Organizational History," SOS SPA, 1 Apr to 30 Jun 44. RG 338.

finance office in turn forwarded a check for that amount to the disbursing officer involved.[38]

The China theater presented finance officers with detailed instructions on currency disposition in January 1945. Before funds were destroyed, the finance officer was to consult the senior officer present. Then he had to make a list of the bills by type, such as silver certificates or Federal Reserve Notes, series, and denominations. He did not have to record serial numbers unless they were readily available. If three distinterested officers were present, they witnessed and certified the destruction. The same procedure prevailed when Chinese currency was destroyed, except that serial numbers had to be recorded for the benefit of the Chinese government.[39] Considering the great inflation of Chinese money, this requirement seemed suspiciously like Oriental face saving.

Disbursing officers in the IBT had to send unfit paper currency by registered mail to the theater's central fiscal office. Currency was considered unfit if badly burned, blood soaked, or if it had "a repulsive saturation of body fluids." When the finance officer received notice from the currency destruction committee that his funds had been disposed of, he dropped the amount from his accountability.[40]

Although the army's funding responsibilities were fairly uniform in all overseas areas, problems varied according to the type of operation and locale. Long supply lines in the Pacific and Far East, as well as attendant shipping uncertainties, obviously created more funding difficulties for those areas than the European Continent experienced. Even with all the preparation for Continental operations, the theater fiscal officer had to make many adjustments in funding once American troops secured a foothold in France. The dynamics of combat simply did not conform with advance planning, and the result was poor coordination and wastage. Where difficulties were naturally greater, administrative red tape com-

[38] 2d Lt J. M. Taylor, "Monthly Historical Report," Office of the Fin Off, Hq Base Three, USASOS, APO 923, Jul 44, 314.7. RG 338.

[39] "Disbursing Information Number 4," China Theater, 6 Jan 45. RG 338.

[40] India-Burma Fiscal Memorandum 8, 14 Mar 45, IBT. RG 338.

pounded the problems, as in the case of AFWESPAC's delaying approval of a disbursing officer's bond.

Notwithstanding specific inadequacies, Finance handled its funding responsibilities reasonably well. Disbursing officers were naturally frustrated when they lacked needed currency, but for the most part, the lack of funds was a minor problem. When considering shipping priorities among munitions, food, and currency, one can readily agree that the last was least important to the troops' welfare; therefore it is understandable that the cause of most funding difficulties was beyond Finance's control. Funding requirements for invasions and intelligence operations logically commanded a high priority and thereby received special attention from finance offices.

CHAPTER *5*

Funding for Invasions and Intelligence

WHEN American soldiers stormed foreign beaches in World War II, they carried along with their weapons and other equipment a special kind of money, termed invasion currency, which assured them a negotiable medium of exchange on the local market. The army, as an organization, also used invasion currencies because it had to have an adequate supply of money. A liberated populace would be much more likely to furnish needed goods and labor if the army could pay in a readily acceptable currency.[1]

Since the army could never be certain of the currency situation in an invaded territory, it had to furnish its own funds. According to international law, the Hague conventions, and decisions of the U.S. Supreme Court, an occupying power can decree the legal tender. Any currency the army chose to use in an invaded country therefore became legal tender by authority of the military commander.[2]

The army used two types of invasion currencies in World War II: currencies denominated in the monetary units of invaded countries and currency denominated in American dollars. Examples of the first type were Allied military lire, Allied military marks, and supplemental military yen. Yellow seal and Hawaii overstamped dollars represented the latter.

Those invasion currencies denominated in lire, marks, and yen became legal tender through the decree of the military commander and not that of the U.S. government. The government consequently claimed it was not liable for their redemption.[3] Before the

---

[1] Statement of the Treasury Department on Invasion Currency, 14 Mar 45. RG 338.

[2] Dooley vs U.S. (1901), 152 U.S. 222.

[3] Ltr, Secretary of the Treasury, to Senator Robert Taft, 17 Dec 45. RG 338.

armed forces started using invasion currencies denominated in foreign monetary units, the secretaries of War, State, Treasury, and Navy wrote a memorandum for President Roosevelt proposing the government's policy. They stated that the American government at the outset of invasions should make no move to compensate foreign governments for invasion currencies. With the liberation of friendly countries, restored governments were to give full compensation to the liberating army. When the army conquered enemy countries, the economy of the vanquished nation was supposed to support the occupying force. The secretaries thought that if the president volunteered compensation from the beginning, the administration would be a "perfect target for 'hind-sight' critics." Postponing settlement would give the government, rather than its critics, the "advantage of 'hind-sight' and also make possible appropriate consultation with Congress if that should be deemed necessary or desirable."[4] The president followed the suggestion of the secretaries. With dollar-denominated currencies, the American government was the issuing agency and was hence responsible for redeeming these currencies.

Before the outbreak of World War II, the Japanese had pioneered the use of military scrip in China. In 1938 the Japanese army initiated yen notes exclusively for its Chinese operations. This yen currency circulated at par with CNC dollars, but was neither redeemable in Japan nor exchangeable with other foreign money.[5]

The Nazi government, in contrast with the American, issued a German invasion currency that had a fixed rate of exchange with local currencies but that was not redeemable in Germany. This currency, first used in Poland, was called Reichskreditkassenscheine (Reich credit treasury notes), and the notes were printed in denominations of half, one, two, five, twenty, and fifty marks. When the Wehrmacht entered any foreign country, it issued decrees making Reichskreditkassenscheine legal tender at a certain ratio with indig-

[4] Memo for the president from the secretaries of State, Treasury, War and Navy, re: Position of State, Treasury, War and Navy departments on Negotiations with Exiled Governments Concerning Use of Their Currency for Military Operations, n. d. RG 338.

[5] Harry H. Bell, "Monetary Problems of Military Occupation," *Military Affairs* 6 (1942): 78–79.

enous currency. The rate of exchange was usually the pre-invasion rate between Reichsmarks and the local money. German troops received their pay in Reichskreditkassenscheine. Since they were legal tender only in the occupied areas, soldiers had to spend their money there or forfeit its value. After 1 January 1945, the Wehrmacht adopted another military currency, the Verrechnungsscheine (payment orders or nonnegotiable credit notes; literally "clearing account notes"). This latter currency, denominated in one, five, ten, and fifty marks, was used when troops moved from one country to another and was not legal tender in Germany or occupied lands. German soldiers' currency was converted into Verrechnungsscheine before they moved into another country. After they arrived at their destination, Verrechnungsscheine would be converted to local currency or Reichskreditkassenscheine.[6] Verrechnungsscheine, then, were comparable to the American army's military payment orders.[7] By using these invasion currencies, the German government effectively transferred the total cost of the occupation to the defeated country.[8]

German treaties of occupation with Holland, France, Norway, Greece, Yugoslavia, and Belgium not only forced those countries to shoulder occupation costs, but also enabled Germany to inflate those costs at will. Between 1940 and 1944 the Dutch, Belgians, and

[6] Hans J. Dernberg, "Currency Techniques in Military Operations," 11 Apr 45; Memo, Cmdr Frank A. Southard, Jr., Financial Advisor, G-5, to Fis Dir, 31 May 45, sub: Certain Types of German Military Currency, G-5/123.9. RG 338.

[7] To minimize the use of Treasury checks overseas, Congress legislated that military payment orders could be substituted where servicemen were paid in local currencies. These U.S. Military Disbursing Officers' Payment Orders were issued in exchange for cash, just as Treasury checks had been. The new military payment order had to be used in all individual transactions where checks had been payable in dollars. Use of these instruments, which could be redeemed only by a military disbursing officer, rather than the official Treasury check, which had wide acceptability, aided the control of foreign currency manipulators. With military payment orders, there was less danger of U.S. currency becoming involved in the black market. They were used in situations where local currency was exchanged for dollar instruments, where personal funds were taken from one theater to another or to or from the United States, and as a substitute for spearhead deposits (WD Cir 159, 31 May 45. RG 338).

[8] Thomas Reveille, *The Spoil of Europe*, pp. 115–120.

French had to pay Germany ten times the actual cost of the occupation. A French functionary protested that for the funds extorted from France, Germany could have maintained 18 million troops there. The Reich used its excess credit to divest occupied lands of both raw and fabricated goods. By fixing exchange rates between Reichsmarks and currencies of occupied nations, Germany purchased goods at a fraction of their actual values. It also bought on credit, the redemption of which depended on Germany's winning the war. Thus, Germany held all the economic trumps in its occupation policy.[9]

North Africa

The army's first occasion to use an invasion currency was in the North African operation, beginning November 1942. The army had no way of predicting its reception by the French provisional government, which nominally was loyal to Vichy. Since the army could not depend on using franc currency, some alternative had to be devised. During planning for the invasion, Henry Morgenthau, Jr., recommended that the army use yellow seal dollars as its invasion currency. They could be easily differentiated from standard "blue seal" dollars, so if any appreciable number fell into Axis hands, the entire series could have been declared nonlegal tender. The State and War departments agreed with the Treasury on the adoption of yellow seal dollars as an invasion currency.[10]

The army, in using American money in North Africa, did not face the situation confronting Austria-Hungary when that country used its own currency in occupied countries in World War I. Wartime economic conditions had already made the metallic backing of the Austro-Hungarian currency inadequate, so when the dual monarchy extended the use of its money into occupied territories, the

[9] Gordon Wright, *The Ordeal of Total War, 1939–1945*, pp. 119–120.

[10] Memo, Robert P. Patterson, Under Secretary of War, for the Secretary of War, 5 Aug 42, sub: Money for U.S. Troops in Europe. RG 338. Throughout the war, some confusion existed about the nomenclature of yellow seal dollars. In some quarters, they were persistently referred to as "gold seal" dollars. The gold seal dollar went out with the gold standard in 1933, so any gold seal currency in circulation during World War II was not legal tender, and any reference to the army's wartime invasion currency as "gold seal" dollars was inaccurate.

currency suffered from further inflation. While economic conditions in World War II caused some inflation of the dollar, the use of yellow seal dollars overseas did not contribute notably to this inflation.[11]

Gen. Dwight D. Eisenhower, commander of the North African invasion, known as Operation TORCH, had requested the War Department in July 1942 to use something other than the yellow seal dollar as an invasion currency.[12] But Gen. George C. Marshall, War Department Chief of Staff, informed Eisenhower that since a sufficient supply of French currency could not be depended on, yellow seal dollars would have to be adopted.[13]

In addition to the yellow seal currency scheduled for the North African invasion, the War Department authorized $700,000 in gold coins for the initial phase of the operation. The Twelfth Air Force used the coins in escape kits, and Gen. George S. Patton's forces spent them to reward native informers and collaborators and to speed performance of essential services in cases where natives preferred specie to paper money.[14]

Shortly before the beginning of Operation TORCH, a blunder involving the invasion currency almost sabotaged the secrecy of the mission. Yellow seal dollars were printed in the States, shipped to London, and stored in the Bank of England. One bright morning during the invasion mounting, an armored contingent roared up to the front door of the Bank of England. The commanding officer thought his task was to take the invasion currency from the bank to the ships. His soldiers were primed for action, with rifles loaded and bayonets fixed. Jeeps with .50 caliber machine guns stood ready to guard the transfer. Such a flourish naturally signified a military operation of some moment. Before any soldiers commandeered the bank, the staff of the North African theater fiscal

---

[11] Ernst H. Feilchenfeld, *The International Economic Law of Belligerent Occupation*, p. 76.

[12] Radio, Eisenhower, London, to AGWAR, 13 Jul 42, 317. RG 338.

[13] Radio, Marshall, for CG, U.S. Forces, London, 2 Sep 42, R-331; radio, Eisenhower, to AGWAR, 25 Aug 42, 1498. RG 338.

[14] Radio, Marshall, for CG, U.S. Forces, London, 2 Sep 42, R-331; cable, Eisenhower, to AGWAR, 19 Sep 42, 2415. RG 338.

director persuaded the armored officer to withdraw his force as unobtrusively as possible.[15]

As the date of the invasion, 8 November 1942, drew near, many cables sped between London and Washington to insure sufficient invasion currency at the right points. From London, General Eisenhower requested that the navy transmit an additional $20 million in yellow seal bills to the British at Gibraltar. Marshall cabled Eisenhower that the navy could not deliver the money because such a shipment would require diverting a cruiser or battleship and none could be spared. But he stated further than an unlimited amount of yellow seal currency could be provided in five days plus transportation time. When Eisenhower asked what amount General Patton was carrying with his D-5 force, Marshall informed him the sum was $20 million in yellow seal dollars. On 24 October, Marshall indicated that the War Department had done what it could. He cabled Eisenhower: "The currency situation . . . [is] now in your hands. . . . Upon request every assistance will be furnished from this end."[16]

Shortly after the military operations in North Africa began, it became evident through the cooperation of the French in Algiers and Tunisia that there was sufficient local currency for all disbursing needs. Also, there were presses that could print as much franc currency as might be required. When the American command discovered these conditions, it quickly withdrew the invasion currency in favor of North African francs. In Morocco, too, enough francs circulated so that the American army did not have to rely exclusively on yellow seal dollars. As soon as a private American firm printed sufficient Moroccan francs, the army withdrew the invasion currency and disbursed only francs.[17]

Currency used in any military operation, whether a major invasion or a small-scale raid, was an extremely sensitive factor. Before the invasion of southern France, oss (Office of Strategic

---

[15] Interview with Lt Col T. W. Archer, Office of the Comptroller of the Army, 3 Mar 54.

[16] Cable, Eisenhower, to AGWAR, 22 Oct 42, 3944; cable, Marshall, to CG, ETO, 24 Oct 42, R-2395. RG 338.

[17] *Logistical History of* NATOUSA-MTOUSA, p. 396.

Services) troops staged a raid on the Riviera. Against the advice of the Mediterranean theater fiscal director, the force carried brand new francs. Brig. Gen. Leonard H. Sims thought these crisp bills would certainly betray their source when they appeared in circulation, but his protest was ignored. When the time came for the raiding party to signal an American submarine lying off the coast, the submarine received no message. Possibly the Germans had recognized the new notes when they turned up and surmised their source. In any event, the raiding party was never heard from again.[18]

The Pacific

The second area where the army used invasion currency was in the Pacific, where the Hawaii overstamped dollar was most frequently employed. In July 1942 the U.S. government instituted this special series of American dollars in the Territory of Hawaii as part of a scorched-earth policy. Each bill in the series had "HAWAII" overstamped in large letters. In the summer of 1942, the American government could not predict the success of Japanese aggression. If the Japanese conquered the Hawaiian Islands, the U.S. government wanted to make sure they would not benefit from any currency captured. In the event of a successful Japanese invasion, the entire Hawaii overstamped series would have been voided as legal tender. In October 1944, after the danger of Japanese aggression in the Central Pacific had passed, restrictions on the use of overstamped dollars were lifted. Standard American dollars could circulate in Hawaii once more, but the Hawaii series remained legal tender. The first use of Hawaiian dollars as invasion currency was in the Gilbert Islands operation of November 1943. Thereafter, the overstamped series was used in all Central Pacific campaigns through the invasion of the Palau Islands in September 1944.[19]

In Pacific fighting, the army employed three invasion currencies denominated in the monetary units of the invaded areas: the Netherlands East Indies guilder, the Philippine Victory peso, and Type B military yen. The Netherlands government-in-exile

[18] Interview with Lt Col Archer.

[19] "History of Fiscal Mid Pac," pp. 21–23, 14–15. CMH; Dernberg, "Currency Techniques in Military Operations."

furnished the army with the guilders it used on New Guinea and other islands in the Netherlands East Indies. As of 20 September 1944, the Netherlands Indies Commission had furnished the U.S. Army Forces in the Far East (USAFFE) with 95,336,057.075 guilders. At the existing rate of exchange of 1.8835 guilders to the dollar, the dollar equivalent was $50,616,435.[20] For the return to the Philippines, the army used a new series of pesos. These Philippine Victory peso notes, printed in the United States, were backed by silver reserves held in the U.S. Treasury for the Philippine Commonwealth government.[21] The army prepared Type B supplemental military yen for the invasion of Okinawa. At the time of the invasion, the army announced that these yen would circulate at par with yen notes from the banks of Japan, Chosen, and Taiwan. During the Japanese occupation of the Ryukyus, all three of these yen notes circulated.[22]

The insular nature of Pacific warfare made funding problems in each operation different, yet headquarters prescribed that each invasion force carry with it a three-month supply of money. The size and nature of each landing, as well as the transportation facilities and distances involved, became part of the logistical equation. The reckoning of the amount of currency needed for each island had to be more exact than in Europe, for instance, since in the Pacific it was more difficult to maintain contact with funding centers. On small islands like Saipan and Iwo Jima, there was no supply-furnishing rear area, or Communications Zone, as in the European and Mediterranean theaters. Once an island operation began, it was considered logistically self-contained. The fiscal office at Headquarters, USAFMIDPAC, in Honolulu acted as the central funding agency for most Pacific operations. It furnished currency for units that went into the Marianas, Bonins, Marshalls, Philip-

---

[20] Ltr, G. C. C. J. de Beaufort, Asst to the Chairman, Economic Financial Shipping Mission of the Kingdom of the Netherlands, Board for the Netherlands Indies, Surinam, and Curacao, to Mr. Harold Glasser, Asst Director of the Division of Monetary Research, Treasury Department, 20 Sep 44, File 4.23. RG 338.

[21] Statement of the Treasury Department on Invasion Currency, 14 Mar 45. RG 338.

[22] "Tenth Army Action Report, Report of Operations in the Ryukyus Campaign, Chapter 11, Staff Section Reports, Section XIX—Finance." RG 338.

pines, Okinawa, and Japan. USAFMIDPAC shipped most of its currency from Hawaii to the forward areas by air.[23]

In preparation for the GALVANIC campaign, the taking of Makin Island in the Gilberts in November 1943, the finance officer computed funds required for three months on the basis of the tentative strength of the garrison force. The garrison force finance officer took these funds to Makin in the initial phase of the operation. In his computations, he did not have to give much weight to the problem of resupply, for it was evident that most of the funds would stay in circulation on the island. He arranged with the post exchange and postal officers to exchange Treasury checks for their cash. In this way the finance office could use and reuse currency with only a small need for resupply from Hawaii. Since it was impossible to determine exactly how much currency would be needed on Makin, Central Pacific Area headquarters gave the garrison force commander authority to obligate funds as necessary. Headquarters established sufficient credits in the garrison force account to cover any obligations. After conditions on the island became stabilized, credits were adjusted to actual needs.[24]

Funding arrangements for the Marshall Islands campaign were similar to those used for Makin. The disbursing officer arrived on Kwajalein in February 1944 with $787,050 in Hawaiian overstamped currency and silver. This amount would cover the pay needs of the garrison force for three months. In planning his currency needs, the finance officer considered that most of the funds would stay in circulation on the island and would be available for reimbursement. As usual on the Pacific islands, the silver supply on Kwajalein did not last as long as planned and additional coins had to be flown to the island a month after the invasion. From 16 October 1944 until 22 July 1945, the Kwajalein finance office paid troops in the entire Marshall and Gilbert islands area. Frequently during this period the garrison at Eniwetock radioed Kwajalein for currency to pay transient soldiers aboard the army transports docked at the port. When the finance officer received

[23] Interview with Col T. D. Ashworth, Chief, Budget Division, OCF, 26 Jul 55.

[24] "History of Fiscal Mid Pac," pp. 13–14.

these requests, he flew the money immediately to Eniwetok so that payments could be made before the transports sailed.[25]

As the finance officer for the FORAGER operation planned the fiscal aspects of the invasion of Saipan, he calculated according to the customary three-month supply of currency. After he determined he would need $1,839,600, he asked Hawaiian banks if they had the money. They told him they could not supply the funds at that time and would be unable to do so without four to six weeks' notice. The finance officer informed the commanding general of the Central Pacific Area of the hitch, and the general arranged for the necessary funds to be shipped from the United States by airplane and boat. The money was made up of Hawaiian series dollars up through $20 bills and American coins through the half dollar. In making arrangements for shipping currency from Hawaii to Saipan, the finance officer had to devise weight and space loading tables because of the money's excessive weight. Following the principle of split loading, the finance officer divided his currency into two shipments. He took the first half with him in the first wave to land on Saipan, and the assistant brought the remainder with the second landing. In both cases the money, stored in field safes, had to be guarded twenty-four hours a day. Funding arrangements for FORAGER proved adequate with the exception of the coin supply, for hoarding natives quickly withdrew the silver coins from circulation.[26]

Planning for funding the Iwo Jima invasion anticipated the need for a ninety-day supply of currency, as in the other Pacific island landing. The supply of $2,036,800 was denominated entirely in U.S. bills and coins, in accordance with a directive from the commander-in-chief of the Pacific Ocean areas. The finance office had little demand for $20 and $10 bills because it received in exchange for Treasury checks many large bills from the navy,

[25] Ibid., pp. 15–17.

[26] Ltr, Capt David S. Price, Fin Off, Hq Army Garrison Force, APO 244 (Saipan), to CG, APO 244, 10 Aug 44, sub: FORAGER Operation; ltr, Maj David S. Price, Fin Off, Army Garrison Force, APO 244, to CG, AGF, 20 Oct 44, sub: Supplement to FORAGER Operation Report to Include 30 Sep 44. RG 338; "History of Fiscal Mid Pac," pp. 17–19.

marines, post exchange, and APO. The demand for coins however, was "unexpectedly large."[27] It is hard to imagine how by the spring of 1945 the demand for coins on Pacific islands could be "unexpectedly large"; the only conclusion one could draw is that funding estimates never were revised in light of operating experience.

For the invasion of Okinawa the Joint Chiefs of Staff prescribed use of the Type B, supplemental military yen. Regular Japanese yen, as well as yen from the banks of Chosen and Taiwan, were acceptable for exchange on a one-for-one basis. No other currencies were legal tender on Okinawa. As in the case with occupied European countries, where local economies were developed to some degree, funding on Okinawa was handled through G-5. The primitive economies and governments on islands like Saipan, Iwo Jima, and Makin had not warranted the army's establishing a formal section for civil affairs and military government.

For the Ryukyus campaign, Finance devised partial payments for troops. They would get paid a maximum of twenty-five dollars (250 yen) in May 1945 and forty dollars in June. This June payment would settle pay accounts through that month. Any credits remaining in a soldier's account after the cash settlement were to be converted into some form of savings, such as war bonds or soldier's deposits. In keeping with these plans, G-5 got a request for 200 million yen. Due to G-5's inability to secure the funds, finance officers could not make even these modest partial payments in May. Soldiers drew ten dollars in both May and June; therefore, a larger amount of credits than had been anticipated remained in soldiers' accounts to be converted into enforced savings. Actual funding on Okinawa was handled by one of the four disbursing officers on the island, the finance officer of the 229th FDS.[28]

The Continent

As invasion currencies got thorough testing in the Mediterranean and Pacific areas, the Continental operations begun with

[27] Fis Off, HUSAFPOA, Participation in Iwo Jima Operation, 5 Apr 45. RG 338.

[28] "Tenth Army Action Report, Report of Operations in the Ryukuyus Campaign, Chapter 11, Staff Section Reports, Section XIX—Finance." RG 338.

the invasion of Normandy proved Finance's greatest funding challenge. When the Allied forces invaded France, the operation differed from the earlier invasion of Italy in one notable respect. The Italian operation was against an Axis nation, while that of 6 June was to drive Germans from the homelands of governments-in-exile with which the United States had maintained constant contact. The policy, therefore, was not to use Allied military currencies, as in Italy, but to make arrangements with the governments concerned for the advance production of special or supplementary issues of their national currencies. The American government, which sought to avoid a repetition of its World War I experience in France, was happy that the French Committee of National Liberation concurred in having a special issue of supplementary franc notes printed in America.

In World War I, the U.S. Army had waited until it arrived in France before attempting to procure francs for paying troops and commercial bills. In a White House press conference shortly after the 6 June invasion, President Roosevelt asserted that during World War I, the army had paid soldiers in France in dollars, a sizable number of which had found their way into French mattresses and had been turning up for redemption ever since.[29] Unfortunately, the president's sly comment on wartime manners and morals was not accurate, since the army disbursed francs in World War I. Although the 1944 invasion of France did not occur until June, planning for the French supplemental currency commenced long before then. The Bureau of Engraving and Printing started printing the French currency around 15 February. The Treasury began designing the invasion currency for Germany, the Allied military mark, during the first week of January 1944.[30]

Although the French Committee of National Liberation, headed by Gen. Charles de Gaulle, wanted the supplemental francs printed in America, the refugee governments of Holland and Belgium ar-

[29] Report on White House Conference, Tuesday, 13 Jun 44, from Press Br, Bureau of Public Relations, WD. RG 338.

[30] Minutes of meeting held in Mr. McCloy's office 1 Feb 44—Meeting of U.S. members of ad hoc Committee on Monetary and Fiscal Planning—Western Europe, signed Maj Charles C. Hilliard; minutes of meeting held in Mr McCloy's office, 7 Jan 44. RG 338.

ranged to have stocks of Dutch florins and Belgian francs produced in the United Kingdom. These national currency supplies were at the disposal of the Supreme Headquarters, Allied Expeditionary Forces (SHAEF) G-5 currency section, which transferred requested amounts to disbursing officers of various Allied forces. In World War I when American soldiers exchanged dollars for foreign currencies, they had to reconvert to dollars at the existing rate of exchange. But in World War II the army guaranteed to exchange invasion currencies received as pay into dollar credits at the rate prevailing when the pay was disbursed.[31] SHAEF informed Washington by radio of the advances of supplemental national currencies made to American army disbursing officers. The War Department thereupon charged the equivalent dollar value to applicable appropriations. Periodically the U.S. government made the amounts charged available to governments supplying the currency.

These issues of French, Dutch, and Belgian currencies printed in the United States and England and taken to the Continent by the armed forces and repatriated governments were not technically military currencies, despite their use as invasion currencies. Rather, they supplemented the nations' regular currencies that were circulating at the time the Germans withdrew. The control and full responsibility for such money rested with restored governments in liberated countries.[32]

Any large-scale tactical movement on the Continent upset finance office routine. While the task of funding troops with invasion currencies prior to landings was great, the problem of exchanging one invasion currency for another when troops crossed a national boundary was equally immense. "Supplying a new currency at each border caused more confusion in finance offices than any other single factor," commented Lt. Col. Raymond E. Graham, commander of the Fifty-ninth FDS.[33] In an attempt to minimize the confusion resulting from moving from one country to another, the Eighth Air Force instructed its fiscal officers to study troop

---

[31] Report on House Resolution 150, Appendix A, signed Henry L. Stimson, Secretary of War, 28 Apr 45, p. 1. RG 338.

[32] Ltr, Secretary of the Treasury, to Senator Robert Taft, 17 Dec 45. RG 338; "History of the Fiscal Services," pp. 582–583.

[33] Interview with Lt Col Raymond E. Graham, 3 Feb 54.

allocations so they could determine which units would move to an area where a different currency was used. Using a study made in Italy, the Eighth Air Force was able to predetermine its currency needs for the invasion of southern France.[34]

Finance officers with the air forces also had to estimate requirements for various European currencies used in escape purses. If airmen were shot down over occupied territory, local money and maps in escape purses often enabled them to reach the friendly underground. Escape purses of fliers operating from England usually contained Belgian, Dutch, and French currencies.[35]

Although invasion currencies involved high-level negotiations within the U.S. government and between Allied governments, the army's fiscal operations were rarely as dramatic as any tactical phase of the war. Finance offices performed routine tasks of paying troops and commercial bills, budgeting, and accounting for their expenditures—administrative functions, however prosaic, that facilitated the army's functioning. Toward the end of the war and in the first year of occupation, financial operations were exciting, as currency control broke down and the army incurred a deficit of $530,775,440.[36] Before then, the closest that finance men came to the stimulation and savagery of combat was through supplying soldiers with invasion currency.

Intelligence

After an invasion established the army in a foreign country, the Finance Department needed intelligence reports on several situations so that it could operate with reasonable efficiency. Information as to the availability of banking facilities was of prime importance. The type and quantity of currency used by the civilian population and the capacity of printing presses for further production were also items of major significance. This sort of intelligence, or G-2, information enabled Finance to know what to expect when it entered a new area. The army, as an entity, had

[34] Ltr, Maj Burnis Archer, Asst AG, Hq Eighth Air Force, to CG's, First Bombardment Div, Second Bombardment Div, et al., 19 Aug 44. RG 338.

[35] Ltr, Capt John R. Philpott, Adj, Hq Ninety-third Bombardment Grp, to CG, Second Bombardment Wing, 17 Mar 43. RG 338.

[36] See Walter Rundell, Jr., *Black Market Money.*

to have an active G-2 program so that it could know the conditions under which it would operate. The security surrounding most payments for G-2 activities made this facet of finance work more interesting than ordinary transactions.

Funding for intelligence encompassed a wide range of activities. Frequently intelligence operatives needed gold coins—the most universally accepted medium of exchange—to buy information. Other, more routine needs, such as transportation, clothing, food, drink, housing and supplies, could be covered by paper money.

In London one Sunday afternoon in October 1942, the fiscal director for the Mediterranean theater received a visit from Maj. Gen. Walter Bedell Smith, Eisenhower's Chief of Staff. Smith informed General Sims that he needed several hundred dollars in gold coins right away. All the gold currency Sims had at the time was locked in the subterranean vaults of the Bank of England. Sims went to work immediately. Officials of the banks were aghast when they realized someone wanted admittance to the vault on Sunday. The doors of the vault had never before swung open on the Sabbath, and the English hardly saw the necessity for changing the custom. But when General Sims insisted that he must have the gold, the bank hierarchy relented and the finance officer collected approximately 100 Louis d'ors, worth six dollars apiece. Gen. Mark Clark used these gold pieces in his famous intelligence expedition to North Africa three weeks prior to the invasion.[37]

General Clark and his small party went to North Africa to determine the attitude of the French toward the invasion, which was to begin 8 November 1942. It was imperative that General Eisenhower know whether the French would welcome the Americans as friendly liberators or whether they would retain their loyalty to Vichy and oppose Operation TORCH as an enemy invasion. In case of emergencies, the Clark party wore money belts containing the Louis d'ors. Clark, in trying to rendezvous with a submarine after the mission, had his money belt and all its contents swept away by a giant wave.[38]

[37] Interview with Lt Col T. W. Archer.
[38] Mark W. Clark, *Calculated Risk*, pp. 72, 84. Gen Clark's account differs slightly in detail from that of the Finance Department officers involved. In this book he says that the gold secured amounted to $1,000, denominated in

Certainly not all G-2 activities were as dashing as General Clark's sortie. While the ordinary duties of intelligence troops could hardly have been considered routine, they could be classified sufficiently to permit rough estimates for necessary expenses. In the Mediterranean theater the assistant chief of staff, G-2, recommended to the commanding general that a class A agent be appointed and given a flat sum of $5,000 to cover a list of estimated operational costs for an indefinite time. The most expensive item on his list was motor transportation. For some G-2 operations, army vehicles could be used, but frequently unmarked civilian automobiles were necessary. When the motor pool had no such cars, they had to be bought on the outside.[39]

Another essential item that intelligence and counterintelligence agents needed to remain unobtrusive was civilian clothing. Because few agents had received civilian attire in the United States, a schedule of allowances was constructed for overseas theaters. In 1942 the initial expense of civilian clothes could not exceed $100, with $7 a month allowed for maintenance and replacement. A soldier could collect this sum only by presenting a receipt of his expenses. In 1943 the initial allowance was increased to $125 and the monthly maintenance to $12. Any special clothing needed to accomplish a specific mission could be purchased without regard to these restrictions. Usually these clothing allowance payments came from provost marshal general or military intelligence division confidential funds.[40]

Canadian $5 and $10 pieces. He also mentions that the American dollars he carried on the expedition brought the total currency to around $2,000. News dispatches reported a much greater loss than actually occurred when a wave swept his money belt off the raft. There is no mention in this book of any money being used to purchase the collaboration of Admiral Darlan, a rumor that gained some circulation. George F. Howe's account of Clark's visit to Africa relies on the earliest official documents and is therefore likely the most valuable: *Northwest Africa*, pp. 80–82.

[39] Lt Col D. W. Bernier, GSC, ACofS, G-2, Hq Mediterranean Base Section, Memo for the CG, 30 Dec 42. RG 338.

[40] Ltrs, Maj Gen J. A. Ulio, TAG, to CG, SOS; Defense Commands; Corps Areas; Base Commands, sub: Clothing Allowances for Special Agents, Investigations Division, 8 Jul 42; Brig Gen H. B. Lewis, Actg TAG, to CG's, AGF, AAF, ASF, et al., sub: Counterintelligence Corps Clothing Allowance, 20 May 43. RG 338.

In the Mediterranean theater special equipment needed by intelligence agents had not been provided, so they requested funds for lock-picking devices, moulage, small arms other than those issued by ordnance, blackjacks, fingerprint-lifting equipment, and cameras, as well as intelligence from professional informers. Of one specific request for $5,000, $1,000 was allotted to buy information. Aside from what could be gleaned in this manner, much valuable intelligence could be obtained when an agent loosened tongues with alcohol; therefore, "entertainment" expenses were also a necessary part of G-2 fund requirements.

Recurring operating expenses included maintenance of civilian quarters for undercover agents who could not be associated with other U.S. troops and the costs of meals and travel for these agents. Such undercover agents were in a different category from those who only wore civilian clothes. Hiring civilian interpreters and guides incurred another frequent and necessary expense.[41]

The special equipment, attire, and organization of intelligence agents sometimes caused disbursing officers to forget that they had to be paid just like other soldiers. In the European theater counterintelligence agents registered enough complaints of nonpayment that the OFD issued a special directive stating that agents be paid promptly if they could offer proper identification.[42]

In the course of normal operations, few FDS's reported providing funds for any sort of G-2 activity. But the Twenty-fifth FDS, commanded by Maj. H. A. Miner, frequently paid for intelligence operations. While it was in North Africa, the Twenty-fifth handled secret vouchers connected with the Casablanca conference of Roosevelt, Churchill, Giraud, and de Gaulle in January 1943. When the Twenty-fifth prepared for the Sicilian invasion, it carried $20,000 in Canadian gold earmarked for G-2 agents. The Twenty-fifth performed so efficiently that General Patton wrote its commandant a letter of appreciation.[43]

[41] Lt Col D. W. Bernier, GSC, ACofS, G-2, Hq Mediterranean Base Sec, Memo for the CG, 30 Dec 42. RG 338.

[42] Ltr, Col M. F. Moriarty, Deputy Fis Dir, Hq ETO, OFD, APO 887, 5 Dec 44. RG 338.

[43] T/4 Milton Glazer, "Unit History"; ltr, Lt Gen G. S. Patton, Jr., Commanding, Seventh Army, to Maj H. A. Miner, CO, Twenty-fifth FDS, APO 758, Seventh Army, 27 Nov 43. RG 338.

Finance officers sometimes had to operate on faith when money was requested for intelligence, for the nature of G-2 activities precluded any kind of detailed accounting for the funds. When General Smith instructed General Sims to get gold for Cark's expedition, no questions arose. Once a theater commander called an air forces fiscal officer and told him he had to have $5,000 in thirty minutes. The officer assumed it was for a G-2 operation and delivered the money.[44] In the Pacific finance officers supplying G-2 funds were actually burdened less by these transactions than by ordinary ones. The only accounting necessary was an entry indicating where funds had gone and a supporting receipt from G-2.

A primary use of G-2 funds in the Pacific was for the payment of Filipino guerrillas. Capt. Ralph A. Metzger, finance officer for General MacArthur's staff in Australia, gave the G-2 of USAFFE $10,000 "practically every day." Submarines carried this money, in small denominations, to U.S. commanders secretly working with guerrillas in the Philippines. The commanders used the money to pay troops and buy information.[45]

On at least one occasion, a finance officer's skepticism of a request for G-2 money turned out to be warranted. A man claiming to be a famous general asked a finance officer of the Eighth Air Force to deliver a large sum to his hotel in London as soon as possible, with accountability to be cleared the next morning. Sensing something phony, the finance officer notified the provost marshal. An immediate investigation exposed the man as an imposter. After this incident, finance officers were cautioned to make no payment on irregular or unusual requests, but to report the matter quickly to their commanding officers, who would notify the Criminal Investigation Detachment (CID).[46]

Most finance activities overseas were sufficiently routine that only the locale gave the men much sense of being involved in the war. In funding invasion and intelligence operations, however, they could identify more with the war's tactical and adventurous

[44] Interview with Gen Campbell, 27 Apr 54.
[45] Interview with Lt Col Metzger, 26 Jul 55.
[46] Ltr, Maj Burnis Archer, Asst AG, Hq Eighth Air Force, Office of CG, APO 634, to CG, Second Bombardment Div, APO 558, 25 Sep 44. RG 338.

aspects, whose success depended partly on the finance work having been done efficiently.

From the outset, the army would have preferred to fund its invading troops with foreign currencies, but considerations of time and place frequently prevailed. Since the army could not always count on the availability of the right types and amounts of foreign currencies, it often relied on what was easily available: dollar-denominated currencies, such as yellow seal and Hawaii overstamped. Despite initial misgivings about employing these U.S. issues, they served reasonably well in both the Mediterranean and the Pacific areas. Wherever possible, however, the army used the currencies that were familiar, and hence easily acceptable, to the residents of areas the army entered. The army reasoned that locally denominated currencies enabled it to buy goods and services quickly and also facilitated soldiers' purchases on the local economy. At the time the army issued foreign invasion currencies, the U.S. government had not decided whether it would be liable for their exchange to dollar credits. The foreign invasion currencies therefore represented a hedge against a positive decision.

Despite the efficiency of the army's issuing invasion currencies denominated in foreign units, economists raised the question about the military's prerogative to do so. The uncertainty of the U.S. government's responsibility for redemption of such currencies indicated that the executive branch should not have been able to act unilaterally in this matter. As it turned out, the American government was willing to exchange for dollar credits any foreign invasion currency the army disbursed to its members; and because of the breakdown of currency control, the government bore excessive costs. Unfortunately, economists' somber warning of 1944 went unheeded: "It is a dangerous precedent to let the American army issue its own money without Congress' permission. For centuries Anglo-Saxon peoples have kept the military in hand by their control of the purse strings. This is a sound philosophy for a peace-loving people and should not be abandoned."[47]

Had Congress taken the initiative in determining what military

[47] Donald L. Kemmerer and T. Eugene Beattie, "Allied Military Currency in Italy," *The Commercial and Financial Chronicle* 160 (21 Sep 44): 1269.

currencies the U.S. government would exchange for soldiers, it would have borne the responsibility that the military shouldered alone. Congress obviously found it easier to rely on legal precedent and let the army make unilateral decisions, some of which proved unsound. The practicality of congressional involvement in this issue is debatable, but as long as Congress gave the army free rein with military currencies, it could complain only after the fact.

CHAPTER *6*

Paying Troops

THE most important responsibility of the Finance Department was to pay the soldier. When World War II began, pay rates were still those established in 1922. Monthly rates ranged from $21 for a private to $126 for a master sergeant with less than four years' service. A second lieutenant with less than five years' service drew $125, while a lieutenant colonel with less than twenty years' service made $250 per month. Soon after the war began, it became obvious that the pay scale for a peacetime army would be inadequate during the emergency. Since wages and prices through the nation were higher, the soldier was entitled to a proportionate increase. In addition, wartime civilians-turned-soldiers needed more money to support dependents than their traditionally bachelor counterparts. The Pay Readjustment Act of 1942 provided substantial increases for all grades. The pay of a private increased to $50 per month and that of a master sergeant to $138. A second lieutenant with less than three years' service earned $150 monthly, and a lieutenant colonel with less than thirty years' service, $291.67. Rates set by this act, with a few minor exceptions, remained in effect throughout the war.[1]

One exception related to overseas service. On 7 March 1943 Congress legislated increases in base pay for foreign service. Enlisted men, warrant officers, and nurses got a 20 percent increase of their base pay for all time in foreign areas subsequent to 7 December 1941, while commissioned officers received a 10 percent increment.[2]

---

[1] PL 235, 67th Cong., "Army, Navy, etc. Pay Readjustment," Approved 10 Jun 1922, *Acts and Resolutions Relating to the War Department*, 24 (Washington: Government Printing Office, 1922); PL 607, 77th Cong. "Pay Readjustment Act of 1942," Approved 16 Jun 42, *Laws Relating to the War Department*, 49 (Washington: Government Printing Office, 1942).

[2] PL 490, 77th Cong., "Pay and Allowances of Certain Military and Civilian Personnel," Approved 7 Mar 42, United States Statutes at Large, 56

For the performance of hazardous duties, soldiers earned special bonuses. They received "incentive" pay for flying, gliding, and parachuting. Officers and enlisted men required to fly as an essential part of their military assignment got a 50 percent increase in base pay. Officers on glider duty also received a 50 percent increase in base pay, provided the increase did not exceed $100 per month. Enlisted men on glider duty likewise got a 50 percent boost, with the stipulation that the increase not exceed $50 monthly. A straight $100 per month for officers and $50 for enlisted men were awarded as incentive pay for paratroopers.[3]

Similar to incentive pay for hazardous duty was the provision during wartime for additional pay for officers who exercised a command calling for a higher grade. For example, if a major performed duties that a T/O&E usually assigned to a lieutenant colonel, he would be entitled to pay for the higher grade. The service had to be with troops operating against an enemy; the officer had to assume a command above one appropriate to his grade; and the exercise of the command had to be authorized in orders before the assumption of the command. Increments of this nature could go only to those with the rank of colonel and below.[4]

Pay branches in finance offices handled military pay. The organization of the enlisted and officers' pay branches was similar in both division and separate finance units. A warrant officer supervised the enlisted pay branch, headed by either a staff or a technical sergeant and manned by eight enlisted men of lower grades. The composition of the officers' pay branch differed only in having six fewer enlisted men. These pay branches figured all pay and allowances in American dollars, as required by the legislation that fixed rates of pay. After the branch computed payrolls in dollars,

(Washington: Government Printing Office, 1943). Memo No. 33, Puerto Rican Department, 19 Mar 42, sub: Increased Pay for Foreign Service. RG 338.

[3] PL 607, 77th Cong.; PL 409, 78th Cong., "Amendment to Pay Readjustment Act of 1942," Approved 1 Jul 44, *Laws Relating to the War Department*, 51 (Washington: Government Printing Office, 1945).

[4] Ltr, Maj Norman Johnson, Office of the Fin Off, 202d Fin Sec, AAF Station 107, APO 557, to Fis Off, Eighth Air Force, APO 634, 12 Mar 45. RG 338; "Act of 26 Apr 1898," *The Statutes at Large of the United States of America from Mar 1897 to Mar 1899*, 30 (Washington: Government Printing Office, 1899), p. 365.

it converted them to the appropriate foreign currency for payment.[5]

Payrolls for Enlisted Men

Many variations in pay procedures existed at different times and among diverse organizations, but through general practice, two principal systems for paying enlisted men evolved. In the more traditional system, personnel sections typed payrolls in triplicate by the tenth to fifteenth of the month and sent them to the companies for signatures. By signing the payroll, a man indicated his willingness to receive pay. Signed payrolls went to the finance section, which computed them and put the money for each roll in a bag. The personnel section published names of Class A agents who would come to the finance office for their payrolls and money. At the organizations, agents paid their men, usually on the last day of the month. In combat it sometimes became impossible to pay on the final day of the month, but usually finance offices had payrolls ready then.

An agent had no standard time limit in which to pay his men. If he paid a Transportation Corps truck company or armored reconnaissance unit, it might take a week to locate the last man because of wide deployment of such groups. On the other hand, he could pay a field artillery battery or infantry line company in a relatively short time, since they were clustered in a small area. If a man could not be located or decided he wanted no pay, his name was "redlined" on the payroll. After the agent had completed his mission by paying as many as possible and redlining the remainder, he returned the unpaid money and the payroll, which he signed as a witness to the payments, to the finance office. Technically, class A agents were to close out their accounts in twenty-four hours, but this frequently was not possible. When agents turned back money along with witnessed payrolls to clear their accounts, many finance officers required a comparison of all three copies of the payroll so that the copy from which the service record entry was made agreed with the original.

The other method of paying enlisted men streamlined payment

[5] "Joint Statement of the War and Treasury Departments," 2 Jan 45. RG 338.

procedures. The personnel section did not send payrolls to the company for signing, but sent them directly to the finance office for computation. Figuring every name on the roll for payment eliminated the time required to send the roll to the company for signing, but it also resulted in some wasted time and labor, since frequently men on payrolls had been transferred or hospitalized and therefore were unavailable for payment. Sometimes men just did not want their pay. Each time a man was redlined, it meant that the work involved in computing his pay had been wasted. Another part of the procedure that made this system less exacting than the former was that one class A agent would sign for the payrolls and money for several organizations. He would then issue money to other agents and get their receipts. All agents would go to the finance office to obtain their individual clearances. The one agent who had drawn the money would present his own signed payroll plus receipts from other agents to close his account. This method of payment caused an initial waste of time, but it saved some time since payrolls did not have to be sent to the company to be signed prior to computation. The system also resulted in conservation of gasoline and rubber.[6]

The Seventy-third FDS used this latter system at the Second Reinforcement Depot at Bad Godesburg, Germany, from January through April 1945. Although time was saved in computation, from 50 to 90 percent of those on the payroll might be unavailable for payment. The commandant of the section, Maj. W. M. Cavin, considered that percentage "satisfactory," since the primary task of the depot was to move men and finance service was only secondary.[7]

When a personnel officer opened a service record for an enlisted man, he issued the soldier's individual pay record (SIPR). Only the personnel officer having custody of the service record could issue a duplicate SIPR. Commanding officers bore responsibility for requiring men to carry their pay records with them habitually. Each SIPR listed the following information: name, serial number, grade, years of service, insurance premium, other allot-

---

[6] Col Ralph A. Koch, Lt Col Harold W. Uhrbrock, and Lt Col Maynard N. Levenick, "The Activities of the Finance Department in the European Theater of Operations," pp. 46–52. RG 338.

[7] Maj W. M. Cavin, "Unit History."

ments, technician grade, name of the person to be notified in case of emergency, and date the book was opened. The SIPR proved extremely useful to enlisted men separated from their parent organizations. As a good means of identification, it served as authorization for payment when the holder had not been paid on the last regular payday.

Personnel officers of units picking up a "casual," a man unassigned or separated from his organization, used his SIPR to prepare a voucher for the casual payment. Then the personnel officer recorded payment in the SIPR and returned it to the man. Finally, the personnel officer notified the man's commanding officer of the casual payment.[8] Although SIPR's were supposed to enable casuals to be paid, some cases of nonpayment occurred because personnel officers would not accept the data in SIPR's.[9]

Vouchers for Officers

Entirely different from the payroll method of figuring enlisted pay was the system used by Finance to pay officers: a separate voucher for each officer each month. This system, in comparison to the enlisted pay system, required excessive paperwork. One harassed fiscal officer in Europe termed it "the most outstanding abortion that I can think of."[10] Improvement came in 1944 when finance units could group officers' monthly pay vouchers on one summary voucher, a procedure that led to a significant saving in time and energy.[11]

The Twenty-ninth FDS made some innovations in officers' pay procedures that enabled it to handle an unusually large number of casuals arriving from the United States. The section persuaded the casual company to establish a clearinghouse to process all pay vouchers, allotment papers, and personal transfer accounts. A class A agent appointed from the company consolidated the flow of

[8] AR 345–155, 15 Jan 43; WD Cir 93, 5 Apr 43. RG 338.

[9] WD Cir 114, 5 May 43. RG 338.

[10] Ltr, Col William P. Campbell, Fis Off, Hq ASC, U.S. Strategic Air Forces in Europe, APO 633, to Col Andrew Stewart, Hq ASF, OFD, Washington, D.C., 24 Dec 44. RG 338.

[11] CWO Merton G. Jefts, "Unit History."

documents to the finance office and handled monetary transactions. Casual officers and enlisted men worked in the clearinghouse.[12]

Finance offices had many more difficulties with officers' pay than with enlisted pay, because officers were paid individually and could contest differences of opinion. When the finance office overpaid or underpaid enlisted men, it merely adjusted on the next payroll. Legitimate complaints were considered, but enlisted men did not have the opportunity to argue a point. In 1944 an officer was involved in two cases of overpayment of his rental allowance. The twelve-dollar overpayment case ran from 13 April through 14 June; the eighteen-dollar case, from 11 May through 30 October—and twenty endorsements on the basic correspondence! The officer's grounds for holding out against repayment were that an ex post facto law was invoked. He contended he was charged with over-payments that were not overpayments when he got them. In one of the many endorsements in the case, the officer said he would repay only when ordered to do so by the Secretary of War or when the GAO disallowed his voucher. Before hearing from either of these authorities, however, the officer made both repayments.[13]

Ordinarily officers were paid by check. Sometimes, though, a shortage of checks forced finance offices to make cash payments. After January 1943, headquarters, Tenth Air Force, located in New Delhi, had to stop paying its officers in rupee checks. Subsequently, both basic pay and allowances were paid in cash. The finance office requested officers to sign vouchers by the twentieth of each month so that payments would be ready on the last day of the month.[14] By April 1945 in Manila, the SWPA General Headquarters, a short-age of check facilities forced a revision in pay procedures. All GHQ lieutenant colonels and ranks below that were paid in cash, while colonels and generals continued to receive checks.[15]

[12] Lt Col Catesby ap R. Jones, "Unit History."

[13] Ltr, Capt W. H. Phillips to 1st Lt David P. Mason, 13 Apr 44, sub: Overpayment of Rental Allowance, 241.2x201, 6 Inds; ltr, Capt J. H. Reed, Jr., to 2d Lt [sic] David P. Mason, 11 May 44, sub: Overpayment of Rental Allowance, 241.2x201, 20 Inds. RG 338.

[14] Office Memo 4, Hq U.S. Air Forces in India and China, Tenth U.S. Air Force, New Delhi, India, 19 Jan 43. RG 338.

[15] Info Bul 3, GHQ SWPA, 27 Apr 45, AG 240. RG 338.

Most finance offices assisted officers in preparing their vouchers. The post finance office at headquarters, CPBC, prepared initial vouchers for those certifying their own pay and allowances. Officers could keep a copy of this initial voucher to use in the future, and model vouchers were available to other officers. The post finance office continued to prepare individual claims for mileage and per diem, which could be complicated.[16]

Officers received subsistence allowances in lieu of free meals, but in turn had to pay for meals at field messes. Until 1 October 1943 the rate for the field ration was seventy cents, but after that date it increased to seventy-five. When a finance unit computed officers' pay vouchers, the disbursing officer making individual payments entered the cumulative value of field rations. In case officers did not mess in the field, the voucher certified this fact. When officers ate at field messes without paying, the disbursing officer listed the amount due on their pay vouchers.[17]

Field Problems

An unresolved question concerns the pay of troops during combat. One position holds that it was unnecessary to make full cash payments while troops were engaged in the line. Col. George R. Gretser, finance officer for the Eighth Armored Division, observed that the typical comment of men in his division was, "What the hell do I want with money in a foxhole?" The only pay they wanted was a little pocket change to buy items from the post exchange truck. The remainder they wished to send home in various allotments.[18] A consideration equal to that of the convenience or desires of the GI's was the impact of soldiers' pay on foreign economies. The inflation and currency speculation that resulted from soldiers' money being spent in foreign economies both ultimately redounded against American economic interests. To reduce

---

[16] Ltr, Lt Col H. S. Thatcher, Actg AG, CPBC, to All Personnel Who Certify Their Own Pay and Allowance Accounts for Payment by Finance Office APO 956, 30 Jun 45, sub: Preparation of Pay Vouchers, CPFIS 241. RG 338.

[17] "History of Peninsular Base Section, NATOUSA," Jan 44; ltr, Capt C. S. Davis, to Fin Offs, Thirteenth, Forty-seventh, Forty-ninth and Fiftieth FDS's, 12 Oct 43. RG 338.

[18] Interview with Col George R. Gretser, 30 Mar 54.

cash in soldiers' hands, the army vigorously promoted savings programs, especially buying war bonds through payroll deductions. An important advocate of pay restrictions to curb speculation, Col. Bernard Bernstein, chief of the SHAEF G-5 currency section, urged the army to establish full pay credits for soldiers overseas but to disburse only limited sums. He saw this as a practical way to solve the army's difficult problem of speculation, while not infringing on the soldier's basic entitlements.[19]

Another contention is that the American soldier had earned his pay and deserved the full amount in cash if he wanted it. Regardless of the disposition a soldier might make of his pay, he still expected to see his name on the payroll once a month. If he were only drawing a small portion of his pay, he could ascertain by seeing the payroll that his savings program was in effect.[20] Those ultimately responsible chose this position. The Judge Advocate General ruled that any compulsory withholding of pay would violate the law,[21] and the army refused to approach Congress for legislation to authorize restricted payments.[22] Maj. Gen. John J. Hilldring, Chief of the Civil Affairs Division of the War Department special staff, and Maj. Gen. George J. Richards, War Department budget officer, commented that any limitation on payments "would be contrary to the ingrained rule that a soldier's pay is inviolate and that he can spend it as he considers best."[23] Lt. Cmdr. Frank A. Southard, Jr., an economist and financial adviser to the Mediterranean theater, declared that "neither the troops themselves nor American public opinion would tolerate a pay-withholding system which limited troop pay-withdrawals for local expenditures" to a small percentage.[24]

Whether allowing each soldier to make his individual decision

[19] Minutes of meeting held in office of Assistant Secretary of War, 30 May 45. RG 338.

[20] Koch, Uhrbrock, and Levenick, "Activities of Finance Department," p. 49.

[21] Maj Gen J. A. Ulio to Commanders, Theaters of Operations, et al., 14 Jul 44, AG 123 OB-S-E-M. RG 338.

[22] A. J. Rehe to CG, ETO, 4 Nov 42, AG 242 (10-27-42) OB-S-A. RG 338.

[23] Minutes of meeting held in office of Assistant Secretary of War, 30 May 45. RG 338.

[24] Frank A. Southard, Jr., "Some European Currency and Exchange Experiences," p. 12.

on how much pay he wanted each month was the best method of wartime operation remains debatable. Certainly it would have simplified paperwork to have set an arbitrary sum to be paid in the field. Of course, Finance could not have made such a decision independently, since several members of the War Department staff had significant influence in the matter. Congress fixed soldiers' pay and allowances and the army could not, without Congress' approval, limit the amount a man could actually receive on payday. Totalitarian nations could make such limitations to disencumber their fighting machines, but the War Department thought this democratic government would refuse to restrict soldiers' pay. The War Department assumed congressional hostility to pay limitations, but the intense interest of Congress in the breakdown of the army's currency controls in 1945 and 1946, resulting largely from earlier decisions not to restrict pay, indicated that it might not have been so ill-disposed toward wartime limitation as the War Department imagined. The soldier's option to draw full pay overseas was a burden imposed by the War Department's questionable appraisal of American social ideology.[25]

By far the most telling complaint registered against the army's pay system overseas was its design for peacetime operations at installations in the States. Before the war began, those in the Finance Department responsible for planning had failed to foresee that the existing method of payment was not fitted for overseas. They had also neglected to provide finance service for nondivisional troops, as well as suitable office equipment and transportation. A tremendous difference existed between figuring a payroll in a stateside finance office with electric adding machines and on the North African desert where the wind kept whipping papers about. "You just don't put a man under a palm tree to figure a payroll" declared Colonel Gretser. When troops were stationed in the United States, a class A agent had little trouble in paying them all at once. But overseas, agents had to "chase around all over the countryside looking for their men when they should have been free to command them in the field. That the job got done over there was a credit

---

[25] For a fuller exposition of this topic, see Walter Rundell, Jr., *Black Market Money*, pp. 9–11, 36, 89–90, 94 n. 17.

to the men running the system, not to the system itself," said the colonel. "They were hard working men who simply made the inadequate system work."[26]

That the stateside pay system did not operate satisfactorily overseas in the early part of the war was evident from the many recorded instances of nonpayment. In the Aleutian Islands some units of the Amulet Force went unpaid for six months, and at the beginning of 1943 some enlisted men in the Hawaii Department had not been paid in four months.[27] In August 1943 the situation was sufficiently grave for Gen. George C. Marshall to make an official comment. He notified all theater commanders that "large numbers" of the enlisted men who were returning to the United States from foreign theaters had not been paid for months. Their accounts could not be settled upon arrival because they did not have the necessary records with them. General Marshall also commented on delays in payment of those who remained overseas. He urged all theater commanders to give special attention to correcting pay deficiencies.[28]

Conditions existing in Rabat, Morocco, in December 1942 gave further evidence that men overseas were not being paid properly. When the Twenty-fourth FDS arrived there, it found that men had not been paid in three months. The section's immediate task was to get them paid as quickly as possible. Maj. Gen. Lucian K. Truscott requested that the Twenty-fourth attempt to pay all troops by Christmas. Although the section worked every night for almost a month, it had completed only three-quarters of the payrolls by Christmas Day. By 1 January 1943, however, it had brought all payments up to date. After this task had been accomplished, the Twenty-fourth aided the Third Division finance section in catching up with its own troop payments.[29]

One obvious reason for lapses in pay procedures was the physical conditions under which finance units operated. In North Africa

[26] Interview with Col Gretser, 30 Mar 54.

[27] "Historical Report, Detachment Finance Section, Alaska Department"; ltr, Col R. E. Fraile, AG, Hawaiian Dept, to Distribution D, 22 Jul 43, sub: Prompt Payment of Troops, FIN 241. RG 338.

[28] Marshall, to Hq USAFIME, AMSME, No. 6233, 12 Aug 43. RG 338.

[29] Capt R. A. Alexander, CO, "Unit History."

the Twenty-fifth FDS found that wind and sand severely hampered disbursing operations. As soon as papers were laid out for a payment, a flurry of wind scattered them. Finance staffs operating under such handicaps had to develop a great deal of equanimity. The mission of the Twenty-fifth was such that it had to disburse in different locations. The frequent moves accustomed the staff to dismantling and setting up the office in very little time. On one occasion it operated in Casablanca in the morning and by late afternoon it was ready for business in Rabat.[30]

After General MacArthur returned to the Philippines in late 1944, finance officers experienced considerable difficulty in paying troops under combat conditions. During the Mindanao campaign, a four-man detachment from the 195th FDS joined the 108th Infantry Regiment to provide finance service. Lt. Evo Domenici, commander of the detachment, found the units so widely dispersed that they could not be grouped for payment. The finance detachment therefore had to travel to pay the men in their respective areas, frequently using a light plane to reach the front lines. This detachment did its work without any office equipment, buildings, or electric lights. It received a commendation from the regiment for its "untiring efforts," which contributed materially to soldier morale.[31]

Lapses in efficient pay service continued through the war, despite the concerted efforts of overseas theaters. As late as April 1945, reports circulated on the nonpayment of enlisted men with the U.S. Strategic Air Forces in Europe. Surveys to determine causes for nonpayment uncovered a large assortment of reasons, some justifiable, others not. Legitimate causes for nonpayment included a man's having no pay due because of fines, assessments for government property lost or damaged, or allotments being withheld. When a soldier was absent without leave or confined awaiting a court martial, he was not accruing pay. If a soldier did not want to draw pay, he could request that. Sometimes, contrary to regulations, men were not paid while on furlough, detached service, or temporary duty upon being transferred, hospitalized, or absent on payday.

---

[30] T/4 Milton Glazer, "Unit History."

[31] Ltr, Capt Bernard R. Cohn, Personnel Off, 108th Infantry, to Fin Off, Eighth Army, 12 Jul 45, sub: Commendation. RG 338.

Some finance offices would not pay men when their records were incomplete, although regulations provided for the construction of a temporary service record upon which to base payment. Men serving a sentence imposed by a court-martial could be paid the amount specified in the court-martial order; upon occasion, however, they were not paid at all. When allotments were not properly executed or payrolls were either not signed or signed incorrectly, finance offices might mistakenly refuse to compute pay.[32] In replacement depots in the Mediterranean theater, casuals sometimes did not get paid promptly simply because there were not enough finance men to do the work. The T/O&E for a finance section had not been designed to provide service for 56,000 men a month, the average strength of the Mediterranean Replacement and Training Command.[33]

In the North African theater an investigation revealed that the primary reason for nonpayment to enlisted casuals was the lethargy of personnel officers. To remedy the condition, the theater organized personnel sections to ascertain the pay status of arriving casuals and appointed class A agents to draw funds in advance so they could pay arriving troops without delay. The Seventh Replacement Depot did not have facilities to safeguard the funds a class A agent would require to pay his constantly large flow of casuals, so a class B agency was established there. One officer and three enlisted men from the Thirty-first FDS staffed the agent office, located in the same area.[34]

Field Expedients

Finance offices recognized that under adverse conditions in foreign countries, pay procedures often did not "follow the book." The trouble was that the book had been written for peacetime disbursements in the States, and the Office of the Chief of Finance

[32] Ltr, 2d Lt Montie Thompson, Jr., Asst AG, Hq U.S. Strategic Air Forces in Europe, Office of the CG, AAF 379, to CG, Hq Eighth Air Force, APO 634, 24 Apr 45. RG 338.
[33] Ltr, Brig Gen R. P. Hueper, Deputy Dir, Hq ASF, OFD, Washington, D.C., to CG, Hq ComZ, MTOUSA, APO 512, Attn: Fis Dir, 9 Jan 45, and 2d Ind. RG 338.
[34] Report of Operations, Eastern Base Sec, NATOUSA, 43. RG 338.

had not made the proper adaptations for overseas operations in war-time. That the army got paid at all is a tribute to the ingenuity of finance officers who made necessary alterations in the field. Some adaptations were peculiar to time and place, while others had general applicability. In many instances, of course, these adaptations did not guarantee satisfactory service for all, but they represented Finance's desire to accomplish its mission.

To alleviate complaints, finance offices devised several procedures. When unusual circumstances prevented regular payments, USAFIME authorized payment on supplemental payrolls or separate vouchers.[35] Considering the potential for work of unmanageable proportions, finance offices had to use great discretion about when a separate voucher was justified. At the Peninsular Base Section in Italy, the Twenty-fifth FDS expedited pay of soldiers and civilians by having personnel officers of regular organizations submit at least a portion of their payrolls well before payday so that the section could have ample time for computations. Such arrangements relieved the pressure of processing payrolls and diminished the attendant errors that occurred too frequently under rushed conditions.[36]

Finance offices always sought means for improving service or simplifying operations. The man in the Eighty-first FDS who devised the following plan for figuring franc denominations necessary for paying thirty or more men must have been a devotee of *Alice in Wonderland*.

> "Write that down," the King said to the jury, and the jury eagerly wrote down all three dates on their slates, and then added them up, and reduced the answer to shillings and pence.

According to the Eighty-first's imaginative plan, one figured the number of 2-, 10-, and 100-franc notes required by multiplying the number of men by two; and the number of 5- and 50-franc notes, by dividing the number of men by two. "To determine the number

[35] Brig Gen V. H. Strahm, Acting cofs, Hq USAFIME, Cairo, Egypt, Cir 53, 10 Sep 43. RG 338.
[36] Southard, "Some European Currency and Exchange Experiences," p. 12.

of 500-franc notes, subtract the total amount of the other notes from the total amount of the roll and divide the difference by 500." The section admitted that on the surface their system appeared more cumbersome and time consuming than other methods of change listing. But actual tests in the office proved that the plan was more accurate, saved more time, and required a smaller number of franc notes. When the Eighty-first devised this plan in 1944, it operated as the finance office for headquarters, Channel Base Section, Communications Zone, European theater. The theater's office of the fiscal director took official notice of the Eighty-first's system and disseminated the information as a possible aid to all finance officers in the theater.[37]

Finance offices responsible for paying hospitalized personnel recognized that they presented special problems. Payment regulations and directives applicable in the field sometimes could not be followed in hospitals. For instance, had hospitals in USAFFE followed theater regulations strictly, patients would have had to be retained until their accounts were current—regardless of the extent of injury. Since regulations ignored men who did not want pay because of their conditions or who were unable to give complete personal data for figuring payments, some hospitals adopted their own rules for payment.

The 118th General Hospital at Tacloban, Leyte, paid according to the following rules: (1) Patients with service records were paid in full. Those without service records but who wanted money received partial payments promptly. If they were to be hospitalized for longer than seven days, temporary service records could be opened for them so they could be paid in full. Comparatively few made use of this service. (2) Men too ill to manage their affairs or those not desiring payment were not paid. (3) All patients returning to the States were given fifteen dollars to cover miscellaneous expenses en route. The hospital made payments according to these rules for six months without any complaints from the patients. Headquarters, AFWESPAC did not subscribe entirely to the hospital's methods, but did allow the commanding officer to make

[37] Ltr, Lt Col M. P. Patteson, Adm Off, to OFD, Hq COMZ, ETOUSA, APO 887, 29 Sep 44. RG 338.

individual determinations on payments. When a patient was in no condition to be paid, theater directives would not prevail.[38]

Partial Payments

The fluidity of the military situation and the fact that the pay system was not geared for overseas operations made a measure for intermediary payments essential. Frequently an individual or an entire unit might be separated from service records for several months. So that a man could receive some pay, partial payments could be made on the basis of the SIPR, temporary service records, or the actual records. Most often men were separated from their records when in replacement depots or hospitals. Sometimes when men first arrived overseas they drew partial payments for spending money. Such payments usually served to boost morale more than to fill any real monetary need. When Col. William P. Campbell was the fiscal director for the U.S. Strategic Air Forces in Europe, Lt. Gen. Ira C. Eaker, commander of the U.S. Army Air Forces in the United Kingdom, told him that when a group of new fliers arrived in England he wanted them to get some English money immediately. The finance office prepared partial payments equivalent to five dollars per officer. At the time, there were no vouchers, payrolls, or receipts, but within three weeks all papers relating to the payments were assembled and "not a cent" was lost in the transaction.[39]

Colonel Campbell's action was consistent with the policy established by the European theater's chief finance officer to facilitate payments wherever possible. The chief finance officer authorized payment of officers on the basis of previous entries on their pay data cards, rather than the substantiating papers required in regulations. Thousands of officers arrived in England without travel orders, official statements of service on which to claim longevity pay, or flying pay certificates. Most officers who belonged to organizations had no travel orders, since orders were not issued individually for overseas movements. To have denied payment because of the

---

[38] Ltr, Col James Bordley III, CO, 118th General Hospital, to CINC, Hq AFPAC, 20 Jul 45, sub: Payments to Hospital Patients, 4 Inds. RG 338.

[39] Memo, Lt Col R. E. Odell, Fin Off, Hq USAFIME, to Personnel Officers and Detachment Commanders, Incoming Troops, 9 Oct 42. RG 338; interview with Brig Gen William P. Campbell (Ret), 27 Apr 54.

absence of such documents would have been unfair.[40] Men going on pass or furlough could usually draw a partial payment if they desired.[41]

Since partial payments were designed to fill immediate financial needs, most finance officers assumed that those applying would actually have legitimate requests. Experience proved that such was not the case. The chief abusers of partial payments were flying officers. Their mobility made it easy to appear at any number of finance offices and request payment, often giving fictitious units to prevent detection of their fraud. In the Mediterranean theater such dishonesty was once discovered quite by accident. The fiscal director's office centralized all pay data from the theater so that it could simplify legitimate entries such as collections for field rations. When the office consolidated pay records, it uncovered the fraudulent requests for pay.[42]

Casuals and hospitalized soldiers were the chief recipients of partial payments. When certifying vouchers for payments, USAFIME officers were pecuniarily responsible for the truth of the vouchers and had to send notices of partial payments to the personnel officer holding the casual's service record.[43] Anyone hospitalized in the Central Pacific Base Command (CPBC) who was not paid within the month prior to hospitalization received a partial payment within ten days after his admission. If the patient's pay account had not been settled in full within fifteen days after the partial, he received a second. CPBC hospitals never delayed partial payments because of the lack of service records. Even if a temporary service record was being opened, payments were not held up until the record was completed. As long as a patient wanted pay and could make an affidavit, CPBC hospitals made complete payments within thirty days after the patient's admission.[44]

Replacement depots used partial payments as much as any type

[40] Col N. H. Cobbs, Chief Fin Off, Fin Cir Ltr No. 20, Hq SOS, ETOUSA, 9 Oct 42. RG 338.

[41] Report of Operations, First U.S. Army, Annexes 1–3, 1 Aug 44–22 Feb 45, p. 37. RG 338.

[42] Interview with Lt Col T. W. Archer, 3 Mar 54.

[43] Cir 32, USAFFE, 4 Apr 45. RG 338.

[44] Administrative Order 1, CPBC, 11 Mar 45. RG 338.

of military installation. Casuals passing through the Twenty-third Replacement Depot on Saipan in May 1945 included battle returnees, fresh troops, and soldiers on reassignment. Many of these lagged from three to eight months behind in their pay. Since a quick turnover was the rule at the depot, payment of casuals took precedence over other types of pay. While service records were brought up to date, casuals received partial payments. The 237th FDS used two methods to pay casuals at the Twenty-third Replacement Depot. At first it employed that procedure traditional with regular monthly payments—sending payrolls for signatures and then computing signed rolls. But men were quartered in such scattered areas on Saipan that this method proved too time consuming. Consequently, an alternative procedure was developed by which a class A agent picked up the payroll from the personnel section and took it to the finance office for computation. He would then set out with the payroll and the money, looking for his men. This saved much time and resulted in a greater percentage of men being paid.[45] The similar alternative method with regular monthly payrolls also saved time, but resulted in a smaller percentage of payments.

The 184th FDS, located at Hollandia, New Guinea, made a further refinement in the method of paying casuals. It began, as the 237th had, by computing signed payrolls. But due to rapid turnover, 90 percent of the men whose pay was figured would be shipped out before they could receive payment. To eliminate this waste, the 184th began preparing a voucher for each man on his day of arrival. These individual vouchers were ready for payment on the following day. By using this method, the 184th eliminated excessive redlining and got everyone paid prior to departure.[46]

Undoubtedly the most widespread use of partial payments during the entire war came as part of the preparation for the Normandy invasion on 6 June 1944. Mounting plans for Operation OVERLORD included the mandatory payment to every participant of four dollars in French francs. Finance officers in the Twelfth Army

[45] "Unit History," 237th FDS, 14 May 45 to inactivation. RG 338.
[46] Capt Samuel Dame, "Unit History."

Group regarded this payment as gratuitous, since most soldiers did not need the money.[47]

The Finance Department's mission in the mounting operation was far more extensive than simply making partial payments. It exchanged American and English money into invasion currency, accepted unit and personal funds as spearhead deposits, and encouraged all field forces to reduce their funds through personal transfer accounts. To accomplish this varied mission, teams of one officer and one to three enlisted men moved into each staging camp on 1 May 1944. Their equipment included one typewriter, one listing adding machine, and three field safes. The morning after the sealing of the camps, seven days before D Day, payrolls came in. Of the 598 processed in the Western Base Section, 526 came in the first day after sealing, 55 the second, and 17 the third. Finance teams reported preparing payments for 41,300 of the 42,449 troops in the Western Base Section camps (97.3 percent). They packed these partial payments (denominated in invasion currency) in bags that unit commanders carried aboard the ships. Craft commanders ordered distribution of the partials en route to Normandy.[48]

In the gigantic operation of handling all financial matters in the marshaling area, finance officers were bound to make some mistakes. Maj. B. M. Rogers, who disbursed in the Southampton region prior to 6 June, overpaid on three occasions. Twice he was lucky enough to catch the agents he had paid on the dock or ship before it departed and recover the money. But once the party was gone before he discovered an overpayment of $380. A board of officers handled this case and many others like it. The board cleared him of accountability. "There was hardly a single disbursing officer in the area who had not made similar mistakes," Rogers commented.[49]

A more dramatic overpayment was made by a finance officer shortly after the invasion began. Replacements funneled across the channel from the Southampton port in great numbers. One night a

[47] "Report of Operations (Final After Action Report)" Twelfth Army Group, vol. 10, p. 11. RG 338.

[48] Col Fenton S. Jacobs, "History of the Western Base Section, APO 515," vol. 2. RG 338.

[49] Interview with Maj B. M. Rogers, 16 May 53.

disbursing officer worked by candlelight to prepare the standard partial payments of 200 francs for each of 500 enlisted men scheduled to sail early the next morning. When the officer balanced his cash later that night, he discovered that he was short 450,000 francs. In the dark he had mistaken 500-franc notes for 50-franc notes. Being strictly accountable, the finance officer crammed his briefcase with 50-franc notes, grabbed the payrolls, and sped toward the quay. He scrambled up the gangplank just as it was being lifted. During the voyage across the English Channel the disbursing officer worked feverishly to make the adjustments. By the time the craft hit the beach, he had finally balanced his accounts. He then faced only the minor problems of getting back to England and convincing his superiors that he had not gone AWOL.[50]

Irregularities

Usually finance officers scrupulously followed the rules when handling huge sums of public funds, mostly for paying troops. With human nature as it is, however, a few rebelled against strict procedures and others were simply careless. Regardless of motivation, their actions resulted in different types of irregularities, with various results. The latitude that disbursing officers sometimes allowed themselves in deciding whose pay they would figure also extended to other phases of their operations. The most common violations involved keeping too much cash on hand and the attendant manipulation of accounts to avoid detection. When finance officers refused to follow regulations and were caught with shortages, their careers were ruined.

According to regulations, they could keep only enough cash to meet requirements of the command. If they kept more cash on hand than was sufficient for their immediate needs, especially if adequate local banking facilities existed, they were warned that the IG (Inspector General) would report them.[51] In the Mediterranean theater, disbursing officers, despite warnings, sometimes had enough currency to pay a division twice. But little official notice was taken of such matters, since fewer than one-half of 1 percent of the com-

[50] Maj Alfred A. Abbott, "The Army as Banker," p. 37.

[51] Ltr, Beeland to Fin Offs, Forty-seventh, Forty-ninth, Fiftieth FDS's, 123.4 BGFIN: AG 131/015 FO-M, 10 Nov 43. RG 338.

plaints received by the IG in the Mediterranean theater concerned pay.[52]

When a disbursing officer had more than the authorized cash at the end of the month, he could make certain manipulations to cover himself. He could show on his account current, a monthly consolidated report reflecting the status of public funds for which he was accountable, a deposit in transit on the last day of the month. Actually he would not send the money to a bank, but hold it in the safe. Then on the first day of the following month the disbursing officer would report drawing a check on the depositary to bring the money into his working funds. In reality, the money never left his hands. A disbursing officer who used this deception could be liable for intent to defraud the government if fire or bombing destroyed the funds, for the money supposedly in transit would never register in the depositary's accounts.[53]

Occasionally finance officers made the mistake not of having too much cash on hand, but of having too little. The specter that consistently haunted a disbursing officer's life was that of a shortage in his account, since any loss of public funds became a matter of official inquiry. In the case of the 175th FDS, laxness in office procedures caused losses and resulted in an administrative admonishment from the commanding general of the Luzon Area Command (Provisional). A payment to a Philippine army disbursing officer led to the discovery of the procedural deficiency. The cashier of the 175th mistakenly gave the Filipino a stack of 20-peso notes, rather than 2-peso notes, resulting in a shortage in the 175th's accounts of 18,000 pesos or $9,000. The investigating board decided that had a proper office procedure been followed, such a mistake would have been discovered the day it occurred rather than at the end of the month. The disbursing officer did not exchange receipts with his cashier at the close of the business day. He did not limit the amount of cash handled by cashiers to the penalty value of their bonds, and he allowed cashiers to have full access to funds in the vaults. This negligence contributed to the loss of funds, stated

---

[52] Interview with Lt Col T. W. Archer.

[53] Ltr, Capt Raymond E. Strong, Asst AG, Hq Second Bombardment Div, AAF 147, APO 558, to Accountable DO's (thru: CO, AAF 104, 114, 115, and 123, APO 558), 7 Apr 44. RG 338.

the board. The disbursing officer also violated army regulations by not requiring a daily settlement with the cashiers and by not personally counting their cash. But these violations were not direct causes of his loss. In this particular case, the funds were recovered. The Filipino had lied about receiving the overage. Under pressure he admitted his guilt and restored the money.[54]

Sometimes losses of funds were not only a matter of lax procedures. In the case of the finance section of the Sixth Infantry Division, losses resulted from the finance officer's unwillingness to follow regulations. When a loss was discovered, a board of officers investigated the officer's operations and found damning evidence against the disbursing officer. He tried to foist off his responsibility for public funds onto his deputy, even to the extent of instructing the deputy to put an IOU in the safe to cover a shortage of $119. When the Sixth Infantry Division began operations on New Guinea, the disbursing officer brought in over $1 million and gave the money to his deputy without any kind of verification or receipt.

This particular disbursing officer made his own rules for operating a finance office. He refused to make proper partial payments to officers, even when shown current army regulations authorizing them. He did not check the cash at the close of each day's business; in fact, on one occasion he did not check his funds for five days. This major used such abusive language with class A agents, most of whom were second lieutenants, that they registered protests against him. His manner of dealing with agents carried over to his own enlisted men, whom he browbeat so constantly that the unit's morale was extremely poor. When a board of officers investigated the finance section's operations, it queried the enlisted men. Each man stated that if given the choice, he would not work under this officer again. Among the grievances of the enlisted men were the officer's cursing them and calling them bastards and sons of bitches. The outcome of the investigation was that the deputy was transferred to another unit, as he had requested. The disbursing officer was relieved from his assignment and transferred outside the Sixth Army.[55]

[54] Report of Proceedings of Board of Officers, Hq AFWESPAC, Office of the Fis Off, 5 Nov 45, p. 71. RG 338.

[55] Report of Investigation of the Finance Section, Sixth Infantry Div, 11 Apr 44, 333.5/09. RG 338.

Just as office procedures sometimes resulted in a loss of funds, they could also produce overages. 1st Lt. J. C. Saladino, an agent for the 156th FDS on New Guinea, found after paying troop units that he had $27.77 surplus from four payrolls. Following the instructions of the OFD, he credited the excess to Miscellaneous Receipts Unexplained Balance in his cash account.[56] In similar situations, some finance officers might have covertly retained the overage to offset possible deficits in the future.

Throughout the war, the payment of soldiers constituted Finance's central concern. The immense problems it faced in paying enlisted men and officers around the globe revealed the inadequacy of prescribed procedures. A great variety of means existed whereby payments could be made, but these often pointed up the absence of a satisfactory standard of payment. Finance offices expended great time and effort, for instance, in sending out payrolls for signature before computing them. They followed this procedure simply because it had been routine at installations before the war. Fortunately, some finance officers realized that static peacetime procedures had to be abandoned in fluid overseas situations; and luckily army regulations permitted sufficient leeway to enable them to modify operations as needed.

As the finance officer for the Eighth Armored Division indicated, the peacetime procedure of making a full settlement of a soldier's pay account at the end of each month manifestly ignored the conditions and demands of wartime operations overseas. Much more feasible would have been the practice of standardizing partial payments during service in foreign theaters, with the remaining pay transmitted home in allotments. Since the army provided all the necessities, no cash was needed for basic expenses, and partial payments could furnish ample pocket money. Such a system would obviously restrict soldiers' private business ventures, but it would recognize that overseas operations demanded administrative alterations akin to those tactical innovations required by combat.

Had the Finance Department planned for wartime conditions or had it had imaginative leadership after the war began, field oper-

---

[56] 1st Ind, 1st Lt J. C. Saladino, Agent Fin Off, 156th FDS, Hq U.S. Forces, APO 323, to Fin Off, 175th FDS, 29 Nov 44. RG 338.

ations could have been more economical and efficient. The wartime record indicated that in the important area of paying troops, Finance relied on a considerable array of field expedients, lacking a unified and workable program adapted to overseas needs.

CHAPTER 7

Paying Civilians

THE payment of troops clearly dominated overseas disbursements, but others also had to be paid in order for the army to function sucessfully: commercial vendors, native laborers, and dependents. Payments of commercial accounts, and native laborers often went hand in hand, because vendors would contract to supply workers. The army used more native workers in the United Kingdom and on the Continent than elsewhere, but national authorities in those areas paid them under reciprocal aid and Finance handled only the accounting aspects of the transactions. In such noncombat areas as PGC, AMET, India, and Australia, the army paid local workers directly, as it did in the Philippines before, during, and after combat. Only in these cases did the records show the procedures the army used and the kinds of problems faced. Most of these payments were routine, but some proved unusual and challenging. The morale of the troops overseas depended to a significant extent on the welfare of families and sweethearts back home. While the army could do nothing to enhance the financial condition of the girlfriends left behind, its dependency allotment system enabled servicemen to insure the financial well-being of their families.

Commercial Accounts

Besides paying military and civilian members of the War Department, disbursing officers overseas also had to pay commercial accounts. Before a finance officer could pay a vendor for goods or services delivered to the army, he needed complete procurement papers and receiving reports, so contracting, receiving, and finance officers had to work together closely to pay commercial bills.[1] Rules governing payments to commercial concerns and civilian employees were more flexible than those pertaining to military forces. In Italy, for example, when the issuance of 1,000-lire notes

---

[1] Col Clyde D. Keith, cofs, Hq USAFIME, Cir 23, 16 Mar 44. RG 338.

to soldiers was suspended so that more control could be exercised over currency transactions of the military, finance officers could still receive the notes and issue them to pay civilian payrolls or commercial vouchers.[2]

During the early days of the war in England, the Finance Department paid many commercial accounts to speed the growth of an effective fighting machine. In 1942, for example, Lockheed Aircraft Corporation had contracted with the government to repair airplanes. Since skilled mechanics were in great demand, they commanded an unusually high wage. Finance did not pay the Lockheed payrolls, but did pay the government's contract. In addition to his regular salary, a Lockheed mechanic in England drew $25 per diem. It was possible for such a man to earn more than $14,000 a year—more than General Eisenhower's salary.[3]

Finance offices in Australia handled a large volume of commercial accounts, since the army depended on the local economy for much of its logistical support. To satisfy local firms supplying goods and services, the army tried to pay commercial accounts quickly. Purchasing and contracting officers (P&CO's) were to send invoices and supporting papers to a finance office within forty-eight hours after delivery. The finance office then made payment within twenty-four hours.[4]

In Sydney, maladministration by P&CO's frequently caused extra work in finance offices. P&CO's would delay sending their accounts until after the thirty-day discount period had expired. Yet when they did submit their papers, they would still certify vouchers for the 2.5 percent discount allowed by commercial firms. The businesses would naturally complain, and the P&CO's would acknowlege their mistakes, whereupon the finance office would have to cancel the old checks and write new ones.[5]

[2] Ltr, Davis to DO's, Sixth Port Hq TC, Twenty-fifth, Forty-seventh, Forty-ninth, Fiftieth FDS's, Agent Fin Offs, Hq Staging Area, and Second Repl Depot, 26 Dec 43. RG 338.

[3] Interview with Brig Gen William P. Campbell (Ret), 27 Apr 54.

[4] Ltr, Col L. S. Ostrander, AG, USASOS, to CG, Advance Base, Base Sec CO's, et al., 11 Dec 42, sub: Procedure for Expediting Payment of Accounts, CSD 120.1. RG 338.

[5] Check Sheet, Purchasing and Contracting Branch, USASOS, to Fin Off, APO 927, 21 Apr 44; ltr, Clinton-Williams Pty Ltd, to Control Br, Procurement Div, APO 927, 3 Apr 44; ltr, Capt E. F. Armstrong, Fin Off, USASOS,

Native Labor

No doubt the most interesting commercial accounts paid in the Pacific, Asia, and Middle East involved native labor. In those places the army encountered people and customs entirely different from its own. Recognizing the power of folkways, the army paid for services in manners quite alien to the procedures used when dealing with Americans. But if the army wanted work done by Tonkinese or Iranian laborers, it had to pay in ways that insured their willingness to perform. The army used natives for a variety of tasks: construction work, rescue of downed fliers, driving trucks, and running railroads, among others. Usually it was much cheaper and quicker to employ native labor for such work than for the army to do it. The following instances represent the highly diverse situations in which the army paid for native labor. They reflect the adaptability of the army's payment procedures to secure needed services. If the army had any consistent policy in such matters, it was this adaptability to diverse situations.

In the most underdeveloped regions where the army operated, native workers, still accustomed to bartering, had little concept of money. Such was the case in the northern forward base sections of Australia. There the army paid for services in beads, mirrors, colorful cloth, and cosmetics.[6] Bedouins in Morocco also frequently preferred and received payment in cloth.[7]

Elsewhere, such as in New Caledonia, where the French had lent their civilizing influence, the army established an elaborate scale of wages for construction workers. It employed three classes of labor: supervisory (all French), per diem, and indentured. The last category was composed of natives. Supervisors worked on a daily basis, forty-five hours a week; natives worked under a contract, fifty-four hours a week. They could work overtime up to seventy hours. A married supervisor with no children earned 3,700 francs per month. If he had six children, he would draw 7,125

Base Sec 7, to CG, USAFFE, 3 May 44, sub: Discount Lost on Commercial Accounts, BSGF 120.1. RG 338.

[6] "History of the U.S. Army Forces in the Far East, 1943–1945," p. 99. CMH.

[7] Memo, Col O. W. DeGruchy, Chief Fis Br, Hq PGSC, to Command Signal Off, PGSC, 18 Jan 43, FO 230.14 230.341. RG 338.

francs. Per diem laborers got 15.5 francs a day during their first month and 20.5 subsequently. Each day half a franc was deducted for their tribal chief. The indentured male employees, Tonkinese for the most part, got 190 francs per month. Compulsory savings of 20 francs per month were deducted, as well as a repatriation charge of 90 francs a month, leaving a net pay of 80 francs. A Tonkinese woman grossed 125 francs per month. From her pay, 10 francs were deducted for savings and 55 for repatriation, leaving a net of 60 francs per month. Obviously, in this situation the army did not see itself as an instrument of social melioration. When the finance office at Noumea ran short of French currency, it had to pay with American money. This arrangement was not wholly satisfactory to the French because they had trouble following the computation of allowances and feared they were being cheated.[8]

Similarly, the army set up specific rates of payments for natives who performed rescue work in the IBT. In 1944 in cooperation with the Indian government, the IBT established rates for rewards. A native could draw up to 100 rupees for each person rescued alive on land, sea, or a river; and up to 500 rupees for each body recovered. At that time, one rupee equaled $.301875. Between 3 and 5 rupees (with a maximum of 25) could be paid for salvaging equipment from crashes on land. A worker could get from 1 to 3 rupees (with a maximum of 10) for recovering equipment lost in training. Individual fliers forced to bail out could pay these rewards from funds in their money belts, or rewards could be paid by the nearest finance officer. Each air-ground or air-sea unit had an agent officer to pay rescue expenses.[9]

Finance officers in Egypt, as well as the rest of Africa, faced some unusual problems connected with paying natives employed by the army. Among these were the payment of workers who left the government's employ without having accounts settled, the desire not to draw pay in the country where work was performed, the unwillingess or inability of some workers to sign payrolls, and the graft often attending the employment of illiterate workers. For

[8] Agreement between the United States of America and the Colony of New Caledonia, 1 Sep 43; ltr, Lt Col George W. Studebaker, Fin Off, Hq Sv Com, APO 502, to the QM, Sv Com, APO 502, 17 Jun 43, sub: Shortage of French Currency. RG 338.

[9] Memo AAF 145–6, Hq IBT, 4 Dec 44. RG 338.

example, in 1943 one Josef Skarabat, a truck driver for the American army, had driven in a convoy from Asmara to Heliopolis. While in Cairo waiting to return to Asmara, he met a Yugoslav who persuaded him to enlist in Tito's Partisan army. Josef was so taken with his new venture that he entirely forgot to collect the pay due him from the Americans. By August 1944 Josef had remembered his omission and applied to the American embassy in Cairo for payment. Finance records verified his claims and he was paid.[10]

To accomplish its construction mission in the Middle East, the army needed skilled native workers as well as truck drivers. It had to make special payment arrangements with trained native engineers to secure their services, such as allowing those in Saudi Arabia to send pay wherever they wished via the intertheater PTA.[11]

When native laborers in Africa, Iran, and Italy could not sign their names on payrolls, several alternatives were used. Moroccan bedouins could mark the payroll with thumbprints.[12] In Italy illiterate workers received pay in the presence of a responsible government official who formally witnessed the payroll. The disbursing officer often certified payment as usual.[13]

The more educated native employees in Iran exhibited great pride in their signatures and took umbrage if asked to sign a payroll with a thumbprint. The word "signature" to these people was not a synonym for "name." A man's signature could consist of his initials or one or two words of his name. He would write this signature with a studied flourish that would make duplication difficult. Such signatures sufficed in legal and business transactions in Iran. All Iranians who could write their signatures were happy to use them, but many Muslims refused for religious reasons to write out the full names required on payrolls. In their way of thinking, their last name was not something to be recorded on public documents.

[10] Ltr, 1st Lt William H. McNeill, CAC, Assistant Military Attaché, American Embassy, Near the Governments of Greece and Yugoslavia, Cairo, Egypt, to USAFIME and 3d, 6th, and 11th inds, 29 Aug–18 Nov 44. RG 338.

[11] Ltr, Col Dale L. Thompson, AG, Hq AMET, APO 787, to Cairo Military District, APO 787; Area Engineer, Dhahran, Saudi Arabia; Eritrea Base Command, APO 843, Attn: Fin Offs, 8 Sep 45; WD Cir 330, 44. RG 338.

[12] Memo, Col O. W. DeGruchy, Chief Fis Br, Hq PGSC, to Command Signal Off, PGSC, 18 Jan 43, FO 230.14 230.341. RG 338.

[13] Ltr, Col D. R. Nimocks, Fin Off, PBS, to Fin Offs, 6th Port Hq TC, Thirteenth, Forty-seventh, Forty-ninth, and Fiftieth FDS's, 12 Oct 44. RG 338.

The PGC and the GAO did not insist that natives conform to ordinary payroll procedures. They could use their "signatures," executed in the Roman alphabet, or they could sign in Arabic, Persian, or Armenian script. Finance clerks spelled native names phonetically on payrolls.[14]

The Ahwaz Service District of the PGSC developed its own system of paying native laborers. Paymasters were former civil service employees of the Corps of Engineers, who had been placed on the payroll of the Foley Brothers construction firm at the request of the Chief of Engineers. Coolie laborers received a brass tag when they reported for work in the mornings; in the evenings they traded these tags for chits. On each payday, the coolies surrendered chits they had accumulated during the pay period. Two soldiers and the civilian paymaster counted chits and the latter made payment in the presence of a witnessing officer. While one basic wage rate existed for coolie labor, there were many for artisans. Consequently, these skilled workers were paid on the basis of time cards. The Ahwaz District found this method of payment the most satisfactory and the most economical of personnel. It estimated that to follow conventional methods, a minimum of three finance officers, along with a full staff of enlisted men, would be required.[15]

With such unorthodox pay procedures, some irregularities inevitably developed. To accomplish its mission, the PGSC had to depend on the use of the Iranian State Railway, so the PGSC paid the salaries of railroad workers. An investigation revealed that railway paymasters demanded a fifty-rial kickback from each coolie per payday. Cashiers and paymasters conspired to credit coolies with overtime but not pay them. The conspirators then split the proceeds. They also padded payrolls. Since paymasters did not carry small change with them, they paid laborers to the nearest even

---

[14] Ltr, Capt Jack A. Dabbs, Class B agent, U.S. Truck Assembly Plant 2, Khorramshahr, Iran, to CO, Port of Khorramshahr, Attn: Fin Off, 7 Aug 44, sub: Signatures on Native Pay Rolls, FD 248.2; 2d Ind, Maj R. E. Burch, OFD, Hq PGSC, to Fin Off, Port of Khorramshahr, Khorramshahr, Iran, 15 Aug 44. FD 248.2. RG 338.

[15] Ltr, Capt Leon Zwicker, Adjutant, Hq Ahwaz Service District, PGSC, Ahwaz, Iran, 4 Mar 43, to Chief Fis Br, PGSC, Teheran, and Chief, Civilian Personnel Branch, PGSC, Teheran, sub: Pay Roll and Timekeeping Procedure for Native Personnel, A-1 FO 230-05 (Civ Employees). RG 338.

amount under their rightful wages.[16] A later generation of American corporate leaders would have recognized such irregularities as the cost of doing business overseas.

Another departure from standard payment methods was the way the PGC settled accounts of deceased natives who had been in the employ of the U.S. government. Army regulations prescribed that the GAO make such settlements. Because this was obviously impractical in the PGC, the command based settlements on a Comptroller General decision. The disbursing officer paid wages due the deceased to the nearest of kin on a separate payroll. The recipient had to certify that he was the next of kin, and the payment had to be witnessed by two disinterested people.[17]

Philippine Accounts

Many pay problems that were peculiar to the Philippine Islands deserve special attention. Since the Spanish-American War, the United States had maintained a military establishment in the Philippines. The functioning of the American army therefore mystified few Filipinos. Many men of the islands belonged to the Philippine Scouts, the Filipino arm of the U.S. Army. Commercial firms in the islands had done business with the army for years, so the army had virtually the same footing in the islands that it had in the United States. Despite the independence movement, few Filipinos considered the army an occupation force. A spirit of mutual cooperation in financial matters consequently existed between Filipinos and the army.

Immediately after the Japanese bombed Pearl Harbor, the army in the Philippines accelerated preparations for defense of the islands. The army leased privately owned buildings and occupied public property. It took over radio, cable, and telephone systems. All transportation facilities, including spare parts, repair shops, equipment, and employees, came under military control. The army bought new cars and trucks outright. But where large businesses were involved, such as fleets of buses and ships, commercial plants,

[16] Ltr, Capt Henry Dawes, Public Relations and Labor Off, Hq Military Railway Service, PGSC, to Col John B. Stetson, Fis Adviser to CG, PGSC, 11 Jun 43, sub: Irregularities in pay, accounts, and food departments, Iranian State Railway, 248. RG 338.

[17] Cir No. 20, PGC, 15 Feb 44. RG 338.

and real estate, it made no immediate settlements. Many owners were satisfied as creditors of the U.S. government throughout the war, since any property they had was vulnerable to confiscation by the Japanese. The army made regular, short-term payments for most personal services.[18]

Since army units had been stationed in the Philippines for many years and since Filipinos could serve in the army, some soldiers lived in the islands after retirement. When the war began, approximately 1,000 retirees were paid from the Manila finance office. The office found it impossible to continue paying these people by check, yet it realized that nonpayment would work a great hardship on them. The office therefore directed provincial treasurers to pay up to one-half of retirees' claims that would be presented by affidavit. A local justice of the peace or priest had to witness such affidavits.[19]

Payments to most officers and men in the Philippines became irregular after the November 1941 payday. The few organizations receiving regular pay until the islands fell were located around Manila and Subic Bay and on Cebu and Mindanao. Most Americans on Bataan neither received nor wanted any pay, but the Philippine army on Bataan drew pay through 31 March 1942, just nine days before the surrender. Civilian employees on Bataan also got paid through 31 March and those in the harbor defenses of Manila Bay, through 30 April.[20]

When the war broke out, some individuals in the Philippines received temporary commissions, but few of these officers drew pay. They seemed to feel they were fulfilling an obligation for which they wanted no pay. Their reluctance to accept pay hindered finance offices in settling accounts and jeopardized the position of their dependents.[21]

Although all official finance activity ceased with the fall of the Philippines, American intelligence funds continued to sustain

---

[18] Vance, "Report of Operations, Finance Officer, USFIP," pp. 6–7. RG 338.

[19] Interview with Col Royal G. Jenks (Ret), 17 Aug 55.

[20] Radio, Allied Supply Council, USAFFE to Washington, 6 Mar 43, 1634 Third; Vance, "Report of Operations," p. 7. RG 338.

[21] Vance, "Report of Operations," p. 7.

guerrilla warfare while the Japanese held the islands. Submarines from Australia supplied these funds. Immediately after the invasion of Leyte, disbursements resumed, several finance officers landing with the assault phase. As soon as tactical units employed natives for construction work, disbursing officers began paying them daily. These quick payments encouraged large numbers of Filipinos to work for the army.[22] They also helped to boost the natives' confidence in the new Philippine Victory currency. The increase of purchasing power through the injection of sound money into the local economy was another beneficial aspect of daily payments.[23]

While paying Filipino workers daily proved advantageous, it did require some administrative innovations. A new voucher had to be devised to eliminate paperwork. Tenth Corps disbursing officers designed the emergency payment voucher to pay Philippine Civil Affairs Unit (PCAU) civilian employees. As Col. J. C. Kovarik, finance officer for the Tenth Corps, described the voucher, it "was a very simple form and only required average intelligence in its preparation." The voucher was streamlined in every respect. It did not specify the using agency nor the purpose of the labor. Laborers' names were omitted in favor of serial numbers. Each worker was supposed to get an identification tag, but a shortage demanded some improvisation. One PCAU tried to substitute paper slips with the serial number written in ink, which worked fine until a rain washed the numbers away!

As operations in the Philippines progressed, the trials of PCAU disbursing officers multiplied. The military situation demanded an increasing number of workers, so the areas of the PCAU's were extended. With this extension, disbursing officers had more people to pay and a wider area to cover. They had to travel on traffic-choked roads for eight and ten hours a day from village to village to pay laborers. Frequently workers would not appear for their pay for days on end, and they demanded more money for carrying supplies to troops in the mountains. Finance officers could not catch

[22] Report of the Leyte Operation, 20 October 1944–25 December 1944, Sixth Army, p. 276. RG 338.
[23] Ltr, Col J. C. Kovarik, Fin Off, Tenth Corps, to Fis Dir, USAFFE, 1 Jan 45, sub: Disbursement Vouchers, 132.2-N. RG 338.

up on their records at night because combat conditions demanded a complete blackout.[24]

Payment to guerrilla forces was also a constant problem. Early in the Luzon campaign guerrilla units had not been fully recognized, yet their cooperation was important in expelling the Japanese. To maintain their support, the Sixth Army paid guerrillas as civilian laborers and interpreters. When they gained recognition as military units, the Philippine Army Finance Service assumed obligation for their payment. No U.S. Army disbursing officers were to pay guerrillas, but Philippine army officers with guerrilla units were used as class A agents to disbursing officers of the Sixth Army. In this capacity they enabled guerrillas to secure provisions and labor quickly.[25]

The Philippine army prescribed rates of pay and allowances for members of guerrilla units. All individuals, including members of the U.S. armed forces who had not been returned to American control, received the rates of their guerrilla grade specified by the Philippine army. Retired Philippine Scouts could draw pay as guerrillas and as retired members of the U.S. army. Guerrillas' "current" pay (as opposed to pay due for service during the Japanese occupation) dated from the time the commanding general of USAFFE confirmed a guerrilla band as an operating unit under the Eighth Army.[26]

South of Luzon, the Eighth Army reorganized guerrilla forces and integrated them into the Philippine army as organic units. Part of this task was devising a pay system. The greatest problem involved forcing a settlement of guerrillas' pay. Although the Philippine army, cooperating with the Eighth Army, listed 15 August 1945 as the last day a man could get paid as a guerrilla, it tried to make settlements earlier. After 15 August 1945, guerrillas became ineligible for inclusion on regular payrolls. Many guerrillas did not

[24] Ibid.

[25] Operational Report, Fin Sec, Hq Sixth Army, 25 Jan 43–24 Jan 46. RG 338.

[26] Ltr, Col R. E. Fraile, USAFFE, to CG, Sixth and Eighth armies, 15 Apr 45, sub: Payment of Recognized Guerrilla Units, FEPA 242; Check Sheet, GHQ, USAFPAC, to Theater Fis Dir, 25 Jul 45, sub: Pay of Retired Philippine Scouts, AG-KF. RG 338.

want settlement of their accounts. By avoiding the Eighth Army processing teams who were visiting the small islands, they hoped to stay on payrolls as guerrillas indefinitely. They wanted neither discharge nor release. Philippine army finance officers made final decisions on guerrilla pay.[27]

The pay of some guerrilla units, even after they had been integrated into the Philippine army, was irregular. Maj. Ramon Magsaysay, commander of Magsaysay's Forces and later president of the Republic of the Philippines, informed the commanding general, U.S. Army Forces in the Pacific (USAFPAC), of the pay troubles of his unit. According to the agreement between the army and the Filipinos, Magsaysay contended, guerrillas should get paid in full until the time of their discharge. He protested that his men got paid only for time actually spent in tactical operations against the enemy. The Filipino leader said that if his men were to be paid only for time devoted to direct support of U.S. Army operations, rather than on a full-time basis, their status as members of USAFFE would be that of mere laborers. He thought their efforts entitled them to more consideration. Headquarters, AFWESPAC investigated this case and supported Magsaysay's position. His officers and men won pay for their entire service.[28]

Confusion about the military status of Filipinos existed on all levels. As long as questions arose about the status of such recognized bands as Magsaysay's Forces, it was inevitable that individual Filipino soldiers became confused as to their status. Although most Filipinos were probably inclined to claim membership in the U.S. Army because of the monetary advantage, evidence indicates that many could have had honest doubts. The case of Cpl. Loreto Comora illustrates the uncertain status of Filipino soldiers. Comora enlisted in a guerrilla unit that had formerly had status with USAFFE. He thought that his enlistment made him a member of the Army. Consequently, he filed a claim for accrued pay, family allowances,

[27] Ltr, Col E. S. Graham, Asst AG, Eighth Army, to CINC, USAFPAC, 29 Jul 45, sub: Limiting Dates for Processing and Payment of Guerrillas, AG 230.145. RG 338.

[28] Ltr, Maj Ramon Magaysay, Commanding Magaysay's Forces, USAFFE, to CG, AFPAC, Attn: Guerrilla Affairs Sec, 4 Nov 45, sub: Information, Request for. RG 338.

insurance premiums, and compensation for property damaged by the enemy. The Eighth Army ruled that the corporal was mistaken in assuming he was a member of the U.S. Army and therefore had no valid claim. But as a member of the Philippine army serving with a recognized guerrilla force, the Ninety-fifth Infantry Regiment of the Ninety-second Philippine Division, Comora could register his claim with headquarters, Philippine army.[29]

One of the objectives of the American army when it returned to the Philippines was to help establish the civil government. While the Philippine government assumed final responsibility for paying its functionaries, the army made interim payments as the government resumed operations. Col. A. H. Miller, commanding the 172d FDS, stated that these payments to the officials of the Philippine government represented a major problem. Finance officers had to improvise a payment voucher acceptable to both parties. After the Philippine government audited the paid vouchers, it reimbursed the U.S. government. The president of the Republic of the Philippines sometimes sat in on the reimbursement conferences.[30]

The American army also aided local government agencies to resume operations. The Fortieth Division CIC (Counterintelligence Corps) entered a town in Pampanga Province after the Japanese retreated and set up a school system. Since no civil official had authorized the reopening of the schools, various civilian agencies were reluctant to pay teachers. The provincial governor would not pay them because his budget would not stand the strain. A PCAU refused payment since it had not appointed the teachers. Finally, the American army resolved the differing points of view and arranged pay for the teachers.[31]

After American forces reentered the Philippines, they recovered many soldiers and War Department civilian employees who had been captured by the Japanese. Finance officers would give these ex-prisoners of war, as well as members of the Philippine army, partial payments equal to three months' pay of the grade

[29]Ltr, Cpl Loreto Comora, to TAG, 7 Dec 44, sub: Status of Enlisted Man of Philippine Constabulary. RG 338.

[30]Interview with Col A. H. Miller, 15 Aug 56.

[31]Ltr, Col Paul Oed, AG, Eleventh Corps, to CG, Sixth Army, 3 Jun 45, sub: Pay Rolls in Pampanga Province, AG 230Y, 8 Inds. RG 338.

held when captured, but payment depended upon positive identification.[32]

After American forces returned to the Philippines, finance officers resumed paying retired members of the U.S. Army, including Philippine Scouts. The Washington FOUSA had no record of payments having been made to retired personnel living in the Philippines after November 1941, but in December 1944 the OFD sent SWPA a list of 839 retired Philippine Scouts to be paid, along with a photostatic copy of the Adjutant General's certification of their length of service. SWPA settled these accounts. The War Department directed the USAFFE fiscal director to designate a disbursing officer to settle retired pay. This disbursing officer could bring payments up to date, provided the retired members could produce proper identification and certification of service.[33]

Selected to handle retired pay was the 180th FDS, located in Brisbane until March 1945. The 180th operated as part of the USAFFE OFD, in both Australia and Manila. On the basis of records sent by the Adjutant General, the 180th established and maintained retired pay files. When a retired member could not produce immediately all the requisites for full payment, he could present an affidavit to any finance officer and draw a partial payment equal to one month's retired pay. Finance officers paying these partials sent completed vouchers and all supporting papers to the 180th.[34]

The principal reason the 180th FDS was chosen to handle this function requiring extensive study was because it had the necessary staff and reference library. To make a current payment to a retired person, the 180th had to have affidavits stating retired status, grade, date of retirement, date of last payment, by whom the last payment was made, the amount of pay and allowances received from American sources since the date of last payment, and the address to which retired checks should be mailed.[35] By December 1945 the 180th

[32] Ltr, Maj M. B. Kendrick, Asst AG, USAFFE, to CG, Sixth Army, et al., 19 May 45, sub: Partial Payments for Recovered U.S. Military Personnel (Including Philippine Scouts), Philippine Army Personnel, and Civilian Employees of the War Department, FEGARP 241. RG 338.

[33] Radio, Carter, WD, to CINC SWPA, 21 Dec 44, 2-79992. RG 338.

[34] Cir 8, USAFFE, 22 Jan 45. RG 338.

[35] Ltr, Col C. W. Stonefield, Deputy Fis Dir, USAFFE, to Fin Off, Hq

had cleared practically all cases where retired pay was in arrears and was paying only current retired pay.[36]

Allotments for Dependents

The nature of the army in World War II greatly influenced the congressional legislation that determined its pay. This was not an army of professional fighting men; it was an army of citizen soldiers, of civilians who had left their normal pursuits to fight aggressors. The government, remembering that its soldiers were fulfilling the highest obligation of citizenship, as it was then interpreted, strove to pay them adequately. Not only did legislation make the pay of American soldiers the highest in the world, it also provided for the care of dependents. Peacetime soldiers, as a rule, were bachelors with few outside obligations. No allotment was designed expressly for the support of those dependents they may have had. But if the citizen soldier of World War II had dependents, Congress authorized means for their support.

Even though support of dependents and building soldiers' financial future represented the chief aims of the extensive allotment system administered by the Finance Department during World War II, reduction of soldiers' money in foreign theaters was also a most important consideration. Since the American soldier always had more money to spend than either a native population or other Allied troops, the danger of disrupting local economies was tremendous. Americans' potent buying power, by inflating prices, created antagonism on the part of those who had to compete with it in local markets. So it behooved the American government from a diplomatic standpoint to drain soldiers' earnings away from foreign economies.

A number of devices reduced the quantity of money that crossed pay tables. Allotments, taken from military pay for a variety of purposes, were identified alphabetically: B, D, E, F, N, and X. The army also provided devices other than allotments for withdrawing money from circulation, such as the soldier's deposit and the personal transfer account.

USAFFE, Attn: Col J. B. Rothnie, 6 Mar 45, sub: Pay of Retired Personnel, FETF 242.18; Check Sheet, OFD USAFFE, to Chief Fin Off, USAFFE, 24 Feb 45, sub: Retired Pay Rolls, 242.18. RG 338.

[36] 2d Lt R. E. Hensen, Semi-Annual Report, 180th FDS, 11 Dec 45–3 Jul 46. RG 338

The first important wartime legislation providing family support was the Servicemen's Dependents Allowance Act of 1942, which became effective 1 June of that year. Before this act, all support of dependents came through the class E allotment, which was any specified sum from a man's pay. The government added nothing to the allotment. This 1942 act set up allowances for the dependents of enlisted men exclusive of the first three grades, i.e., master, technical, and staff sergeants. Since that portion of the soldier's pay going toward dependent support was not liable to forfeiture through any type of legal process, it was not known as an allotment, but rather as a class F deduction, and it was paid regardless of a man's pay status. Types of dependents were divided into two groups, A and B. Those in the first category were wives, children, and divorced wives whom soldiers were legally obliged to support. In the latter were parents, brothers, sisters, or grandparents who depended upon the enlisted man for a substantial portion of their support. The government's contribution varied according to the number and type of class A dependents. For a wife it allowed twenty-eight dollars. If there was one child, forty dollars, and ten dollars for each additional child. When there was a child but no wife to support, the government contributed twenty dollars. For two children, but no wife, the amount was thirty dollars, and ten for each additional child. A divorced wife received twenty dollars from the government, plus twelve for the first and ten for each additional child.

For the support of class B dependents, the government contributed fifteen dollars for one parent and twenty-five for both. Additional dependents such as brothers, sisters, or grandchildren would raise the government's contribution five dollars apiece. If a serviceman had no parents to support, his other dependents received five dollars each. In none of these class B cases could the aggregate government contribution total more than fifty dollars. The enlisted man's contribution to all allowances amounted to twenty-two dollars per month, plus five dollars extra if he had dependents in both class A and class B categories.[37]

In October 1943 Congress amended the Servicemen's De-

---

[37] PL 625, 77th Cong., "Servicemen's Dependents Allowance Act of 1942," Approved 23 Jun 1942, *Laws Relating to the War Department*, 49 (Washington: Government Printing Office, 1943).

pendents Allowance Act to liberalize family allowances. The amendment made families of all enlisted men eligible for support and increased the classes of dependents to three by creating a class B-1. Those covered by classes A and B remained the same, but class B-1 was established for parents, brothers, or sisters depending on the enlisted man for the "chief," rather than "substantial," portion of their support. The enlisted man's contribution to the family allowance remained the same, twenty-two dollars per month. The category of "wife with no child" stayed the same, fifty dollars. A wife with one child got eighty dollars, plus twenty dollars for each additional offspring. When the soldier had a child but no wife to support, the allowance remained forty-two dollars per month, but the amount for additional children was increased by ten dollars per child. A former wife with no child still received forty-two dollars, but such a woman with one child got an increase to seventy-two dollars, and twenty more for each additional youngster.

Allowances for class B dependents remained the same or were cut. A maximum of thirty-seven dollars was placed on the stipend any one or group in this category of dependents could get. This sum was payable only while there was no class B-1 dependent to draw an allowance.

Class B-1 was created to give greater support to those the 1942 act placed in class B. A single parent got fifty dollars, and both parents would draw sixty-eight dollars. One parent and one brother or sister received sixty-eight dollars, with an extra eleven dollars for each additional brother or sister. Both parents and one brother or sister got seventy-nine dollars, plus the eleven dollars for additionals. When there was only a brother or sister, forty-two dollars was given, plus the eleven dollars. The provisions of this 1943 amendment to the Servicemen's Dependents Allowance Act remained in effect for the remainder of the war.[38]

When the war began, Congress had authorized only three types of allotments. The principal one was the class E, which could be used to send any desired amount of money to individuals, banks, or commercial life insurance companies. Class D allotments were for premiums on U.S. Government Life Insurance, and class N, for

[38] PL 174, 78th Cong., Approved 26 Oct 1943, *Laws Relating to the War Department*, 50 (Washington: Government Printing Office, 1944).

premiums on National Service Life Insurance. By the end of the war's first year, the government realized that some provision was necessary to support dependents residing outside the United States, and therefore devised the class X allotment. The effectiveness of this allotment for alien support, first used in the United Kingdom, was decreased by frequent delays in delivery, which, of course, produced genuine hardships.[39] By September 1944 army regulations provided for the purchase of war bonds with a class B allotment.

Personnel sections instituted allotments, with the serviceman signing for a particular allotment and the personnel clerk entering the amount on the soldier's service record. Then the form went to the certifying officer, who signed and returned it. The personnel clerk retained one copy of the allotment form and one copy of the letter of transmittal in his files. The original allotment form and three copies of the letter of transmittal then went to the finance office, which put the allotment into effect. Some offices varied this procedure by having the personnel clerk wait until both the allotter and the certifying officer had signed the allotment form before entering the amount on the service record.[40]

Allotments continued in effect as long as a soldier was entitled to his pay and allowances. The fact that a man was missing, missing in action, beleaguered, besieged, interned in a neutral country, or captured by an enemy did not affect his allotments. Under certain circumstances of this nature, however, allotments could be terminated. When a disbursing officer had a document signed by a soldier stating his allotment was to be stopped in the event he entered into a casualty status, the cancellation was automatic upon receipt of such notice. If the disbursing officer received a request for stoppage from a soldier formerly in a missing status, the allotment was ended. The determination of the Secretary of War that allotments should be stopped for the best interest of the soldier and his dependents was another cause for cancellation.[41]

[39] AR 35-5520, Change 3 (29), 22 Dec 42. RG 338.

[40] Ltr, CWO C. W. Hogsett, Asst Fin Off, Hq Middle East Service Command, USAFIME, APO 678, to CO, MESC, USAFIME, Camp Russell B. Huckstep, Egypt, 6 Jun 44. RG 338.

[41] AR 35-5520, Sec 8, 30 Sep 1944; ltr, Carter, to Eighth, Tenth Ports, Twenty-fourth, Twenty-fifth, Twenty-ninth, Thirty-first, Thirty-fourth, Thirty-fifth, Thirty-seventh, and Forty-seventh FDS's, Staging Area, 1261 AAFBU, 27 Nov 44. RG 338.

Local situations frequently altered the usual system of paying family allowances. In North Africa, the Twenty-fourth FDS had the responsibility of handling allowances for American soldiers' native wives residing in Morocco, Algeria, and Tunisia. The section was located in Algiers, so the wives who lived in the city called at the office for cash payment. Wives living outside the city received monthly checks drawn upon the Banque de l'Algerie. All correspondence pertaining to the allotments had to be in French. The Office of Dependency Benefits (ODB) in Newark, New Jersey, prepared vouchers for the payment of these family allowances. After they were paid by the Twenty-fourth, it mailed the vouchers back to the Newark office, which reimbursed the Twenty-fourth's account. The ODB was the central War Department agency for mailing monthly family allowance checks to millions of dependents of servicemen.[42]

Had the ODB's contribution to the war effort been appraised on the basis of its performance through 1943, the appraisal could hardly have been enthusiastic. The ODB's percentage of error in 1943 was exceedingly high. One of its common practices was to acknowledge the discontinuance of a class E allotment and then maintain payments to the allottee. The disbursing officer in the field who received ODB's acknowledgment of discontinuance naturally terminated deductions from the allotter's pay. In some cases, ODB continued payments for as long as ten months, and as long as ODB made payments, lump sums had to be deducted from the erstwhile allotter's pay. Brig. Gen. L. S. Ostrander, adjutant general for USAFFE, reported that ODB's performance created "a serious morale lapse" in his theater. "The average enlisted man, as well as many officers, lost all confidence in the present allotment system."[43]

Col. Louis W. Maddox, chief finance officer of SWPA, termed dependency allotments "the most painful thing we have had to contend with." Late in 1943 there were between 4,000 and 6,000 allotment cases from SWPA that the ODB had not acted on for from six to twelve months. Colonel Maddox protested, "I realize ODB has

<hr />

[42] Capt R. A. Alexander, "Unit History."

[43] Ltr, Brig Gen L. S. Ostrander, AG, USAFFE, to TAG, 6 Sep 43, sub: Discontinuance of Class E allotments. RG 338.

its problems, but when those problems become a year old, it's very hard to explain . . . to a soldier in the combat area."[44]

Not all allotment trouble was traceable to the ODB. Slovenly administration in the field also gave rise to complaints. In the CBI personnel officers complicated procedures by not routing letters of transmittal through proper channels, by sending an insufficient number of copies of letters of transmittal or too many copies of the allotment forms, by grouping officers and men on the same lists, and by allowing forms to slip by without the signature of commanding officers. The theater explained to administrative officers that while the prosecution of the war should certainly have first consideration, the handling of allotments was "entitled to more attention" than it received in the CBI.[45]

Allotment problems can be best explained through a representative sampling of individual cases. In two instances where officers were not supporting their dependents properly, the army forced the officers to increase allotments. The army contended that as long as an officer was legally married, he was obliged to support his dependents "in a manner consistent with army standards of honor." In one case, an officer cut his allotment in half when he suspected that someone else had impregnated his wife. The reason that he maintained a $75 allotment was for the maintenance of his son by this woman. Although the officer had requested a divorce, the IG held that he was still legally responsible for the family's support. As a result, the officer increased his allotment to $150. Another case concerned a medical officer who had sent his wife only $200 over the period of a year. When the wife complained to the Adjutant General, the physician had to initiate a class E allotment of $111 per month.[46]

In contrast to the army's concern over insufficient support for dependents was a case in which a finance office thought a captain was allotting an excessive amount for his mother's support. The captain claimed that his mother needed a large sum each month to

[44] Ltr, Col L. W. Maddox, Chief Fin Off, SWPA, to Fis Dir, ASF, 8 Dec 43, sub: Progress Report of Fiscal and Finance Activities in SWPA. RG 338.

[45] Cir 29, Rear Echelon, CBI, 14 Mar 44. RG 338.

[46] Ltrs to TAG and Inds. RG 338.

maintain her standard of living. The money he was contributing constituted the majority of her income. The finance office considered this sum more than necessary to keep a mother's body and soul together. After the case was referred to the OFD in Washington, the OFD informed the headquarters that it was not the duty of a finance office to determine the necessary living expenses of any officer's parents. Not only was it not the finance office's duty, but the office was without any authority to make such determinations.[47]

Servicemen's dependents living outside the United States and receiving class F allotment checks from the ODB sometimes had trouble cashing them. The class E allotments that replaced the class X for support of dependents in foreign areas were paid by local disbursing officers in native currency. But all class F allotment checks coming from the ODB were denominated in dollars. Mrs. B. B. Hassani was the Indian mother of an American soldier who had taken out a class F allotment for her. Nowhere near her village in Assam was there a bank that would cash the dollar checks for Mrs. Hassani. The ODB referred her case to the IBT fiscal director, who arranged for a disbursing officer only ten miles from the woman's village to cash her checks in rupees.[48]

Fairly unusual was the case of a woman receiving class F allotment checks from two American soldiers. This New Caledonian citizen had two natural children by an enlisted man who took out a class F allotment for their support. Then another enlisted man married her and was willing to assume full responsibility for her illegitimate children, so he also took out a class F allotment. When he began supporting the children, she refused further aid from their

[47] Ltr, Lt Col Stuart T. Friant, Fin Off, USASOS, to Chief of Finance, Washington, D.C., 19 May 43, sub: Payment of Increased Allowances on Account of Dependent Mother, GSF 245.7; 1st Ind, Lt Col H. C. L. Feast, Asst, Receipts and Disbursements Div, WD ASF OFD, 22 Jun 43, to CG, USAF, APO 501, Attn: Fin Off, SPFED 245.81. RG 338.

[48] Ltr, Miss Doris L. Bushnell, Chief Correspondence Unit, Home Service, Red Cross, to ASF OCF, Attn: Col E. J. Bean, 2 Nov 44; ltr, Lt Col Ralph G. Langley, Asst Actg Theater Fisc Dir, IBT, to Mrs. B. B. Hassani, Monsur Village, Kaulaura Post Office, Sylhet District (Assam), 29 Nov 44. RG 338.

father. She returned an allotment check of $126 to the finance office of the South Pacific Base Command in Noumea. The finance office, upon advice from ODB, cancelled the check and terminated the father's allotment.[49]

The confusion that existed in the minds of Filipinos concerning their relation to the U.S. Army extended to dependency allotments. Many members of the Philippine army tried to use the American allotment system to support their families. These men learned that they were ineligible to participate in the American army's allotment program, but that disbursing officers of their own army could initiate allotments for them.[50]

The informal motto of the Finance Department in World War II was "Get 'em paid!" This was obviously more circumspect than the bold "Pay the troops and fear nothing!" Had the latter been the slogan, Finance would obviously have had something to fear, for troops, contractors, civilians, and dependents were not always paid efficiently. All of the blame, however, cannot be attributed to finance offices. Sometimes finance units simply were not available to handle all the army's payments and the payment of commercial accounts had to be coordinated with contracting officers. Despite inadequate peacetime planning for various pay procedures in war, finance offices overseas regularly sought to improve their methods of paying commercial accounts, native labor, the reconstituted Philippine government, and dependents.

Because of the peculiar relationship of the Philippine Islands to the United States, the army willingly assumed responsibility for furnishing various kinds of payments that helped revive the Commonwealth and enabled the establishment of the Republic on 4 July 1946. Had the army not furnished the money, the reconstitution of normal life in the Philippines would have been much slower and arduous. Life in the United States during the war would similarly have been much more difficult had it not been for millions of

---

[49] Ltr, Maj R. A. Mislock, Fin Off, Hq SPBC, APO 502, to ASF OFD, ODB, 5 Jun 45, sub: Class F Family Allowance, SPFIS 246.7, 4 Inds. RG 338.

[50] Ltr, Col C. W. Stonefield, Deputy Fis Dir, USAFFE, to Chief Fin Off, USAFFE, 25 May 45, FETF 240 (p). RG 338.

depedency allotments paid through the Finance Department. That the Office of Dependency Benefits performed badly can be attributed to its hasty conception, gigantism, and the usual inefficiencies of the makeshift wartime bureaucracy.

CHAPTER *8*

Paying Prisoners of War

PAYMENT of prisoners of war during World War II was supposedly regulated by an international treaty. The U.S. Army scrupulously abided by the provisions of this treaty in paying Axis prisoners of war. The Axis powers, on the other hand, were not so meticulous in following the provisions of the treaty when paying American prisoners of war. In addition to having the responsibility for paying enemy prisoners, the American army also faced a large task in paying its own members who had been Axis prisoners.

The Prisoners of War Convention Between the United States of America and Other Powers, 1929, signed in Geneva, outlined the basic procedures belligerents would use in making payments to prisoners of war. Subject to any private agreement between powers, officer prisoners would receive from the capturing power the same pay as officers of corresponding rank in the capturing army. The condition was added that the pay should not exceed the amount an officer would be paid by his own government. In other words, when American forces captured a German second lieutenant, that prisoner would be entitled to as much pay as an American second lieutenant or his own normal salary, whichever sum was less. In this illustration, the German officer would be paid at his own rate, since American officers' pay was considerably higher than that of corresponding ranks in the German army. The Geneva Convention stipulated that officers be paid monthly, if possible.

At the end of hostilities, the government for which prisoners of war had fought was to reimburse the detaining power for payments made to those prisoners. Internees working for the detaining nation were to receive wages, in addition to any pay that might accrue while in captivity. The wage rate would be fixed by agreements between the belligerents. All money credited to the accounts of prisoners was due them at the end of their captivity.[1] Nations

[1] "Prisoners of War Convention Between the United States of America

signing the Geneva Convention manifestly subscribed to the notion that prisoners of war should work during captivity. Each captor nation understood that idleness fomented discontent and furnished time and energy for escape attempts—the devil's workshop motif. Working prisoners usually enjoyed better health, stayed out of trouble, and earned a little nest egg. They moreover provided cheap labor for the captor. What better justification of the work ethic?

Around the basic frame of this international treaty the U.S. government developed its program for paying prisoners of war. Initially, it established a trust fund in the Treasury as the central depository for all prisoners' accounts. Any American currency a prisoner might have had at the time of his capture was forwarded to his account, where it was held pending his release. Col. Bickford E. Sawyer reminded finance officers in the Pacific that Japanese prisoners could not be credited with American currency stolen from wounded or dead American prisoners. Each case had to be determined individually. Japanese with American money were not automatically to be treated as if they had come by the money illegally. "But," continued Colonel Sawyer, "surrounding circumstances could easily establish lack of ownership. The prisoner could admit having stolen the money or having taken it from a dead or wounded soldier. Others might have seen the prisoner commit the unlawful act." When it became apparent to the captors—apparently semi-automatically—that the prisoner possessed currency illegally, they were to confiscate the money and hold it in trust for the lawful owner.[2] To the central account in the Treasury were also credited monthly allowances and work pay. Any foreign currencies that prisoners had were collected and sent to the Provost Marshal General in Washington.

---

and Other Powers, 1929," Treaty Series No. 846, 47 Stat 2021, in *Treaties, Conventions, Internal Act, Protocols, and Agreements Between the United States of America and Other Powers, 1923–1937*, 4 (Washington: Government Printing Office, 1938).

[2] Memo, Col B. E. Sawyer, Fis Off, USAFPOA, to See Distribution, 19 Dec 44. RG 338.

Entitlements

As soon as a prisoner arrived at an internment camp or hospital, a personnel officer opened a pay record for him. This record would accompany the prisoner until his release, when final settlement was made. All prisoners' accounts were credited with a monthly allowance, which accrued from the first official date of custody. A prisoner who escaped was not entitled to his allowance until he was returned to American military control. The only other cause for nonentitlement was punishment.

Enlisted prisoners received a monthly allowance of three dollars. Since the Geneva Convention made no stipulation for the pay of enlisted prisoners, the allowance was a gratuity of the American government. No Axis power reciprocated with uniform rates. The monthly allowance of an officer was determined by his grade and the army in which he served. German and Italian officers received the same allowances. All lieutenants got twenty dollars; captains, thirty dollars; majors and above, forty dollars. Japanese officers drew five dollars less per month in the equivalent grades. Late in the war, allowances for Japanese officers rose above those for German and Italian prisoners.[3]

In addition to the automatic monthly allowance, prisoners who chose to work received compensation. Again, no Axis nation paid a uniform rate for work comparable to the American rate. The type of work performed by prisoners determined their pay status. Class I labor included all services connected with the management, administration, and maintenance of the camp. Since this work was largely for the benefit of the prisoners, no pay accrued for its performance. Class II labor consisted of projects performed for agencies of the U.S. government other than the War Department, as well as projects for states, municipalities, and private parties. For this work, the War Department and the hiring party entered into a contract. Prisoners employed at class II labor initially received a credit of $.80 a day. This figure approximated the wages of an American private—$21 per month. If an enlisted Japanese prisoner of war performing class II labor was injured on the job, he was

[3] Cir no. 10, wd, 5 Jun 43; tm 19-500, chap. 4, sec. 3, par. 9, 20 Apr 45. RG 338.

entitled to a compensatory allowance of $.40 a day if his injury was not caused by misconduct. When the prisoner returned to work, this compensation stopped and the $.80 rate resumed.[4] In 1944 Prisoner of War Circular No. 29 provided an incentive for extra labor by allowing prisoners to earn up to $1.20 a day for piece work.[5] Officer prisoners were not required to work, according to provisions of the Geneva Convention. But if they requested suitable work, it was given them. Noncommissioned officers were assigned only supervisory jobs unless they made a specific request for another type. All prisoners doing class II labor—officers, noncommissioned officers, and privates—were paid at the same rate. Men performing class I labor could be compensated only when they were required to devote so much of their time to camp work that they were unavailable for remunerative jobs. In such cases they, too, received $.80 a day. Work pay accounts were kept subsidiary to the regular monthly allowance records.

Prisoners could receive canteen coupons rather than having all their pay credited to their accounts. The total value of coupons issued could not be greater than the sum of the regular allowance and work pay earned in the preceding month. When a prisoner elected to receive coupons, they were charged against his account on the same payroll or individual voucher on which his monthly earnings were recorded.

Personnel officers in prison camps prepared monthly payrolls for internees. They submitted separate rolls for each nationality and paid officers on different rolls from enlisted men. Revisions of procedures in April 1945 enabled finance officers to pay officers and men on the same roll, with officers grouped at the top of each list.[6] Payrolls reflected amounts accrued as monthly allowances and work pay. From this total came the prisoner's indebtedness for canteen coupons. When disbursing officers received the payrolls, they computed them and prepared vouchers. They drew checks in favor of the camp canteens for the coupons previously issued, and they

[4] POW Cir no. 1, 24 Sep 43, USAFFE. RG 338.

[5] Prisoner of War Operations Division, Office of the Provost Marshal General, *Historical Monograph* (n.p., n.p., n.d.), pp. 99–100; TM 19-500, chap. 5, sec. 5, par. 25, 31 May 45.

[6] TM 19-500, chap. 4, sec. 6, par. 23, 20 Apr 45.

credited by name any unused allowances to the Treasury trust fund account. When disbursing officers had completed their work, they delivered checks, triplicate copies of the payrolls, and individual vouchers to camp commandants.

While it was illegal for prisoners to have American currency at any time, they could make withdrawals from their trust fund accounts in special instances, but only with the approval of the camp commander. When a prisoner had a legitimate desire or need for goods or services he could not obtain through camp canteens, he might withdraw money. For example, if a prisoner wanted to buy a musical instrument or take an extension course from an American university, he could use his money from the trust fund. The amount withdrawn could not exceed total credit in the account, and an enlisted man could use only thirty dollars in any one month. The first step in the procedure for making a withdrawal was a letter of application from the prisoner to the camp commander in which he stated his reason and purpose. If the commander approved, the finance office prepared a voucher. The check drawn would be made payable to the prisoner, who would endorse it in the presence of the camp commander to the agency for which it was intended. Then the check would be delivered or mailed to that agency.

When German prisoners were repatriated, they took the balances in their trust funds. This final settlement could be by cash or check.[7] On the other hand, Japanese prisoners being repatriated were restricted in the amount of currency they could take. Officers could return with 500 yen; enlisted men, with 200; and civilians, with 1,000. Fiscal officers collected any funds an individual had in excess of his quota. They kept records of the amount of excess currency each prisoner had, along with the prisoners' permanent addresses. Japanese could not return to their homeland with jewelry, precious metals, securities, or other financial instruments. Records of such property were turned over to the custodian of enemy property.[8]

[7] POW Cir no. 1, WD, 24 Sep 43; Fin Cir Ltr no. 62, Hq ETO, OFD, 1 Mar 44. RG 338; interview with Lt Col Merlin Nelson, POW Br, Office of the Provost Marshal General, 29 Oct 54.

[8] TWX, CG AFWESPAC SGD STYLER, TO CG BASE M, CO BASE K, CG OBASCOM, 30 Oct 45, 311.23. RG 338.

Variations in Payment

Although War Department instructions for paying prisoners of war intended to provide a uniform system, local variations existed in the way prisoners were paid. Reasons for the variations included lack of relevant army regulations, forcing finance offices to estimate appropriate payments. When the American army worked closely with the British, as in the Middle East, it generally followed British procedures for paying prisoners, which were considerably less generous than the American. Commanders elsewhere assumed responsibility for varying the prescribed rates of compensation to prisoners, depending on their needs and circumstances. The repatriation of large numbers of Italian and German prisoners after hostilities revealed that the army had not followed usual pay procedures during their captivity. In some cases, the army had not paid prisoners at all, awaiting a final payment to settle accounts. In others, the army had co-opted German prisoners to handle the payments of fellow internees.

In the Eastern Base Section of the North African theater, the problem was evolving a workable method of paying military prisoners, since the only circular available dealt with enemy civilians interned in the United States. Lacking any other material, the finance office based its program of paying military prisoners on this document. Even after the Eastern Base Section received the proper circulars, the office found it necessary to deviate from War Department instructions to cope with local conditions.[9]

In the African theaters, where most American military activity had to be coordinated with the British, prisoner of war administration was no exception. Headquarters, USAFIME, at Cairo confirmed the policy of using the British work pay scale as the basis for American payments. Another distinct departure from War Department instructions was making cash payments directly to prisoners every month. While Americans disbursed work pay to Axis prisoners in their employ, the British continued to handle their base pay. The reason for this procedure was that in Egypt the British government assumed responsibility for all Axis prisoners. American

[9] Report of Operations, Fin Off, Eastern Base Sec, NATOUSA, Sep 43, RG 338.

commands that needed prisoners as laborers could employ them, but in so doing they had to conform with British administrative procedures. In one instance, during the construction of the John H. Payne Air Field, Italian prisoners were needed as painters, brick-layers, carpenters, plasterers, electricians, plumbers, and general la-borers. At most American installations the Italians could be used profitably as cooks, waiters, launderers, and kitchen police. The employment of Italian prisoners in routine jobs released enlisted men to perform essentially military duties.[10]

Following the general trend of making American policy con-form to the British policy in Africa, the Provost Marshal General (PMG) authorized theater commanders to prescribe a work pay rate of less than eighty cents a day. The British in Egypt paid prisoners of war anywhere from ten to twenty cents a day for their work. The PMG also allowed USAFIME to issue any instructions necessary to supplement prisoner of war circulars and to insure uniform Allied policy.[11]

According to the Geneva Convention, governments that pris-oners served before their capture had to reimburse the detaining power after repatriation. When both the British and the American governments had responsibility for Axis prisoners in Egypt, the question arose of who was to reimburse whom. The British paid all prisoners their regular monthly allowances, and those prisoners released by the British to the Americans received work pay from the United States. The War Department took the position that any reimbursements for monthly allowance pay would be strictly a matter between the British and Italian governments. American re-sponsibility extended only to work pay. Since work pay was in addition to monthly allowances, it was over and above the amount for which the British could claim reimbursement from the Italians. But when the British paid Italian prisoners for work done for the

[10] Ltr, Brig Gen Gilbert X. Cheves, cofs, Hq USAFIME, to AG-5, GHQ MEF, 17 Dec 43, sub: Italian Prisoners of War; 3rd Ind, Maj H. Kunzler, Asst AG, Hq USAFIME, to CO, Deversoir Air Dept, 8 Feb 44; ltr, Maj Ned Sanger, AG, Hq USAFIME, to the PMG, 28 May 44; 1st Ind, Col Francis Howard, Hq ASF, PMGO, to CG, USAFIME, 9 Jun 44. RG 338.

[11] Ltr, Col H. H. Wild, AG, Hq USAFIME, to the PMG, 14 May 44; 1st Ind, Hq ASF, PMGO Washington, to CG, USAFIME, APO 787, 31 May 44. RG 338.

Americans, AMET reimbursed the British in cash. In areas where reciprocal aid was in effect, the British were credited for payments they made to Italians working for the United States.[12]

Just as theater commanders had a great deal of latitude to make American policy conform to the British, they enjoyed similar latitude in areas where the degree of coordination was not so great, illustrating again their power to vary fiscal procedures significantly from theater to theater. For Oran, Algeria, the War Department established pay rates for Italian prisoners in service units, which it was using for the first time. These service units were organizations of Italian prisoners who volunteered to perform special duties. They had a minimum of American military supervision, and they worked at such places as ordnance and quartermaster depots.[13] Service unit members received monthly pay in francs at the following rates: majors, 1,300; captains, 1,200; first lieutenants, 1,100; second lieutenants, 1,000; first three graders, 400; privates first class and corporals, 300; and privates, 250.[14]

After hostilities ceased in Europe, the problem of repatriating Italian prisoners from Africa arose. So that Italians could be turned over as quickly as possible to their government, AMET was to close records and settle pay accounts prior to prisoners' embarkation for Italy. When AMET made all payments, the Mediterranean theater was spared administrative responsibility other than actually delivering the repatriated prisoners to their government.[15]

In areas where prisoners had not received monthly cash payments, the final payments in lire of their accumulated allowances and work pay proved to be a large item. In Casablanca, 3,000 Italian prisoners were repatriated during October 1945. Settling their accumulated pay increased gross disbursements from $3,333,005 in September to $5,363,139 in October.[16]

---

[12] Ltr, Col Dale L. Thompson, AG, Hq AMET, to cinc, Middle East Forces (British), 18 Jun 45. RG 338.

[13] Office of the Provost Marshal General, *World War II—A Brief History* (n.p., n.p., n.d.), p. 434.

[14] Memo, Col C. A. Frank, Fin Off, Hq Mediterranean Base Sec, APO 600, 8 Jun 44. RG 338.

[15] Ltr, Maj Alan M. Clack, Asst AG, Hq AMET, to CO, North African Service Command, APO 600, 2 Jun 45. RG 338.

[16] Ltr, Hq, AMET, OFT, APO 787, "Bi-Monthly Report of Operations for Months September and October," 23 Nov 45. RG 338.

An examination of the practices used in paying German prisoners of war reveals that, as with the Italians, many deviations from
the wartime norm existed both before and after hostilities ceased.
Sometimes American finance units would actually pay German
prisoners, and sometimes they would just maintain German records
in anticipation of final settlement. In other cases the army used
Germans themselves to pay German prisoners. With the situation
fluid in Europe immediately after the German surrender and the
war still going on in the Pacific, it was illogical to use American
finance men to pay enemy prisoners. Most finance sections prepared
for redeployment and so were not available to pay German prisoners. By 15 May 1945, when headquarters, Communications Zone, of
the European theater had formulated the policy of paying released
German officer and enlisted prisoners eighty and forty Reichsmarks
respectively, it had devised a plan to utilize German prisoners in
twelve finance offices to make the payments. The German officer
in charge of each group was taken to a Reichsbank, where he
signed for and received funds. This payment occurred without the
use of Americans and without having any funds charged to the
U.S. government.[17]

The Twelfth Army Group executed Operation ECLIPSE, a
large-scale plan for paying German prisoners after hostilities. After
months of study, the Twelfth Army Group headquarters devised
a method of using German finance personnel to administer the
program. In general, the plan followed the standard procedure of
paying released prisoners their accumulated pay and allowances.
Except for limited supervision by American finance men, the Germans did the work. To provide necessary supervision, Twelfth
Army Group headquarters established a Wehrmacht fiscal branch
to inspect all records.[18]

As late as the first week in June 1945, there was still some
question in the Fifth Army regarding the policy for paying prisoners. Although AFHQ (Allied Forces Headquarters) was "concerned"
about paying surrendered German troops, it took the position of

[17] "History of the Fiscal Section," Hq AdSec, ComZ, OFD, APO 113, U.S.
Army. RG 338.
[18] "Report of Operations (Final After Action Report)," Twelfth Army
Group, vol. 10, p. 12. RG 338.

making no payments until the prisoners were repatriated and discharged. At that time, the prisoners received "whatever the Allied Governments agreed upon as a discharge stipend." While it is remarkable that AFHQ was uninformed on what "discharge stipend" the Germans were to get, it seems to have followed the standard policy for paying prisoners.[19]

In July 1945 the Chanor Base Section in France busily processed German prisoners to turn over to the French government. The Forty-third FDS at Le Mans made 20,000 final payments to prisoners during that month.[20] In February 1946 the U.S. Army initiated a program to transfer to the French government 700,000 German prisoners suitable for labor. This move caused the finance office handling prisoners' pay to close their accounts and to issue certificates of credit for any remainder that might be due. Under no circumstances did the Forty-third make any cash payments to either prisoners or their agents.[21]

When the time came for settling prisoners' accounts, confusion reigned concerning the interpretation of War Department instructions. Directives dated September 1945 stated that certificates of credit given prisoners should be redeemed in the currency of the country of prisoners' origin. Redemption would be at the official rate of exchange. Finance offices quickly pounced upon the vagueness of these two statements about settling accounts. Since members of the Wehrmacht captured as prisoners of war came from practically all European countries, were settlements to Hungarians to be made in pengös and were Danes to be paid in kroner? And was the official rate of exchange to be interpreted as the prewar or the postwar rate? Until these basic questions were answered, no satisfactory settlements could be made.

By January 1946 the War Department had clarified its position. A prisoner's country of origin was the nation in whose armed forces he served, and the military rate of exchange of ten Reichsmarks to the dollar was the official rate. This latter determination immediately caused a protest from American authorities in Europe.

[19] Col H. F. Chrisman, Fin Off, "Report of the Army Commander's Weekly Conference," Fifth Army, 2 Jun 45. RG 338.

[20] "Historical Report of Operations," Chanor Base Sec, p. 7. RG 338.

[21] Ltr, SHAEF file AG 383.6-12, Transfer of Prisoners of War to the French, 14 Feb 46. RG 338.

The OMGUS (Office of Military Government, United States) objected, since that rate would give the returned prisoners disproportionate buying power on the German economy. Article 23 of the Geneva Convention of 1929 stipulated that in the absence of a specific agreement between belligerents, the prewar rate would be used, and there had been no agreement between the United States and Germany. Hence, OMGUS recommended that the prewar exchange rate be adopted. While the War Department was deciding what course of action to take, the European theater grew restive over the delay, since ex-prisoners' inability to cash certificates of credit reflected on the desire of the United States to fulfill commitments. By June 1946 the rapidly increasing number of released prisoners made a decision from the War Department imperative. Finally, in July, the War Department, basing its decision on the Geneva Convention, authorized redemption at the prewar exchange rate of one Reichsmark to $.3997. For Austria, the rate established by the Germans after the Anschluss, 1 schilling to $.2665, obtained.[22]

The source of marks used to settle prisoner of war accounts in Germany relates directly to the story of currency control in Europe. Since an American soldier's pay was always figured in dollars, he was entitled to have his account credited in dollars, regardless of the medium in which he was paid. Although he could not draw his pay in dollars overseas, through various means he could receive dollar credits at home. Or if he chose, he could be paid in whatever currency was used in the overseas area. When payments were made in other than American currency, the government was beholden at some future date to convert those payments back into dollars.

As a result of excess conversions of marks into dollar credits in the period immediately following cessation of hostilities, the army sustained a "long position" of $270 million in marks, which means that the army converted $270 million in marks that was not

---

[22] "Budgetary and Financial Aspects of the Occupation. 1946–1947," pp. 101–104. The Hon Howard C. Petersen, Asst Sec of War, testified that the rate of exchange was one mark to $.30, rather than $.3997 (*Occupation Currency Transactions*, Hearings before the Committee on Appropriations, Armed Services, and Banking and Currency, U.S. Senate, 80th Cong., 1st Sess. [Washington, D.C.: Government Printing Office, 1947], p. 44).

covered by pay appropriations from Congress. Not eager to accept this loss, the army began to search for some methods of recoupment. The prisoner of war situation proved the ideal vehicle. Credits totaling $150 million had poured into the Treasury prisoner of war trust fund throughout the hostilities, consisting of work pay and monthly allowances. Also, private concerns contracting with the War Department for prisoner labor had made payments into this trust fund. The government had made a good profit from prisoners' labor, since the price charged private contractors always exceeded the compensation given prisoners for their work. To partially recoup its long position in marks the government decreased that loss by the $150 million in the prisoner of war trust fund account. Then German prisoners received their final payments with highly inflated marks from the long position that did not begin to equal the value of their American-denominated pay credits.[23]

Repatriated GI's

The payment of foreign prisoners of war went on throughout the war, but the problem of paying Americans who had been prisoners of Germany was confined to the last few months of the European war and the post-hostilities period. As soon as the army recovered Americans in Europe, it established fiscal records for them. These records were as complete as the information individual prisoners could furnish. Rosters forwarded to the adjutant general in Washington included the prisoner's name, grade, army serial number, and name and address of next of kin. Any other facts a recovered prisoner could furnish were sent to the Adjutant General. These could include original organization, date and place of capture, names of other American or Allied personnel captured at the same time and place, names and locations of various prison camps, and details concerning other prisoners.[24]

By the end of March 1945, large numbers of liberated American and British prisoners had been moved to the rear of the European theater. The Twelfth Army Group had planned to pay repatriated Allied prisoners as they passed through its area, but their

[23] *Occupation Currency Transactions*, pp. 3, 12; see Walter Rundell, Jr., *Black Market Money*, pp. 88–89.

[24] Ltr, TAG, Repatriation, Recovery, and Rehabilitation of American Prisoners of War in Europe, AG 383.6 OBSAM, 3 Oct 44. RG 338.

movement to the rear was so rapid that no payments were possible.[25]

On 30 April, 14,174 U.S. nationals had been recovered by American forces. Some Americans held prisoner in eastern Germany were freed by the Soviets. When this happened, they obviously could not be turned over directly to the American army, since the Red and American forces had not met at that time. So the Russians sent the Americans back through the Soviet Union to the port of Odessa.[26] The Soviet foreign commissar, V. M. Molotov, ordered these ex-prisoners released to the United States. As soon as they entered American control at Camp Arimabad in Iraq, they received partial payments of $200 for officers, and $100 for enlisted men. Disbursing officers making the payments gave each man the opportunity to exchange $5 into rials for local spending money.[27]

Up to February 1945, the Russians had liberated approximately 1,000 American prisoners. The Germans made every effort to evacuate prisoners westward so they could maintain custody of them, but the power and speed of the Soviet drive in the spring of 1945 made these attempts futile.[28] As the number of American prisoners liberated by the Red army increased, the size of their partial payments was limited to an amount deemed appropriate by the PGC fiscal director. Those who departed the PGC within twenty-four hours received mostly yellow seal dollars, with a small amount in local currency. Those who arrived in the PGC with American dollars could exchange enough to cover their immediate needs in the PGC. Final settlement of accounts was made in the United States from temporary records created in the PGC.[29]

[25] "Report of Operations," Twelfth Army Group, p. 12. RG 338.

[26] "The First Year of Occupation," Occupation Forces in Europe Series, 1945–1946, Office of the Chief Historian, European Command, Frankfurt-am-Main, Germany, 1947, p. 66. CMH.

[27] "Plan for Hall Project No. 1," "Plan for Hall Project No. 2," and Radio, Tuck for Morris, 20 Oct 44, Molotov. RG 338.

[28] Radio, Booth for Thomas, Hill for Hampton, and AGWAR for Info from Crockett, 18 Feb 45, MX 22773. RG 338.

[29] Memo, Lt Col C. F. Fowler, Actg Fis Dir, PGC, for AG, Hq PGC, 5 Mar 45, sub: Finance Services for Ex-Prisoners of War Arriving in PGC, FD 383.6. RG 338. For a perceptive treatment of how the issue of Soviet treatment of American POW's exacerbated Cold War relations, see Russell D. Buhite, "Soviet-American Relations and the Repatriation of Prisoners of War, 1945," pp. 384–397.

Many GI's captured by the Germans were so ill when they came back under American control that they had to be hospitalized. In such cases, finance units adapted their service to fit the patients' needs. During January and February 1945, the 113th FDS made partial payments aboard hospital ships to recovered American prisoners. When the unit arrived at a repatriation area, it would confer with G-1 about prisoners' conditions, whether litter or ambulatory, and the volume and types of currency they might want exchanged. The section would then go to the returnees' vessel and arrange with the medical administration office for a time and place for payment. The ship would assign the section working space, as well as tables and chairs. Crew members would assist in the operation by calling payees from their wards and controlling traffic at the pay tables.

The ambulatory patients lined up for payment according to the alphabet. At the pay table each man identified himself, signed the payroll, and received a fifty-dollar partial. Payment of litter patients was a bed-to-bed procedure. The unit took payrolls, money, and exchange currencies to each man. So that no one desiring payment would be overlooked, a final call for payees would be made over the ship's public address system each day before the finance unit debarked. In making such partial payments, the 113th FDS operated more efficiently when it could secure an advance payroll list to use as the basis for preparing partials.[30]

The machinery set up for paying repatriated prisoners was based on the system of partial payments. Returnees were paid enough money to tide them over until complete settlements could be made on the basis of reconstructed records. The amount of a partial depended on the man's grade and length of captivity. The maximum cash payment was $100, unless the net amount due was less than $125. Any remainder was paid by check. As a rule, finance offices tried to settle prisoners' accounts in full within seven days after they arrived at stateside reception stations or hospitals.[31] Any pay that ex-prisoners had received from the enemy did not offset

[30] Maj A. E. Blumberg, "Unit History."
[31] Change No. 1 to WD Ltr AG 383.6 OB-S-A-SPGAM-M, sub: Procedure for Processing and Reassignment of Recovered Personnel, 2 Jun 45. RG 338.

the regular military pay accruing to their accounts. Such amounts (except for work pay) were entered on individual fiscal records.[32]

Captured GI's

The German and Japanese governments had no uniform policy on the payment of prisoners of war. Rates and conditions of payment differed from time to time and from one prison camp to another. In some camps prisoners received regular monthly allowances without working. In others, there was no pay at all. Unlike the Americans, the Germans often paid their prisoners directly in either camp money or Reichsmarks, which they spent in camp canteens. Currency in excess of specified amounts went in communal funds or prisoners' accounts. After the autumn of 1944, all cash payments stopped. The most common scale of monthly allowances for officers was as follows:

Second lieutenants	72 Reichsmarks or $28.80
First lieutenants	81 Reichsmarks or $32.40
Captains	96 Reichsmarks or $38.40
Majors	108 Reichsmarks or $43.20
Lieutenant colonels	120 Reichsmarks or $48.00
Colonels	150 Reichsmarks or $60.00

These allowances were comparable to the salaries of corresponding ranks in the Wehrmacht. Obviously, they were more liberal than those the U.S. government gave German officers in its captivity.[33] But from these amounts deductions were usually made for food and clothing, so in reality American officer prisoners of the Germans were probably no better off financially than German officers captured by the U.S. Army. The most common rate of work pay for enlisted men was seventy pfennigs a day. At the prewar rate of exchange, this equaled twenty-eight cents, substantially less than the American work pay allowance of eighty cents per day for German prisoners. Usually when American enlisted men did not work, they got no pay directly, if they were allowed any credit whatso-

[32] Ltr, TAG, "Repatriation, Recovery, and Rehabilitation of American Prisoners of War in Europe," 3 Oct 44. RG 338.

[33] See the discussion of the monthly allowances for Axis prisoners of the United States on p. 181.

ever. In one camp, Stalag 17-B, the Germans did not require prisoners to work, since they were all noncommissioned officers. Yet they were credited with seven and a half Reichsmarks monthly, or three dollars at the prewar rate, the same pay the United States allowed its prisoners.[34]

Pay credits received by American prisoners of the Germans were the source of a great deal of legalistic inquiry. Even though no amount either paid directly or credited to Americans in captivity could be deducted from their American pay and allowances, ex-prisoners could not use these German credits as the basis for claims against appropriated funds in the U.S. Treasury. Ex-prisoners were advised to retain their certificates of credit until some determination was made as to the liability of the German government for redeeming them.[35]

Although the 1929 Geneva Convention specified certain minimum allowances for all prisoners, the pay American prisoners received from the Japanese usually did not meet these standards. Nor was Japanese pay uniform from one prison camp to another. In many cases, U.S. Army finance officers maintained pay accounts for fellow prisoners.

On Mindanao just before the island surrendered to the Japanese, the American finance officer set his accounts in order. Because of the uncertainty of the situation around 3 May 1942, Col. W. A. Enos, Visayan-Mindanao Force finance officer, directed Capt. S. R. Franks, the disbursing officer, to prepare a synopsis of his accounts. Colonel Enos inspected and approved the account, which he then buried. On 8 May 1942 instructions were received on Mindanao to destroy all funds. Captain Franks, in the presence of Colonel Enos, burned all the bills in his possession and threw his coins into a creek. The total amount disposed of was $252,739.38. A few days

[34] American Prisoners of War in Germany, prepared by Military Intelligence Service, WD, 1 Nov 45, pp. 1, 19, 28, 38, 47, 54, 71, 90, 96, and 105; Prisoner of War Information Manual, AAF Manual 39-1, Feb 45, Hq AAF, Washington, D.C., p. 57.

[35] Memo for the Fis Dir, from Lt Col Willard B. Cowles, Actg Ch, War Plans, JAGO, 23 Mar 45; Memo for the Record, Col E. J. Bean, FFA 16, x Sub 27 Sec 2, "Procedure for Handling Requests Submitted by American Soldiers Released from Internment in Germany for Pay Earned during their Period of Internment," 2 May 45. RG 338.

later the Japanese captured Mindanao, but did not establish a prisoner of war camp immediately. From the time the Japanese captured the island until the middle of July, when they set up prisoner camps, Americans were not furnished food. The senior American officer directed Captain Franks to provide money for Americans to buy food from the Filipinos, so he fished coins out of the creek. Around the middle of July when the Japanese established a permanent prison guard, they began to provide subsistence and Captain Franks ceased his activities as a disbursing officer.[36]

At the Cabanatuan Prison Camp in the Philippines, the Japanese began paying prisoners according to the Geneva Convention. Officers got the same pay as Japanese in corresponding ranks, but they were charged for quarters and subsistence. Pay remaining in their accounts went in Japanese postal savings. Enlisted men got ten centavos each work day. As inflation decreased buying power, the Japanese increased pay rates slightly. When runaway inflation ruined the pay schedules, the Japanese began to "forget" payments and refused to give transferees their pay cards. After September 1944, all payments ceased.[37]

The Cabanatuan prison finance officer from September 1942 to October 1944 was Lt. Col. J. E. Brinkmeyer, who made monthly payments based on the Japanese rates to army, navy, and marine personnel. Warrant officers could earn twenty-five centavos a day for six hours' labor; noncommissioned officers, fifteen centavos; and privates and civilians, ten centavos. On 1 August 1944 these work pay rates increased ten centavos a day. Colonel Brinkmeyer paid approximately 1,600 officers and 2,500 enlisted men per month in Japanese military scrip, or "Mickey Mouse money."

In addition to handling these disbursements, the colonel was custodian of two welfare funds. Each month 100 American field grade officers (majors and above) contributed 50 pesos to the fund. These donations came from their Japanese postal savings accounts. After the fund had existed for some time, the Japanese began donat-

---

[36] Ltr, Col W. A. Enos, Force Fin Off, Visayan-Mindanao Force, to Fin Off, USAF in Philippines, POW Camp, Camp Casisang, Malaybalay, Bukidon, Mindanao, PI, 28 Aug 42, sub: Report of Fin Off, Visayan-Mindanao Force. RG 338.

[37] Report on American Prisoners of War Interned by the Japanese in the Philippines, prepared by OPMG, 19 Nov 45. RG 338.

ing 5,000 pesos a month, raising the monthly total of the fund to 10,000 pesos. When the Japanese raised the ante, American company grade prisoners (captains and lieutenants) could contribute to the fund. The second welfare fund of which Colonel Brinkmeyer was the custodian was a secret fund of about 6,000 pesos. Unidentified friendly persons had given this money to American prisoners, who used it to care for the sick and to buy food for the general mess. Each time a man went on a work detail, he received a peso or so for food or tobacco. During the spring of 1944, Japanese intelligence arrested thirty prisoners buying such goods from Manila friends. Colonel Brinkmeyer decided that it was no longer safe for him to administer this secret fund along with his official funds, since a periodic audit of the authorized funds might disclose the extra money. Upon Colonel Brinkmeyer's recommendation, the senior American officer transferred the fund to Lt. Col. Dwight Edison. With the exception of this secret fund, the Japanese supervised all transactions handled by Colonel Brinkmeyer as the prison finance officer. He brought to this work the ingrained characteristics of a good finance officer: meticulousness, circumspection, and conservativeness. "All accounts were regularly audited as I insisted on this for the protection of all concerned, and to my knowledge I disbursed without loss of one cent to the Japanese government or anyone else."[38] The colonel apparently never considered that his causing a loss to the Japanese government might further American war aims.

Administration of financial matters at Japanese prison camps in Manchuria resembled that in the Philippines. Col. John R. Vance, senior finance officer in the Philippines when they fell, became the unofficial finance officer at various prison camps in Manchuria where he was confined between May 1942 and August 1945. He always maintained a small cash disbursing account from money found in the effects of dead soldiers and from funds deposited with him by individuals. He used this money to alleviate the hardships always present in prison camps. Each time he made a disbursement, he opened an improvised service record so that he

---

[38] Ltr, Lt Col J. E. Brinkmeyer, to Hq ASF OFD, Washington, D.C., 28 Jul 45, sub: Philippine Accounts. RG 338.

would know who the recipients had been. When he collected funds, he gave the depositor a receipt.[39] Like Colonel Brinkmeyer, Colonel Vance transferred to his prison work the disciplined habits of a finance officer. The Japanese clearly agreed with Americans in using prisoners to handle compatriots' financial affairs. They saw no reason to assign their own men to tasks that prisoners could perform.

Allowances for American prisoners were fairly uniform in various Manchurian prison camps. Major generals and above were credited with 466 yen per month; brigadier generals, 416; colonels, 310; and lieutenant colonels, 175. Other officers received proportionately smaller amounts. Enlisted men were credited with 30 sen per day, but civilians got nothing. The Japanese charged each field grade officer's account 30 yen a month for the rice allowance, but company grade officers were charged only 27 yen a month for subsistence. Officers were actually paid 50 yen a month; noncommissioned officers, 20; and privates, 10. The Japanese deposited any pay in excess of these amounts in the Bank of Manchuria. When the Russians entered Manchuria on 21 August 1945, they froze all bank assets. Although American prisoners were liberated by the Russians, they could not withdraw their accumulated pay, which totaled 2,880,000 yen, because of the Russian action.[40]

As soon as Colonel Vance was liberated by the Red army, he took control of the finance office, safes, cash box, funds, and records of 2d Lt. E. Misago, the Japanese finance officer at the Hoten prisoner of war camp at Mukden. The cash on hand, 34,101 Manchurian yuan, went immediately for food, and that cash belonging to prisoners went to its legal owners when possible. The remainder was distributed by lottery among the enlisted men. Colonel Vance, acting under verbal orders from Maj. Gen. George M. Parker, Jr., senior American officer at Hoten, received for official use 1 million

[39] Ltr, Col J. R. Vance, to Fis Dir, ASF, 12 Nov 45, sub: Pay Accounts of Americans Held as Prisoners of War by the Japanese. RG 338.
[40] Memo for Record, Maj John F. Baldwin, 30 Nov 45, sub: Col J. R. Vance, SPFBC 300.6 X PI 6; Capt James L. Norwood and Capt Emily L. Shek, "Prisoner of War Camps in Areas Other than the Four Principal Islands of Japan," Liaison and Research Br, American Prisoner of War Information Bureau, 31 Jul 46, p. 35. RG 338.

Manchurian yuan from the Red army on 25 August. The unofficial rate of exchange at that time was 150 Manchurian yuan to one dollar, although no official transactions were made with dollars.[41]

Pay rates in effect for officers in the prisons at Kiangwan, Woosing, and Fengtai, China, were on a par with those for Japanese officers of the same rank. They were somewhat higher than the rates in Manchurian prisons. Colonels got 312.50 yen per month; lieutenant colonels, 230; majors, 170; captains, 127.50; first lieutenants, 85; and second lieutenants, 70.83. The captors paid these allowances in Chinese Reserve Bank Notes (CRB) but deducted 60 yen each month from an officer's pay for food, clothing, furniture, and electricity. At Fengtai, enlisted men were paid nothing. At Kiangwan, enlisted specialists could earn $27 in CRB notes, or about 5 yen, a month. Ordinary enlisted laborers got between $15 and $20 CRB a month. Privates who were prisoners of the Japanese on Taiwan could earn 10 sen a day as work pay; noncommissioned officers, 15 sen; and warrant officers, 25 sen. Those prisoners at the Shanghai Bridge House Jail were never paid.[42]

The U.S. government gave American prisoners of the Axis powers an opportunity after the war to file a claim for compensation for inadequate food allowances; inhumane treatment; and performance of enforced, unpaid labor during their captivity. The War Claims Act of 1948 (PL 896) allowed ex-prisoners $1 per day for each day they were without adequate food. Public law 303 of 1952 amended the War Claims Act so that ex-prisoners could receive $1.50 for each day they were subjected to inhumane treatment and/or forced to work without pay. These two allowances did not exclude each other.

The War Claims Commission conducted a nationwide publicity campaign to solicit claims from ex-prisoners. When a claimant filed, his records were checked at the Adjutant General's St. Louis Records Center. If official records substantiated his claim, he was paid.

[41] Ltr, Col J. R. Vance, to Fis Dir, ASF, 12 Nov 45, sub: Disbursing Account in Manchurian Yuan Operated by Col J. R. Vance at Hoten POW Camp, Mukden, Manchuria. RG 338.

[42] Norwood and Shek, pp. 1, 12, 16; Prisoners of War in Taiwan (Formosa), prepared by Military Intelligence Div, 20 Oct 44, Washington, D.C., p. 4. RG 338.

As of 31 March 1955, when payments ended, 179,725 ex-prisoners had been paid $49,935,899 for inadequate food. For inhuman treatment and/or enforced labor, 178,900 ex-prisoners had been paid $73,492,926. The War Claims Act established a fund for these payments, deriving from the income from Axis property seized in the United States at the beginning of the war.

Altogether, the payment of prisoners of war proved the opportunism of all governments involved. Without question, the American government provided far better care for Axis prisoners than the Axis government offered Americans in their custody. Yet, when time for final settlement of German accounts came, the army used a shady expedient to bail itself out of the currency control deficit it had mindlessly created. German enlisted men had volunteered to work for eighty cents a day and assumed they would receive its equivalent upon repatriation. But when that time came, they did not get the equivalent in buying power, since they received marks at the prewar exchange rate of 2.5 marks to the dollar. But the value of the marks they actually received from the army's long position had been drastically reduced by rampant inflation. So their work pay, as well as allowances, turned out to be a pittance.

Nor is it difficult to understand Axis treatment of American prisoners. In some cases, Japan and Germany specified payments that appeared adequate, if not liberal. The specifications rarely translated into actual payments, especially when the tides of war turned against the Axis. The wonder is that early in the war the Axis did sometimes fulfill its announced commitments to prisoners. One can easily understand how a nation facing military defeat gave little attention to the niceties of paying its enemy prisoners. Americans captured by the Axis powers were lucky to escape with their lives—as many did not—and any pay they received during captivity constituted a somewhat surprising token of intentions to abide by the Geneva Convention.

[43] Interviews with Robert A. Kennedy, Exec Dir, Foreign Claims Settlement Commission, 9 Nov 54, and Wayland McClellan, Office of the General Counsel, FCSC, 29 Sep 72; Foreign Claims Settlement Commission of the United States, *Annual Report to the Congress for the Period January 1–December 31, 1968*, p. 22.

CHAPTER 9

Currency Exchange

For finance offices, currency exchange proved enormously time consuming and exasperating. Even after it became evident that American forces would operate in and use the currencies of many different nations, Finance planners did not consider that as troops crossed national boundaries they would need currency exchanged. The finance T/O&E simply had not provided manpower for this important function. Obviously, finance offices had to exchange currencies, which they did at the expense of their other duties. Compounding the problem was the frequent inadequacy of needed currencies. However well finance offices may have geared themselves for currency exchanges, their preparations counted for little when they lacked appropriate monies.

In many such cases, Finance resorted to the expedient of issuing dollar currencies, the Hawaii overstamped dollar in the Pacific or the yellow seal dollar in the Mediterranean and Middle East. Then it usually exchanged the expedient currency for a local one. The yellow seal, especially, represented a real compromise of the army's stated objective of minimizing the inflation of local currencies. The fact that the army had to use it at various times during the war indicated that either planning was consistently inadequate or that currency problems had a low priority among the army's overall concerns, or both.

Certain parts of the world, such as the Middle East and India, presented peculiar exchange problems involving either the use of relatively unfamiliar currencies or unusual opportunities for soldiers to speculate. While these problems did not match the magnitude of exchange operations on the Continent, they do illustrate the diversity of this aspect of the army's fiscal management.

Fractional rates of exchange during the war and changing rates after hostilities complicated office routines, though in each case the circumstances were beyond Finance's control. The instability of many foreign currencies resulting from the war manifested itself in new exchange rates once fighting ceased. As these currencies depreciated against the dollar, Finance had to convert funds for GI's. In cases involving fractional rates, some theater fiscal officers employed field expedients to simplify operations. Postwar conversions added greatly to the work load of overburdened finance units. as did some individual exchange cases. These cases show that during redeployment exchange services often broke down and individuals became unable to cope with the gigantic bureaucracy. But they also show how individual complaints generated incredible paperwork, thus making their mark on the bureaucracy.

Dollar Currencies

From the time American troops began to arrive in combat zones until the postwar occupation, the army disbursed dollar currencies. Such disbursement reflected the army's uncertainty about foreign currency supplies or the inability to obtain them before invasions. Its alternative was to use dollars, which did not present immediate problems of funding with a foreign invasion currency and so did not require systematic planning for exchanges. By the time Finance had to exchange these dollars, it had enough experience to improvise adequately. The army never offered a coherent plan for using dollars overseas, since they usually were expedients. If employing dollar currencies finessed the issue of proper planning for exchanges, the use of foreign monies highlighted this glaring deficiency, as the next section of this chapter indicates.

The Hawaii overstamped dollar was obviously an emergency measure, and once the emergency subsided, it circulated anywhere the blue seal did. But in its initial period, it presented substantial exchange problems. Although finance offices in the Pacific never dealt with the multiplicity of foreign currencies encountered in Europe, they had some exchange problems peculiar to their area. Introduction of the Hawaiian series of American dollars in July 1942 created the greatest volume of exchange transactions in the Pacific early in the war.[1] By 15 July 1942, all American bills in Hawaii had to be exchanged for the new series. Neither soldiers

---

[1] See the discussion of this Hawaiian series money on p. 120.

nor civilians were allowed to retain standard U.S. currency. Anyone found possessing or disposing of the stateside currency after 15 July could be fined $5,000 and imprisoned for five years. Those arriving in Hawaii after standard American currency had been proscribed had to exchange their money for the Hawaiian series immediately. During this initial phase of overstamped currency, none of it was used outside Hawaii. American servicemen had ample opportunity to exchange their regular U.S. currency at finance offices and post exchanges, but some were obstinate enough to retain regular currency and try to force shopkeepers to accept it. Any time after 15 July that an American soldier was found with standard currency, he was required to make a full report as to its origin.

Before soldiers left Hawaii, they were to exchange their overstamped currency only at finance offices, so as not to disclose troop movements. But again, some dullards insisted on trying to exchange Hawaiian currency at local banks prior to embarkation. Commanding officers of troops on vessels leaving Hawaii were responsible for seeing that their men had exchanged all Hawaiian series dollars before sailing. To assist commanders in fulfilling this obligation, the Honolulu FOUSA stationed a man at the gangplank of each departing ship to make the required exchanges.[2]

Even though overstamped dollars were the only legal tender in Hawaii, they also served as invasion currency in many operations in the Pacific.[3] After one such operation against a target in the Western Carolines had been funded with Hawaiian dollars and the task force had sailed, the target was changed to the Philippine Islands. Disbursing officers therefore had to arrange with supply officers en route to exchange their Hawaiian series dollars for the new Philippine Victory Series pesos. As soon as tactical conditions permitted, finance officers paid the assault forces on Leyte in the pesos they had exchanged for Hawaiian dollars.[4]

After the danger of an invasion of the Hawaiian Islands by the

[2] Ltr, Col O. N. Thompson, AG, Hq Central Pacific Area, to Distribution "B" and "C" wide, 1 Feb 44, sub: Use of Hawaiian Currency, AG (FIN). RG 338.

[3] See the discussion of the use of Hawaiian overstamped dollars as invasion currency on pp. 120, 122–123.

[4] "History of Fiscal Mid Pac," p. 39.

Japanese had passed and American forces had gained an upper hand in the Pacific, restrictions on the use of Hawaiian currency lifted. After 20 October 1944, the Hawaiian series and standard U.S. currency could be used interchangeably by disbursing officers and individual servicemen. Hawaiian money could circulate anywhere in the world that the U.S. dollar was legal tender. Even after headquarters, USAFPOA, made its announcement repealing all restrictions on the circulation of the Hawaii overstamped dollars, it was flooded with inquiries as to whether the Hawaiian dollars could be mailed to the United States as souvenirs.[5]

One common denominator between early exchange problems in the Pacific and in the Mediterranean was that in both areas U.S. currency was involved. In the Pacific, exchanges had to be made among regular American dollars, Hawaii overstamped dollars, and foreign currencies, while in the Mediterranean, exchanges were between American blue seal currency and American yellow seal dollars.[6]

In September 1943, the main job of the Twenty-seventh FDS at Casablanca was exchanging currency for troops arriving in Africa. When soldiers left the United States, they carried blue seal dollars. Port authorities in the States appointed officers aboard ships to collect all blue seal dollars and give receipts for them. Then blue seal dollars could be exchanged for yellow seals when the ships arrived in Africa. As long as company commanders collected their men's money, this system worked acceptably. But when one officer was named to make collections for an entire vessel, the situation was complicated. Frequently, troops would be moved from Casablanca before their exchanged money was issued. With men in one place and their money in another, finance office routine was seldom placid. Another complication caused by port authorities arose from their instructions that receipts given on shipboard could be redeemed at any finance office. Since these were merely hand receipts and not official military payment orders, such a redemption was manifestly impossible. The Twenty-seventh FDS stated that "nasty" situations developed when they had to explain to men

[5] Ibid., pp. 49–50.
[6] See pp. 73–74, 117, for a discussion of the differentiation between blue and yellow seal currency.

holding these hand receipts that they would have to find the officer with their money before they could get any exchange. Usually, the men had little idea of which officer had their funds, and the officers did not know exactly from whom they had collected. Such complications were mild, however, in comparison with the instance when, in the midst of the confusion of docking in Africa, a lieutenant dropped all the money he had collected overboard![7]

In the Mediterranean area early in the war, the standard curcurrency was the American yellow seal dollar. Blue seal dollars also circulated until directives specifically declared them illegal in April 1943. As blue seal money filtered through Spanish Morocco into German hands, it commanded a premium of from 10 to 100 percent. The circulation of blue seal currency during the time it was legal tender in North Africa, however, was limited in comparison with that of the yellow seal. Although the latter was early declared legal tender, it carried no premium in local exchanges and was even refused by many dealers who had doubts about the status of yellow seal dollars. Italians, like North Africans, preferred the "real" American blue seal dollars and hoarded them since the yellow seal was not legal tender in the United States. Later this situation was reversed and yellow seal bills commanded a premium.[8]

Among the main body of troops, yellow seal dollars predominated in North African operations until an adequate supply of francs could be secured; hence, the biggest job of exchange was from blue to yellow seal dollars. Since American forces did not know what currency to expect on Sicily on 10 July 1943, they again used the yellow seal dollar as invasion currency.[9] As soon as Allied military lire were ready for distribution, they were exchanged for dollars. On 19 June 1943, two planes carrying seven tons of Allied military lire for the Sicily operation left the United States.[10] The army supposed that after the Treasury's Bureau of

[7] Capt Robert C. Jackson, "Unit History."

[8] "Narrative History of the Mediterranean Base Section, for the Period September 1942 to 1 May 1944," pp. 30–31; Cir 55, Hq NATOUSA, 9 Apr 43. RG 338; Donald L. Kemmerer and T. Eugene Beattie, "Allied Military Currency in Italy," p. 1268.

[9] *Annual Report of the Secretary of the Treasury on the State of the Finances for the Fiscal year Ended June 30, 1944*, p. 382.

[10] Ibid., p. 381.

Engraving and Printing began producing lire, they would be used exclusively in all Italian operations. But when the supply proved inadequate, the army resorted to the old standby—yellow seal dollars. When the Peninsular Base Section of the North African theater moved from Oran, Algeria, to its headquarters in Naples, the finance section expected to exchange francs for lire, since this move came in the first week of October 1943 and the first shipment of Allied military lire had been sent to the Mediterranean in July. But a lire shortage forced it to use yellow seal dollars.[11]

Other parts of the North African theater experienced the same difficulties with local currencies. In each case they had to fall back on yellow seal dollars. At the headquarters of the Atlantic Base Section in Casablanca, the continued use of yellow seal currency resulted in its disappearing from circulation altogether. The local population grew eager to corner the American currency because of its value on the free market. To conserve yellow seal dollars, the Atlantic Base Section headquarters told finance officers to pay by check when possible. If disbursements had to be made directly, local currency was used until it was exhausted; only then were supplemental amounts paid in yellow seal dollars. American coins were limited to exchanges for those returning to the United States or leaving the North African theater. As a further precaution, the theater urged soldiers to spend American money only in official agencies, such as APO's and post exchanges.[12]

During the occupation in areas with few American troops, the army chose not to set up elaborate mechanisms for paying in foreign currencies. Since the number of troops did not justify the time and expense of establishing exchange rates between dollars and local currencies, the army simply paid in dollars when local authorities did not furnish funds. Then soldiers could make their own exchanges into foreign currencies.

After hostilities ceased in Europe, the exchange picture altered in the Balkans and Hungary. American soldiers going into Romania, Greece, Albania, Yugoslavia, Bulgaria, or Hungary exchanged their

[11] "History of the Peninsular Base Section, NATOUSA, Covering the Period 28 Aug 1943 to 31 Jan 44," vol. 2. RG 338.

[12] Ltr, Capt James K. Clark, Asst AG, Hq Atlantic Base Sec, NATOUSA, APO 759, to all Fin Offs, ABS, 1 Feb 44, AG 123 BASFO. RG 338.

funds for American yellow seal dollars, rather than the British military authority notes used during the war. The army expressly forbade them to use any currency other than yellow seal or currencies of these nations and warned them not to accumulate a surplus of Balkan money. Any Balkan currency soldiers might bring out would have only souvenir value, for the army would exchange not one dinar or pengö. When soldiers returned from the Balkans, they were to trade their yellow seal money for the currency being used in their home theater.[13]

Runaway inflation in the Balkans immediately after the war sometimes worked against the interests of American servicemen with yellow seal dollars. When soldiers dealt with local money changers individually, particularly in Romania, they were likely not to get as much in return as when they pooled their dollars and exchanged them together.[14] Introducing any American currency in Europe was risky because of inflationary conditions. Only because so few troops were involved in the Balkans could the American government afford to employ yellow seal currency. The introduction of a large volume of American dollars might well have disrupted any Balkan economy. But the U.S. government figured that it would cost less to utilize yellow seal dollars than to establish exchange machinery for each Balkan nation, the same reasoning that prevailed during hostilities. Neither the U.S. nor any Balkan government was happy about the use of yellow seal dollars, but it seemed the most logical measure. Although individual American soldiers sometimes were discriminated against by local money changers, they more often benefited because of the greater purchasing power of the American dollar on inflated economies. Individual Balkan citizens who possessed American dollars also benefited, but their governments received no compensation for net troop pay.[15]

On Taiwan, as in the Balkans, American soldiers could ex-

[13] Col R. E. Odell, Fis Dir, Hq, AMET, Fin Cir Ltr no. 8, 11 Jun 45. RG 338.

[14] Radio, CG, MTO, to CO, 1419-4Y Operating Location, Athens, Greece, 20 Dec 45, FX 56817. RG 338.

[15] Frank A. Southard, Jr., *The Finances of European Liberation*, pp. 40–41.

change dollars for foreign money if they wanted to make purchases locally. But they did so at their own risk, for there were no facilities for reconversion. This no-reconversion principle prevented black market profit from being converted into dollar assets. Usually, the Chinese government funded American disbursing officers on Taiwan with Chinese currency for local purchases. But when it was unable to do so, finance officers could use dollars temporarily. The Chinese government wanted to minimize the circulation of dollars on Taiwan because of their inflationary attributes.[16]

Planning for Exchange

Early in the war the army had little opportunity to make long-range plans for currency exchanges. Immediate situations demanded quick solutions, so in 1942 the army introduced Hawaii overstamped dollars for tactical operations in the Pacific and yellow seal dollars for the invasion of North Africa. At least the army knew what a servicemen's pay would be in those issues and it could worry about exchanges into local currencies later. The fact that the army used these currencies at all documents another aspect of the lack of planning in the Office of the Chief of Finance before the war.

But Finance could not continue to take refuge in the lack of prewar planning. As the war progressed, it demonstrated further inadequate planning for currency exchange. Despite the manifest eventuality of the army's fighting in many foreign lands, fiscal planners but slowly recognized that this would involve exchanging currencies. Only in September 1943 did the Office of the Fiscal Director in Washington prepare a foreign exchange guide to standardize and simplify currency exchange problems. Until then finance offices had had to rely on piecemeal information that, when synthesized, did not constitute a consistent, systematic exchange policy. To make the 1943 guide complete, the OFD requested all disbursing officers overseas to send their theater headquarters full details on all local currencies circulating in their respective areas. They forwarded one bill and coin of each denomination to Washington along with the official and free market rates of exchange. Their reports also included particulars on any currency that was not legal

---

[16] Radio, Warcos to Manila, CINCPOA, et al., Sep 45, WARX 60466. RG 338.

tender.[17] Overseas finance offices naturally found this foreign exchange guide helpful. The finance office at headquarters, Base Section Three USASOS, in Brisbane used the guide in preparing its own chart for making conversions when dealing with guilders, pounds, and dollars.[18]

As helpful as the guide was, it did not compensate for the lack of basic planning for currency exchanges. In theaters without rapid movement of troops, finance offices usually could handle exchanges adequately, but when tactical situations dictated the quick mobility of large numbers of troops, provisions for exchanges proved wanting. Exchange problems in the European theater during combat differed somewhat from those encountered in Mediterranean operations. In Africa and Italy, finance offices had been concerned mainly with yellow seal dollars, francs, and lire. Exchanges in these currencies usually did not require great speed because of tactical movements. But in European operations, exchanges were complicated since finance offices dealt with many more currencies and funding had to be coordinated with troop movements across national borders. Pressure on finance offices was so great that strict controls had to be used. Before anyone leaving an area could get an exchange, he had to present official travel orders. Conversions for large groups, however, could be made by roster when certified by a commissioned officer. Finance offices had to retain copies of travel orders and requests for exchange for the IG.[19]

Had there been adequate forethought, currency exchange during combat might not have resulted in overburdened finance offices giving substandard service. But, just as other aspects of planning for finance operations had been neglected, this one was also. No one designing the finance T/O&E seemed to anticipate that one man, the cashier, could not make all the currency conversions demanded of a finance office in Europe. There apparently was no realization that using four or five national currencies simultaneously would impede operations. Since exchanges obviously had to be made, most commanding officers of finance units followed the only available course.

[17] Ltr, Lt Col B. J. Tullington, Fin Off, Hq sos SPA, to Fin Off, APO 721, 5 Sep 43, sub: Foreign Exchange Guide for U.S. Army DO's. RG 338.
[18] 2d Lt J. M. Taylor, "Unit History."
[19] Ltr, Col M. F. Moriarty, Deputy Fis Dir, Hq ETO, 7 Dec 44. RG 338.

They transferred men from duties prescribed in the T/O&E to exchanges. Naturally, this meant that their regular duties still had to be performed after normal working hours. The commandant of the Fifty-ninth FDS never had fewer than four men exchanging currency during European operations.[20]

Despite the inadequacy of the T/O&E, finance units sought ways of meeting the demand for exchanges, in addition to adding manpower. Field experiences on the Continent enabled Finance to devise procedures for simplifying exchanges. The cashier of the Twenty-fifth FDS discovered that if personnel officers prepared lists of currency for exchange, the finance section's job was much easier. The Twenty-fifth persuaded personnel officers to tabulate by denominations all currency offered for exchange and to list what was desired in return. It then became an easy matter to verify personnel officers' computations. In dealing with postal units, which always had much money for exchange, the Twenty-fifth insisted on their listing currencies by denominations, which saved valuable time around paydays.[21]

Problems connected with exchanges did not relate solely to poor planning. Occasionally, finance units simply did not follow clear and logical directives. At other times, especially during redeployment, logistical problems prevented finance offices from having sufficient quantities of dollars to exchange for returning troops. At the time of the Battle of the Bulge, the fiscal director of the European theater realized that a substantial exchange problem demanded solution. In January 1945 many replacements were arriving at the front with American and British currencies. Reinforcement depots covered exchange procedures sufficiently in their standing operating procedures (SOP's), but the SOP's were not followed. The fiscal director instructed all disbursing officers at reinforcement depots to ascertain that troops moving into forward areas had exchanged their funds.[22]

---

[20] Interviews with Col Ralph A. Koch, Office of the Comptroller of the Army, 12 Feb 54; and Lt Col Raymond E. Graham, Office of the Chief of Fin, 8 Feb 54.

[21] T/4 Milton Glazer, "Unit History."

[22] Ltr, Maj W. T. Dent, Hq ETOUSA, OFD, APO 887, to Fis Off, AdSec, ComZ, APO 113, 23 Jan 45, sub: Exchange of U.S. Money for Local Currencies, FD 123.7 (Misc File 312.1); ltr, Col F. M. Hariss, Jr., Hq AdSec, ComZ,

The goal of exchanging currencies for all those returning to the United States after hostilities was not achieved in Europe, in spite of announced plans therefor. One reason was the occasional unavailability of American currency to exchange for European money. The finance officer at the Miami (Florida) Army Air Field reported that servicemen who had been stationed in Europe, Africa, South America, and the Caribbean came to his office with large amounts of foreign currency for exchange. Consistently, their reason for not having converted money while abroad was that overseas finance offices did not have enough American money for exchanges.[23]

The War Department expressed annoyance with theaters that allowed men to redeploy to the United States with foreign currency. When members of the Twenty-seventh and Forty-third divisions returned with "material quantities" of Bank of Japan yen notes, Washington instructed the commander-in-chief of U.S. Army Forces in the Pacific (USAFPAC) to requisition immediately the dollars needed in exchanges for men leaving Japan.[24] Despite Washington's enjoinders, overseas commands sometimes found it impossible to make the prescribed exchanges. The finance office at the Eleventh Replacement Depot just could not keep enough one-dollar bills on hand. One of its requisitions for 150,000 one-dollar bills was cut to 40,000. While waiting for a supply of one-dollar bills, the finance office could exchange soldiers' yen to the nearest five dollars only. If troops were at the depot long enough, they got the remainder by check. Otherwise, they redeployed still possessing their yen.[25]

Because of the endless hours and numerous currencies required to make large-scale currency exchanges on the Continent, the Twelfth Army Group finance section suggested that the entire

---

Office of the Fis Off, APO 113, to CO, 143d FDS, c/o Eleventh Reinforcement Depot, APO 350, 26 Jan 45, sub: Exchange of U.S. Money for Local Currency, Misc File 312.1 RG 338.

[23] Ltr, Maj C. C. Webb, Hq 1105th AAF Base Unit, Caribbean Div ATC, Office of the Fin Off, Miami Air Field, to the Fis Dir, Hq ASF, Washington, D.C., 21 Sep 45, sub: Foreign Currency Exchange, 123.7. RG 338.

[24] Radio, Washington (SPFBC), to CINCAFPAC, 13 Oct 45, WX 75536. RG 338.

[25] Memo, Col Paul A. Mayo, Fin Off, Sixth Army, to COFS, 19 Dec 45. RG 338.

army adopt a currency similar to the German army's Reichskredit-kassenscheine. This military currency was legal tender only outside Germany. Troops could exchange it for local currencies when they wanted to purchase native goods. The Twelfth Army Group posited that such a currency would drastically reduce the amount of conversions necessary. It estimated that had such a currency been used on the Continent during one year of combat operations, at least a million man-hours would have been saved in finance offices. Also saved would have been the packing space required to store tons of various European currencies. The Twelfth Army Group's desire was fulfilled on 16 September 1946 when the army introduced scrip currency in the European area. It was much like the Wehrmacht's Reichskreditkassenscheine.[26]

Areal Problems

The exchange of currencies presented Finance with a greater range of problems than any other aspect of its wartime operations. These differed from place to place and time to time, depending on the number of troops serviced, the kind of currency involved, and tactical situations. Exchange problems were most acute in combat areas with many troops, but the exotic backwaters of the war—areas with supply functions, such as Egypt, Iran, and India—had their own peculiar exchange phenomena. The army was greatly concerned with knowing the origin of all dollars it used, since dollars bought indiscriminately overseas might conceivably include hoarded Axis funds, thereby promoting espionage or collaboration with the enemy. Just as the army was not supposed to exchange currencies it had not disbursed and in amounts no greater than had been issued as pay and allowances, it was not expected to acquire dollars from suspect or unauthorized sources. These were not necessarily pressing problems, but they did contribute to the overall picture of fiscal management.

The exchange situation in Egypt related to the easy availability of yellow seal dollars throughout the Middle East and North Africa. Soldiers were theoretically supposed to exchange yellow seals

[26] "Report of Operations (Final After Action Report)," Twelfth Army Group, vol. 10, p. 10. RG 338; see the discussion of scrip currency in Walter Rundell, Jr., *Black Market Money*, pp. 80–91.

for local currencies if they were in the area for any length of time, but with local vendors eager to have dollars and with exchange facilities inadequate and casual, many troops found it easier to continue to use dollars. These dollars usually gravitated to banks, which would try to sell them back to the American army. Since there could be no proof of the origin of American currency the banks offered in exchange, the USAFIME headquarters finance office in Cairo refused to purchase American dollars from civilian sources, except for Barclay's Bank, its British depositary throughout the English-speaking world. This policy did not mean that civilians holding American dollars had no recourse. They could sell them to the Tripoli branch of Barclay's at the commercial rate, which was only slightly less than the official army rate, and thereby take a small loss. Currency from Barclay's could then be routed back into army channels or sold to the National Bank of Egypt.[27]

Since the American currency purchased by the National Bank of Egypt in July 1944 came to $531,000, it was highly improbable that this sum could have been released by transient soldiers. A CIC investigation report indicated the possibility that this yellow seal money was being used to finance the exportation of contraband gold from Egypt. A logical destination would have been French North Africa, where gold commanded a higher price than in Egypt.[28] These assumptions made by the CIC were substantiated by reports from French Morocco. A syndicate in that area, cooperating with some French officials, collected as many yellow seal dollars as it could and used them to buy gold in Egypt. The syndicate brought the gold back to Morocco, where they could sell it at three to four times the Egyptian purchase price.[29]

By December 1944 the finance officer of the Cairo Military District had purchased $3,049,676 in yellow seal dollars from the National Bank of Egypt. Such a sum was obviously suspect. But

[27] Memo, Hq USAFIME, OFD, Cairo, Egypt, for CG, USAFIME, 15 Aug 44, sub: Report of Operations, FD 301. RG 338.

[28] Report, Counterintelligence Corps Detachment, Cairo, Egypt, 24 Jul 44, sub: Egyptian Pounds, 123.7; airgram, John Gunter, U.S. Treasury Representative, American Legation, Cairo, to the Secretary of the Treasury, Washington, 2 Oct 44. RG 338.

[29] Col Byron R. Switzer, Chairman, JICANA, Military Intelligence Div, WDGS, Military Attaché Report, French Morocco, Report no. 13555, "Speculation in American Currency," 30 May 44. RG 338.

since Egypt was not an occupied territory, the American army could exercise no control over civilians and commercial firms, regardless of their dealings in U.S. currency. In buying dollars from the Egyptian bank, USAFIME could only follow the advice of the ASF fiscal director. It evidently could not even regulate the activities of another command's finance officer in Cairo. The theater left further negotiations to the American State and Treasury departments and the Egyptian government.[30]

If Egyptians were involved in questionable transactions concerning millions of yellow seal dollars, they were not the sole currency manipulators. Some American soldiers also tried to profit from exchanges in local markets. They traded money locally for more francs and lire than they could get at army finance offices. Then they redeemed the francs and lire at a finance office. Since the official exchange rate prescribed fewer francs and lire to the dollar than GI's had received on the local market, they would show a net dollar gain. When soldiers were caught trying to profit at the army's expense, they were turned over to the provost marshal for punishment.

One soldier involved in this currency racket was a finance cashier. This was a rare recorded instance of a finance man becoming embroiled in illicit currency speculation. The Finance Department, as the agency handling currency exchanges, should, like Caesar's wife, have been above suspicion. So it was particularly noticeable when a finance man was caught in an illegal transaction. This sergeant, the cashier for a finance section in Egypt, established the unit's bank account in his own name in September 1944. After the bank notified the USAFIME fiscal director, the investigation revealed that the sergeant had not only erred in establishing the account but he had also employed government funds in excursions into local money markets. With Egyptian pounds he bought large amounts of francs and lire at rates lower than the official army rates of exchange. Then he exchanged his francs and lire for Egyptian pounds at the finance office's more advantageous rate. After the cashier's manipulations were detected, he was court-martialed.[31]

[30] Memo, Col R. E. Odell, Fis Dir, Hq USAFIME, for CG, USAFIME, 22 Dec 44, sub: Report of Operations, FD 319.1 (C.F.O.). RG 338.
[31] Ibid.

Had he been stationed in an area that was more active militarily and had more pressing duties, he would have had little time for illicit exchange manipulations.

Probably no area offered more opportunities and temptations for exchange manipulations than the Persian Gulf Command. Established to funnel American lend-lease supplies to the Soviet Union, this command saw vast quantities of marketable items pouring through Iran. When soldiers diverted goods to the black market, they reaped handsome profits. But their manipulative activities paled in comparison with those of merchant seamen, who had easier access to goods and who dealt freely in dollars. The command made valiant efforts to control the exchanges of both soldiers and sailors in its area.

By 1945 PGC had worked out an elaborate system for recording currency exchanges. Each person making an exchange in the command signed a currency exchange register, listing name, rank, serial number, organization, the amount of American and foreign currency held, and the amount exchanged. The PGC exchanged currency for people coming from USAFIME or the Mediterranean theater when they surrendered certificates from finance officers in those theaters authorizing the funds presented for exchange. Casuals could exchange money upon presentation of travel orders. Anyone leaving the PGC was given a statement as to the source of his funds. Only the total shown on this statement could legally be offered for exchange in another theater.

Departing merchant seamen, the worst offenders of exchange regulations, were allowed to convert into yellow seal currency only what they had exchanged when entering the PGC, according to the army finance officer's currency exchange register. For instance, if a seaman had exchanged $100 into rials when he entered the PGC, he could exchange no more than $100 worth of rials into yellow seal dollars when departing. If a seaman had a certificate from his ship's agent stating that he had been advanced pay during his stay in the PGC, he could also exchange this amount when leaving the command.[32]

A seaman would be unable to "beat" the exchange restrictions by leaving the PGC with more dollars than he had on arrival, but

---

[32] Cir No. 16, PGC, 19 Feb 45. RG 338.

within their limits he could enjoy some pleasures of the black market. If he took desirable goods into the command and sold them for rials, he could indulge in the Persian flesh pots and upon leaving exchange rials into the amount of dollars he had brought in. Without participating in the black market, a sailor would not be likely to leave a port area with as much money as he had when he entered. The PGC restrictions allowed a seaman the advantage of not having to deduct normal shore expenses from the reconversion limit. While some profits could be translated into dollars, possibly any kind of exchange regulations that tried to incorporate a living-expense differential would have been administratively infeasible in the PGC.

In some areas the problems of exchange related to infrequently used currencies. Exchange rates for a currency such as Indian rupees were usually known only in areas where rupees regularly circulated. When such money was presented elsewhere, finance offices ordinarily could not make quick exchanges. Once two fliers from India came to a disbursing office in the Philippines, requesting an exchange of rupees for pesos. Since those were the first rupees the finance officer had encountered, he told the fliers he could not make an immediate exchange but would complete the transaction quickly. After the clerk looked up the rate of exchange, he worked out the conversion and paid the fliers later that day. The next morning a general came in the office, wanting to exchange some rupees. The clerk made the exchange immediately. After the general had his pesos, he told the captain he had never seen such an efficient finance office. He explained that he was an IG, carrying rupees just to test finance offices outside the CBI.[33]

In the CBI only China did not worry about the inflationary impact of foreign currencies. It joyfully countenanced the army's disbursement of dollars there, realizing that dollars had far more buying power than its highly inflated yuan. The Chinese government eagerly seized upon every device to garner dollars. In India and Burma, however, local authorities carefully resisted the inflationary dollar and insisted that exchange be rigorously controlled.[34]

[33] Interview with Gordon D. Osborn, Bureau of the Budget, 24 Jan 55.
[34] CBI Fiscal Memo 15, 12 Sep 44; IBT Fiscal Memo 4, 5 Feb 45; ltr, Lt Col L. E. Wilson, to Hq Rear Echelon, CBI, Hq Tenth Air Force, et al., 25 Jan 43, sub: Exchange of Burma Notes; Cir 44, IBT, 4 May 45. RG 338.

Exchange Rate Problems

During hostilities, an annoying aspect of currency conversion was fractional rates of exchange. These rates made computations exceedingly difficult, given the calculating equipment available. In some instances American commands used different rates, illustrating the prerogative for theaters to manage their own affairs. After the war, several foreign currencies were officially devalued, requiring finance offices to make extensive exchanges for soldiers holding the currency. Such problems added up to a significant part of Finance's exchange difficulties.

In North Africa and the Middle East, British and American finance officers cooperated willingly. Each would pay the other's troops when necessary, as well as exchanging currency. In September 1944 British paymasters found themselves faced with the fact that the North African theater and USAFIME used different rates of exchange between the pound and the dollar. Paymasters in Tripoli, when exchanging yellow seal dollars for GI's, used the North African theater's rate of exchange, $4.00 to the pound. When the British tried to sell American currency they had accumulated to USAFIME at its rate of exchange, $4.035 to the pound, difficulties arose. Such a disparity in rates would have meant an American loss of $.035 on each pound transaction. So that none of the parties would sustain a loss from the exchange, the British agreed to exchange their American currency with the North African theater at its simplified prevailing rate. Another arrangement made it impossible for American disbursing officers to lose in dollar purchases. The Fiscal Director in Washington decided that all further purchases of dollars from the British would be paid for with Treasury checks. By paying for dollars at their par value, instead of with British currency, there could be no possibility of loss.[35]

The invasion of southern France, which began 15 August 1944, pointed up the great difficulty in making currency conversions with fractional rates of exchange. Before the invasion began, the finance officer for the Seventh Army learned the franc ratio that would apply in France: .495665 francs to $.01. While this fractional rate was adopted to conform with British policy, it complicated Amer-

[35] Memo, Hq USAFIME, OFD, Cairo, Egypt, for CG, USAFIME, 27 Sep 44, sub: Report of Operations, File 319.1. RG 338.

ican exchange problems immensely,[36] mandating conversion tables. No adequate tables were available, and printing facilities in Italy were limited. The Seventh Army finance officer could find no printer in Naples who could prepare the tables, so he finally had to get the work done in Rome. Not all finance officers in this operation chose to be tied to the tables. When the Forty-fifth Division landed in France, its finance officer simplified the problem by reverting to the North African technique of figuring all exchanges at .5 francs to $.01, rather than .495665. He took the difference as a loss on exchange. Earlier in North Africa, exchange rates were such that finance sections could make mental computations without having to rely on tables. There the rates had been $.01 equals 1 lira or .5 franc.[37]

Another kind of complication occurred when a government withdrew a particular bill from circulation. The army, of course, had no control over any friendly government's decisions concerning its currency. The army could only protect its men by exchanging the old currency for the new. On 9 October 1944 the Belgian government declared that all large (in design) notes issued by the Banque Nationale de Belgique in 100-, 500-, and 1,000-franc denominations would not circulate and would cease as legal tender. It then issued bills in the same denominations but with smaller dimensions. With the announcement of the change, commanding officers had to collect all old bills and get them exchanged at the finance office within five days, on a note-for-note basis. This decision of the Belgian government to introduce a new series of bills compounded burdens in finance offices, since it came shortly after heavy exchanges from French to Belgian francs as troops moved into Belgium.[38]

The end of hostilities and the occupation in Europe accentuated Finance's exchange difficulties in two ways. With a great deal more movement from country to country, soldiers had more opportunities for manipulation and subsequent currency exchanges than

---

[36] Interview with Col Ross H. Routh, 24 Jun 54.

[37] "After Action Report, Annex No. 217, Finance, U.S. Seventh Army, Jan 1944–May 1945." RG 338.

[38] "Report of Operations, Annexes 1–3," First U.S. Army, 1 Aug 44–22 Feb 45, p. 39; ltr, Col W. F. Moriarty, Deputy Fis Dir, Hq ETO, APO 887, to Fin Offs, 7 Dec 44. RG 338.

during combat. Too, the conversions caused by new exchange rates proved especially difficult. Since most finance men were older than the average soldier, they mustered out quickly, leaving units either shorthanded or with unseasoned personnel. When faced with massive currency exchanges, these offices were hard pressed.

Inflationary trends throughout Europe after the war directly affected currency conversions. As any currency depreciated, new rates of exchange had to be adopted, which proved a major task for finance offices. When currencies of countries where the army had few men were devalued, exchanges were not difficult. The devaluation of the Greek drachma in June 1945, for example, affected only a handful. Even so, the following case illustrates how an exchange even for a single person could involve several finance offices, consuming many hours.

An air forces staff sergeant stopped at Athens on 1 June 1945 en route from Rome to Cairo. So that he could have spending money, he unwisely exchanged all his lire—approximately $400 worth—into drachmas at the finance office of the 1418th AAF Base Unit. This finance office patently ignored the theater fiscal director's warning that soldiers should not accumulate a surplus of Balkan money. During the following night, the drachma was officially devalued. The next day, the sergeant exchanged his remaining drachmas for Egyptian pounds, losing $270. When the finance office made this last conversion, it gave the sergeant a receipt stating the amount of his loss and assured him that at a later date the army would reimburse him for the loss. He surrendered his receipt at the 1263d AAF Base Unit at Benghazi, Libya, upon request of wing headquarters in Casablanca.

When he arrived at Fort Dix, New Jersey, the sergeant appealed for assistance, and the base finance officer forwarded the case to the OFD in Washington. From there it went to the AMET fiscal director. Instructions were that the sergeant's original receipt be located, but if it could not be found, a certificate should be made giving the particulars of the case. This information was to go to the fiscal director of the Mediterranean theater, who in turn, would send it to the disbursing officer in Athens. He would draw a check to cover the sergeant's loss and mail it to him at Fort Dix.[39]

[39] Ltr, S/Sgt Victor J. D'Agnese, to Base Fin Off, 592d AAF Base Unit

More currency exchanges resulted from the revaluation of the French franc on 26 December 1945 than from any other postwar devaluation in Europe. Both the French metropolitan franc and the French West African franc fell from $.020175 to $.00840625. For military purposes of accounting, collecting, disbursing, and transferring funds, the new rate was officially considered as 1 franc equals $.008406.[40] An agreement between the U.S. and the French goverments protected quasi-official funds and authorized personnel from loss by devaluation. All francs belonging to quasi-official funds and individuals were collected at the old rate and exchanged at the new. When the Sixth Corps finance office learned of the devaluation on 26 December, it notified its subordinate offices to turn in all francs by midnight. On the morning of 27 December, the corps finance office began making conversions at the new rate. In accordance with the agreement between the two governments, the only losses reflected were in official disbursing accounts. The loss in the account of the Sixth Corps resulting from the devaluation was $10,269.63.

In each theater, the fiscal director compiled losses. The army presented the total figure to the French government. By the terms of the international agreement, the French reimbursed the American Treasury for the cumulative loss. The Sixth Corps finance office thought the short notice on the devaluation was beneficial, despite the resulting confusion, because it prevented any attempts at profiteering on the exchange. For twenty days after the change in rates, the corps finance office processed late claims for exchange. Those making claims had to execute a sworn statement that they had a legitimate reason for not having their francs converted promptly.[41]

The protection afforded individuals against loss on this deval-

---

(Second MAT Grp) FERD, ATC, Fort Dix AA Base, 26 Sep 45, sub: Loss of Money Due to Devaluation of Drachma, 123.7; 1st Ind from Fin Off, Fort Dix AA Base; and 2d Ind, Maj John F. Baldwin, Chief, Foreign Fiscal Affairs Sec, Fis Control Br, Hq ASF OFD, 7 Nov 45. RG 338.

[40] Radio, Sgd Warbud, to Hq IBT, 24 Dec 45, WARX 87856, WARX 87857. RG 338.

[41] Col H. L. Leighton, "VI Corps History," Hq Sixth Corps, Office of Fin Off, 11–31 May 45. RG 338.

uation of the franc contrasted sharply with the army's policy after World War I. Following the "Great War," the army made no attempt to protect its members from losses arising from the devaluation of Continental currencies. Immediately after the end of World War I, the army gave officers stationed in Germany the option of cashing their paychecks in marks or francs. Because of the instability of the mark, most officers chose to receive their pay in francs. While in France, many officers and men had opened bank accounts, containing most of their liquid assets.

The uncertain value of the mark induced many soldiers in Germany to speculate on its exchange value. To curb this speculation, the army severely restricted exchanges between marks and francs. A man could exchange marks for francs only if he were going to France on orders, and the disbursing quartermaster (the World War I finance officer) refused to cash officers' personal checks on French banks. The combination of these restrictions with an accumulation of assets in French banks meant that those having either French money or money deposited in France were unable to maintain much control over their funds. When the franc was devalued in the summer of 1919, individuals with French money were powerless to escape the loss. They could only stand by and watch while the savings of several months vanished. The lesson to be learned from this "unfortunate" experience, according to the officer in charge of civil affairs, American forces in Germany, was that the American soldier should be paid in dollars regardless of his place of service. Thereby, any loss resulting from currency devaluations would be absorbed by the government, not the individual.[42]

In the Far East variations in exchange rates during the occupation did not cause the serious strains experienced by finance units in Europe. For one thing, this area dealt with only one foreign currency—the yen. Also, because of the insular nature of the occupation in the Far East, soldiers could not move easily from country to country, so they had fewer opportunities for currency speculation and the attendant need for exchanges.

The primary exchange problem on Okinawa involved devalua-

[42] Col I. L. Hunt, *American Military Government of Occupied Germany, 1919–1920, Report of the Officer in Charge of Civil Affairs, Third Army and American Forces in Germany*, pp. 203–204.

tion of the yen. While the initial exchange rate of ten yen to the dollar helped hold the line against inflation on Okinawa, it proved unrealistic after several months. The yen was therefore devalued by one-half. On 4 September 1945, Okinawa's conversion day, the exchange rate changed from 10-to-1 to 15-to-1. So that soldiers would not lose purchasing power on the devalution, all yen in their hands were withdrawn at the old rate. Unit officers collected yen from their men and gave them receipts. Officers presented the yen to a finance officer, who gave them Treasury checks in exchange. On 6 September officers returned these checks to the finance officer, who converted them for yen at 15-to-1. Unit officers issued yen to their men and collected their receipts. Post exchanges and APO's were closed from 4 to 6 September and made their exchanges in the same manner as units. On islands in the Ryukyu area that did not have disbursing officers, commanders were required to have their men's money ready for conversion on 3 September, for the yen had to be at a disbursing office on the next day.[43]

Most exchange problems during the early Japanese occupation resembled those in other areas of the Pacific where the army used yen currency. Occupation troops arriving from the United States needed their dollars converted into yen, and redeploying forces needed the reverse conversion made. Currency revaluations presented common difficulties in all occupied areas. The yen devaluation of 4 September 1945 occurred simultaneously in Japan, Korea, and Okinawa. When the exchange rate was adjusted from 10-to-1 to 15-to-1, the same office procedures were used in Japan and Korea as on Okinawa.[44] On subsequent conversion days, a similar routine was followed. Disbursing officers suspended transactions in local currencies except for collections. While business was halted, personnel officers collected local currency as spearhead deposits and turned it in to a finance office. After the collections were con-

[43] Ltr, Capt James R. Rogers, Asst AG, Hq Tenth Army and Ryukyus Area, to Ascom I, Twenty-fourth Corps, Eighth Air Force, et al., 26 Aug 45, sub: Change in Rate of Exchange, Supplemental Military Yen, Series "B", 123 (TAFIS). RG 338.

[44] Ltr, Col C. F. Fowler, Fis Dir, PGC, to Fin Offs, Abadan Air Base, Port of Khorramshahr, and Amirabad Post, 2 Sep 45, sub: Exchange of Yen Currency, FD 123.7. RG 338.

solidated, the disbursing officer prepared an account current, stating his holdings in the foreign currency at the new rate. In this manner, soldiers holding local currency lost no purchasing power.[45]

Individual Cases

Despite the government's efforts in World War II to protect soldiers' interests in exchange transactions, some inevitably suffered losses. Some of these losses could be recouped, but many could not. Redeploying soldiers, both in Europe and in the States, who could not exchange foreign currency at the first finance office they tried, frequently heard that they could make exchanges "up ahead." But when they got to the stated place, it turned out to be only another link in the "up ahead" chain, another instance of buck passing. In such cases, the Office of the Fiscal Director in Washington was the soldier's last resort. Many congressmen who received complaints from constituents about currency exchanges also routed problems to the OFD. Most of the cases referred to OFD had to be refused because they violated regulations, but those that appeared legitimate and came within the scope of official directives received full consideration. The following cases illustrate the range of individual exchange problems and show how the lack of understanding of regulations in the field produced misunderstandings, acrimony, and extra work all the way up the line to the OFD.

A soldier injured on 15 April 1945 in Hamburg, Germany, was immediately evacuated to Paris. He left 14,200 francs behind in his duffel bag. From Paris he wrote inquiring about the money but received no reply. After he recovered and returned to the States, he went home on pass and found that his organization had mailed him his money. When he certified that the money was derived from pay and allowances and that his injuries had precluded any exchange, the conversion was made.[46]

At times disbursing officers in the field complicated problems

---

[45] Radio, Warbud to CG, China Theater, et al., 12 Dec 45, WARX 87858. RG 338.

[46] Certificate of T/4 Charles E. Rand, Sr., 37727630, 21 Aug 45, 123.7 France; 1st Ind, Maj T. J. Flynn, Asst Chief, Receipts and Disbursements Div, OFD, to CO, Glennan General Hospital, Okmulgee, Okla., Attn: DO, 29 Aug 45, SPFES 123.7 France. RG 338.

by their unfamiliarity with directives governing exchange of currencies. They gave some soldiers the "fast shuffle" and told them to take their cases to the Office of the Fiscal Director in Washington. At Camp Shelby, Mississippi, a staff sergeant awaiting discharge in June 1945 requested the camp finance officer to exchange twenty-three dollars in francs to American currency. The finance officer told him to send the francs to Washington where they would be exchanged. The OFD returned them and told the sergeant the Camp Shelby finance officer was authorized to make the exchange provided the soldier could establish the legitimacy of their source.[47]

At the time currency control books were introduced, a soldier in Austria had accumulated five months' pay in anticipation of a furlough in England. Since only three months' pay could be entered on the books, he had over $200 that he could not exchange. When he shipped to the States for discharge, his battalion told him that he could convert the excess at the port of embarkation. At the port, he was directed to the Camp Kilmer, New Jersey, finance office, which instructed him to wait until he got to the separation center at Camp Atterbury, Indiana, to try to get his money exchanged. The Camp Atterbury finance office advised him to write the OFD, which could make no exchange for the soldier.[48]

When the OFD recognized a valid complaint about currency conversions, it took quick action to correct the deficiencies. A private first class was wounded in France and evacuated to a hospital in England. There a finance officer refused to accept a fifty-franc note for conversion because a corner was torn off. The soldier sent the bill to the Treasury Department for redemption. He wrote that there were many cases of this nature and that one finance officer had flatly refused to exchange a two-franc bill because it was too small. "Are we supposed to throw away this sweat money?" the private queried. The Treasury forwarded the soldier's letter to the OFD, which sent it and the franc note to the fiscal

---

[47] Ltr, S/Sgt Carl A. Budinich, 20425155, to OFD, ASF, 15 Jun 45, 123.7 France; 1st Ind, Maj T. J. Flynn, 21 Jun 45, SPFET 123.7 France. RG 338.

[48] Ltr, S/Sgt George Gast, 35070397, 468th AAA (AW) Bn, to OFD, ASF, 12 Apr 46, 123.7 Austria; ltr, Lt Col G. E. Gross, Asst, Receipts and Disbursements Div, OCF, to George Gast, 22 Apr 46, SPFES 123.7 Austria (1152); ltr, Capt Wayne D. Phillips, RFD 4, Box 288, Norfolk, Va., to Capt Breen, 20 Jun 45. RG 338; "History of the Fiscal Services," pp. 591–592.

director of the European theater, instructing him to make the exchange. Also, the Washington office requested the European theater fiscal director to furnish all disbursing officers with the proper information on the redemption of mutilated currency, since this case indicated a weakness in that area.[49]

The OFD often received requests from civilians to exchange currencies coming in the mail from Europe. A GI sent his wife in Illinois some francs, intended as a souvenir. But she thought the money "to [sic] valuable to keep, so would like to know if cashable. . . ." Since the wife was not "authorized personnel," the exchange could not be made.[50]

A veteran's petition for a currency exchange speaks best for itself. He wrote the OFD on 28 January 1946:

> I was discharged from the Army on Oct. 11. (1945) I had a letter from My Friend oversea's who owe Me Some money. he Sent it from Germany. it is one hundred twenty mark's it is worth $12.00 dollar's. would Yow please exchange this in american dollar's for me.
>
> Your loving friend,
> /s/[51]

When by 8 March 1946 the veteran had not received the check he expected, he wrote Washington, saying:

> I would like to know what the hell is wrong with yow Guy's. If I do not get my check for $12.00 dollars in the Next few day's I am Gone to take action against yow. I am Getting tired of the way yow Guy's give us the Run around. So please send me that check as I need that money Right away. I am not kidding.[52]

The OFD assured the veteran that it had made a "careful analysis" and that "every effort had been put forth to effect the exchange,"

---

[49] Ltr, Pfc John J. Rauscher, 6719863, USAHP 411, APO 314, c/o PM, New York, to Treasury Dept, 20 Oct 44, 123.7 France; ltr, Maj T. J. Flynn, to Pfc John J. Rauscher, 14 Nov 44, SPFET 123.7 France; ltr, Maj Flynn, to CG, ETOUSA, APO 887, c/o PM, New York, Attn: Fis Dir, 14 Nov 44, SPFET 123.7 France. RG 338.

[50] Ltr, Mrs Arvil Daily, Rt 1, Box 941, Granite City, Ill., to OFD, 26 Aug 45, 123.7 France; ltr, Maj Flynn to Mrs. Daily, 31 Aug 45, SPFES 123.7 France. RG 338.

[51] Ltr, from Akron, Ohio, to OFD, 28 Jan 46, 123.7 Germany FINEF, Nov 45. RG 338.

[52] Ltr, from Akron to OFD, 8 Mar 46. RG 338.

but since he was no longer in the category of "authorized personnel," the War Department could not "consummate the conversion." It also informed him that the Allied military marks had to be returned with deep regret. Either the ex-soldier was impressed with the sincerity of Washington's regret or too baffled by the jargon to respond. In any event, he wrote no more letters.[53]

Although some soldiers who brought foreign currencies to this country tried to convert the money while they were still in the army, others tried to do so after separation. As long as those still in uniform could prove the legitimacy of their source, they could, after many delays, get money exchanged. Like the veteran cited above, however, men who waited until they had become civilians fought a losing battle, since they were no longer among the "authorized personnel" for whom the army could make exchanges. The following request for an exchange, like the foregoing petition, would suffer from translation. It reflects the pathetic attempt of an ignorant citizen to cope with his government's bureaucracy.

> I have Been in the European theaters and were Discharged on 7th of Nov. Brought home 10-1000 and 10-mille Francs. Which were paid to me for the time that I have Served in France. And have tried to exchange it in the States But failed to for no banks no the Port of Embarkation will exchange this money unless I write this address the Resion that I never exchanged it over Sea is that the time for me to exchange it i were out working and when I got in they told me the time were expired and I gave it to my company commanding officer Lt. R. Bowls of the 3902 QM truck company and asked him to please have it exchanged and when I were undersigned from the company and I asked him for the money he gave me back the freak money and said that it would have to Be proven by a field marshal that the money were for me and he didn't know any and ether did I. and he were supposed to get one for me But failed to do so and I were paid off in this money for the time I served in France.
>
> thanking you very kindly for any thing that you can do that I might get Some of this money
>
> Signed
> /s/[54]

[53] Ltr, Capt R. E. Leach, Actg Chief For Fis Affairs Section, Fis Control Br, OFD, to Akron, 19 Mar 46, SPFBC 123.7. RG 338.

[54] Ltr, from New Orleans, La., to Hq OFD, ASF, Attn: Receipts and Disbursements Div, 26 Nov 45, 123.7 France; ltr, Maj E. G. Brown, Asst,

The mammoth task of exchanging foreign currencies plagued finance offices throughout the war and into the immediate post-combat period. This problem, as much as any wartime finance operation, highlighted the lack of prewar fiscal planning for a foreign war. The staffing of finance offices did not provide for the physical impact of exchanging currencies. When it became manifest that the job must be done, that task was piled on top of the cashier's normal duties. Even the best cashier could not handle the situation alone, so other finance men were diverted from their duties to lend a hand. Consequently, the entire office work load was thrown off balance, and exchange service frequently was inadequate.

Perhaps under wartime conditions it would have been impossible for the War Department to have provided sufficient information and facilities so that exchanges would have been handled efficiently. But it seems that even an occasional lack of conversion tables and the continuing absence of systematic policies concerning such currency as the yellow seal dollar demonstrate the low priority placed on this aspect of fiscal management. At the root of the problem, however, was the government's willingness for its soldiers to deal in a multiplicity of foreign currencies. The alternatives of allowing servicemen to establish dollar credits in lieu of pay or to accept pay in foreign currencies with no exchange privileges were apparently never seriously considered during the war. Or perhaps the War Department figured that the morale boost of having foreign money to spend outweighed the resulting inadequacies of the army's exchange service. And it may have. But this advantage must be measured against the poor morale caused by inefficient service. In September 1946 the army initiated payment in dollar-denominated scrip that could be exchanged for foreign money, which could not then be reexchanged into scrip or dollar credits. Scrip was instituted to achieve currency control rather than to facilitate exchanges; its effect has been analyzed elsewhere.[55]

Receipts and Disbursements Plans and Operations Div, OFD, 21 Dec 45, SPFES 123.7 France. RG 338.

[55] Rundell, *Black Market Money*, pp. 80–92.

CHAPTER *10*

Troop Life

Novelists and Hollywood have transmitted vivid ideas of what it was like to be an American soldier in World War II. James Jones, Irwin Shaw, and Norman Mailer have portrayed the grimness and horror of combat, the inflexible and merciless autocracy of the military system, and the stupefying futility of the soldier's life. Essentially, these fictitious portrayals focused on the combat soldier as hero or anti-hero. Given the needs and uses of fiction, whether in print or on film, such a focus is understandable. However dramatic and compelling the experiences of the rifleman in the front line, they do not constitute the norm for soldier life. Those on the front line in World War II represented only about one-fifth of the army's strength, the others serving in support or reserve. If "combat-sustaining" forces are included (such as those in transportation, ordnance, chemical warfare, and the signal corps), those at the front accounted for three out of every seven soldiers.[1] Whatever the ratio, the majority of soldiers were not involved in combat. Of course, with rotation of units from reserve, different men would serve on the front lines. The obvious implication of these facts is that the fictitious treatment of the American soldier in World War II is hardly typical. A small percentage of those assigned to combat arms—the infantry, artillery, and armor—found themselves facing the enemy; consequently, for most soldiers the military life was not one of derring-do.

Social scientists have shared the literary preoccupation with the lives of combat troops. In trying to assess the quality of soldier life in World War II, Stouffer et al., the authors of the four-volume *Studies in Social Psychology in World War II*, paid scant attention to those serving in technical and administrative services. The official series published by the Office of the Chief of Military

---

[1] Robert W. Coakley and Richard M. Leighton, *Global Logistics and Strategy, 1943–1945*, p. 839.

History, United States Army in World War II, contains volumes on the support services, but no explicit evaluation of troop life is included. As a consequence, the impact of war on those troops who rarely fought—and rarely expected to—has been little investigated. Such groups included those assigned to the judge advocate general, quartermaster, medical service corps, engineers, adjutant general, chaplaincy, and finance. Because of their slight odds of encountering a militant German or Japanese, finance men were jestingly, and derisively, called "fighting finance."

The nature of troop life in the Finance Department in World War II obviously differed considerably from that of combat soldiers. Both popular and scholarly treatments of the reactions of soldiers to overseas service have ignored differences among various branches of the army; this chapter attempts to compensate for that oversight. It has been natural to generalize on the experience of combat soldiers, but this has been done at the expense of an accurate understanding of the heterogeneity of human reaction to involvement in World War II.

The entire Finance organization was very small, consisting of only 14,800 officers and men in May 1945, when the army's strength peaked at 8,290,000.[2] Not only was the number miniscule, but finance men usually worked and lived within self-contained units, either divisional finance offices or FDS's, which consisted of two commissioned officers, a warrant officer, and approximately two dozen enlisted men. The narrow confines of these units influenced the way finance men perceived and reacted to the war.

Troop life in Finance differed from the norm for several reasons. Finance work was certainly unlike that of the infantrymen, as well as that of the other noncombat branches. Technical and exacting finance duties resembled those of a skilled civilian office worker. To perform such duties proficiently, men of high caliber were required. Those assigned to Finance were considerably more intelligent than average soldiers. During the war the army gave all inductees a general classification test to determine mental ability; this test divided men into five classes, based on their scores. From March through August 1942, a period of accelerated mobilization when most Finance T/O&E's were filled, 89.4 percent of those as-

[2] Figures supplied by Reference Branch, CMH. U.S. Army.

signed to Finance came from classes I and II. During this time, no class V scorers entered Finance, and those designated as class IV constituted only .5 percent. Men considered by the army to have average ability, the class III scorers, represented only 10.5 percent of those assigned to Finance. Manifestly, Finance was staffed by an unusually able group. Reflecting the army's—and society's—attitudes toward the relation between intelligence and race, reception centers sent no Negroes to Finance, on the assumption that they did not have the capacity for highly technical tasks. By the end of 1942, in the entire army, only Finance had no Negro units, but a few blacks came into Finance on individual assignments from other units. There is no indication that their performance differed from that of their white associates. (Later all-black divisions had their organic finance units.) Most finance officers and enlisted men eagerly sought their assignments because the skills gained would transfer easily to such civilian pursuits as banking, bookkeeping, accounting, and management.[3] Finance men possessed very high intelligence among army personnel, and they performed specialized work. As a consequence, their reactions to army life differed considerably from those of other soldiers.

A further reason for this difference was the implicit assumption that finance men were not likely to face the enemy—another aspect of the popularity of Finance assignments. In terms of the sociological concept of differential deprivation and reward, finance men understood that however trying their overseas conditions, they were not nearly so deprived as those facing the enemy. Most were thankful for "escaping the risks of death and the gruelling life of the front lines."[4] Part of this thanks manifested itself in positive attitudes toward work.

Attitudes toward Work

Most finance men took considerable pride in their duty, although a few behaved irresponsibly, such as the previously mentioned major in the Sixth Infantry Division and the cashier in

[3] Robert R. Palmer, Bell I. Wiley, and William R. Keast, *The Procurement and Training of Ground Combat Troops*, pp. 14–17, 107; Ulysses Lee, *The Employment of Negro Troops*, p. 135.

[4] Samuel A. Stouffer et al., *The American Soldier: Adjustment During Army Life*, vol. 1, Studies in Social Psychology in World War II, pp. 172–173.

Cairo. They maintained a professional, critical approach toward their work, not content to grouse about established procedures without thinking of how they might be improved. Intelligent inquiry into operating systems could produce important changes. An example was the introduction of a new audit plan in the North African theater. M/Sgt. Harold S. Childs of the Forty-Seventh FDS developed a procedure for auditing sales officers' accounts that proved so beneficial it was adopted throughout the theater. In recognition of his outstanding work, M/Sgt. Childs won the Legion of Merit and a letter of citation.[5]

Commanders of finance units justly appreciated the work their men accomplished. Naturally, in retrospect after hostilities, they waxed enthusiastic over the quality of their men's work. But enthusiasm in Finance seemed general. In August 1943 Col. R. E. Odell, finance officer for USAFIME, claimed, "The Finance gang, including our friends in the Air Force, are tops and a better crowd was never assembled anywhere! I speak of them as my family and am proud of them."[6]

The close cooperation between officers and men in finance units was responsible for quality performance. Maj. J. W. Wood, commanding the 109th FDS, held periodic discussions with his men. Any ideas that promised an improvement in working methods were thoroughly examined. The major urged all in his command to bring forward any constructive thoughts occurring to them. The section studied systems used by other finance offices and tried to make operational innovations whenever possible. It made studies both officially and independently. Men on pass frequently visited other offices and picked up ideas for improvements. Members of the 109th felt that their greatest motivation in producing superior work was the "intelligent, efficient, cheerful, and fair-minded" approach Major Wood had toward his men. As a result, he had their wholehearted cooperation. "Their determination to do well and accurately each task put before them as individuals or as a depart-

---

[5] "History of the Peninsular Base Section, NATOUSA, 28 Aug 1943 to 31 Jan 1944," vol. 2, RG 338.

[6] Ltr, Col R. E. Odell, Fin Off, Hq USAFIME, to Col Gilchrist, ASF, OFD, Washington, 310.1, 23 Aug 43. RG 338.

ment within the Section was an outgrowth of his manners and his methods."[7]

The men of the 109th FDS reflected accurately the behavior and attitudes of a primary group. Edward A. Shils in "Primary Groups in the American Army" cited strong primary group identification among those whose units were already formed before leaving the States. Virtually all finance units were created at the army's finance school at Fort Benjamin Harrison, so their members were well acquainted by the time they arrived on foreign shores. Those in the 109th FDS had the self-assurance Shils attributed to primary groups, as well as the confidence in and esteem for their officers he described. Although he dealt with combat troops, these characteristics of a primary group transfer easily to a service organization.[8]

The esteem in which finance men held their officers was reciprocated, as could be expected. Maj. James A. Stewart, commander of the Seventy-ninth FDS, called his men "without exception the finest group of men that any commanding officer could have. . . . They served always without thought of their personal welfare, but with the idea of being the best soldiers in the European theater and giving the best service to all who came into the office!"[9]

In some locales, especially on Pacific islands, duty was so demanding that troop life was nothing but work. The situation on Corregidor was one of the most taxing of the entire war. No provisions for a finance office existed on the island. The Japanese bombed the improvised office in the Middleside Barracks on 29 December 1941, soon after its establishment. The finance unit was then assigned thirty linear feet of space in an already crowded lateral of Melinta Tunnel. This space became the office, and the men slept outside on the bushy slopes of Melinta Hill. They dug fox-

[7] "Unit History," 109th FDS, 15 Apr 45. RG 338. Unit histories sometimes have a partisan quality and are therefore suspect as evidence. Since those for finance units are critical and analytical on issues other than those pertaining to work conditions and morale, their comments on those issues may be taken as reliable.

[8] Robert K. Merton and Paul F. Lazarsfeld, eds., *Continuities in Social Research*, pp. 27–28.

[9] Maj James A. Stewart, "Unit History."

holes for protection from frequent air raids and shelling from Ternate. During the four months that the finance unit operated under these conditions, the meager plumbing facilities were frequently put out of operation by Japanese air raids. Because of the shortage of food, men survived on one-third rations.

Toward the end of April 1942 the intensity of the Japanese attack on Corregidor drove everyone inside the tunnels except those directly engaged in the defense of the island.

> By that time the end was approaching. Near bedlam arose in the main roadway, jammed with frightened native laborers, whipped refugees from Bataan and stragglers from our own garrison. There was little relaxation possible during the first days of the war in Manila. There was none on Corregidor. Nevertheless, Filipinos and Americans alike stood up under the strain and displayed a loyalty, devotion to duty, and cheerfulness in the face of daily hardships. The work performed by the Finance Department, all other angles aside, contributed greatly to preserving the morale of a command that knew it was fighting a losing battle.[10]

Although the ranking finance officer on Corregidor may have claimed too much for the therapeutic value of finance work, this work included, among other things, burning 51 million pesos and hundreds of thousands of American dollars.[11]

While the Persian Gulf Service Command never fought a battle, losing or otherwise, working conditions there were formidable. Intense heat took a heavy toll. Col. O. W. DeGruchy, chief of the fiscal branch of PGSC headquarters, counseled his finance officers that hard work was the best morale builder under the circumstances.

> In this part of the world work is a boon. It helps pass the time till we return to God's country and allows the worker no time to mope and have his morale lowered. . . . The morale of finance men will never be anything but high if they put their shoulders to the wheel, keep smiling and never lose their sense of humor. Try it. Cuss—sure, but keep on smiling.[12]

---

[10] Col John R. Vance, "Report of Operations, Finance Officer, USFIP, Dec 8, 1941–May 6, 1942," 30 Sep 44, p. 14. RG 338.

[11] Ibid., pp. 5, 10.

[12] Ltr, Col O. W. DeGruchy, Chief Fis Br, Hq PGSC, to Agent DO's, PGSC, 20 Jan 43, sub: Miscellaneous Administrative Matters, FO 319.2. RG 338.

An excellent means of creating a willing attitude toward work was by keeping men well informed. Capt. John C. Shapton, Jr., commander of the 175th FDS, located on Biak, New Guinea, held monthly meetings with his section to discuss general problems, both technical and military. He kept the men posted on such matters as the theater policy on furloughs and temporary duty in the United States, promotion, and censorship. These meetings fostered an air of understanding and cooperation in the 175th.[13]

Before the days of racial integration in the army, a white outfit, reflecting prevailing societal sentiment, felt that no more degrading fate could befall it than to work under a Negro command.[14] When the 198th FDS drew such an assignment in April 1945, it was particularly irate, thinking it had been "sold down the river," doubtless without appreciating the origin of the expression. This finance unit originally understood that its transfer to Morotai in the Molucca Islands was as a class B agency of the finance office of the Ninety-third Division, a Negro division. Upon arrival on Morotai, the 198th was attached to the Ninety-third's finance office. The eight men of the 198th were the only white enlisted men in the entire Ninety-third. The 198th's commandant, Capt. J. E. Williams, Jr., described the situation as having a "bad odor." The men of the 198th had to sleep in two tents "right in with the colored troops and mess with them. They are under colored officers and noncoms. You know what they think of that and also how I feel about it."[15] Explicitly, Captain Williams stated, "dealing with those niggers isn't a job for a white man."[16]

Aside from the "unbearable" situation of being integrated with a Negro division, Captain Williams protested the way his section was subordinated to the finance office of the Ninety-third. The finance officer of the Ninety-third used Captain Williams and 1st Lt.

[13] cwo P. L. Blanchard, "Unit History."

[14] Stouffer et al. reported in *The American Soldier* that 84 percent of white soldiers thought Negroes should be in separate outfits (p. 568). The percentage of negative reaction would doubtless have been much higher had opinion been sought concerning a white unit being subordinated to a black one.

[15] Ltr, Capt J. E. Williams, Jr., Fin Off, 198th FDS, to Lt Col J. R. Laughlin, Fin Off, Eighth Army Area Command, 18 Apr 45. RG 338.

[16] Ltr, Capt J. E. Williams, Jr., Fin Off, 195th FDS, to Maj E. E. Harris, Fin Off, Southern Island Area Command, 10 Oct 45. RG 338.

A. B. Wrench, also of the 198th, to deliver money to out-of-the-way units. Williams complained, "sounds like a class A agent job to me. . . . The division office should be able to more than take care of all the troops. As for our working as part of the division office, that is entirely uncalled for. It appears that the 93d's finance officer just isn't too sure of the ability of his men and wants us to do the work for them."[17]

Morale

After work was done, troop morale to a large degree depended on the availability of recreational opportunities. Finance men, enthusiastic about their work, also attacked recreation with zest. In this enjoyment of diversion from military duties, finance men reflected the norm of soldiers' behavior. Their enjoyment of sports, women, parties, good food and drink, and other amenities nonetheless seemed more intentional and creative than that of combat soldiers who were likely to be more reckless and exploitative in their diversion because of the "here today, gone tomorrow" philosophy.

Sports played an important part in the recreation of soldiers. The Thirty-second FDS sent M/Sgt. Harold Mostkoff to Rome to compete in an Allied track meet shortly after the city's liberation,[18] but most finance athletics were intramural competitions that doubtless provided more general benefit than having a few stars distinguish themselves. The chief recreational activity of the 119th FDS at its home base in Tidworth, England, was tennis. Favorite attractions for the section were the doubles matches played between the officers and enlisted teams. Spectators, usually enlisted men from the section, naturally wanted their buddies to beat the officers. During the summer, the men of the 119th enjoyed swimming, but with the coming of the usual bad weather of the English autumn, they abandoned that recreation.[19] On Leyte basketball, swimming, table tennis, and volleyball proved the most popular sports with the men of the 171st FDS. On one occasion an ocean swim led to a finance man's being decorated for bravery. M/Sgt. Ralph Parrino of

---

[17] Ltr, Williams to Laughlin, 18 Apr 45.
[18] Lt Col Ivy J. Schuman, "Unit History."
[19] T/3 Nathan Sale, T/5 Paul N. Sutton, and CWO Edward M. Lesley, "Unit History."

the 195th FDS received the Soldier's Medal for rescuing a man from drowning in the Pacific. Although decoration for heroism in battle was usually denied finance men, Parrino proved his mettle in another kind of life-or-death situation.[20]

Parties thrown by finance units were as important a part of their play as athletics. One of the main requisites for a good party was the right type of women. Usually the mainstays were local women, wherever finance units happened to be. When the 2974th Finance Detachment and the 586th Army Postal Unit, both located at Bungay, England, decided to have a joint dance, they pooled their contacts and produced the desired number of women. The postal men brought women from an English post office they dealt with, and the finance men brought women from Barclay's Bank. In addition, there was the female staff of the Red Cross Club. The Finance Detachment, which "knew that man does not live by dancing," arranged to feed the "inner man"—twenty-seven gallons of ale, grapefruit juice, and sandwiches. The dance was held in three barracks, which, for the occasion, had been stripped of clothing and equipment and was suitably decorated. "The affair had a deeper significance than merely that of social success. To the dance came young women of a class rarely seen or met by American soldiery in the course of their normal operations in the neighborhood." It established Anglo-American relations on a new level, with implications expected to be "no less than profound."[21]

On Pacific islands, spirits took a decided turn upward when cold beer became available. 1st Lt. A. B. Wrench, commander of the 198th FDS on Mindanao after it had been separated from the Ninety-third Division, was ecstatic when he found fifteen cases of beer left behind by the Marines.[22] On Leyte, too, the issuing of beer was equated with the arrival of WAC's next door as a morale builder.[23]

The WAC detachment provided, in addition to the welcome

[20] Ltr, 1st Lt E. Domenici, CO, 195th FDS, to CG, Eighth Army Area Command, 21 Jul 45, sub: Soldier's Medal, 220.5. RG 338.

[21] 1st Lt H. Greenberg, "Unit History."

[22] Ltr, 1st Lt A. B. Wrench, Fin Off, 198th FDS, to Maj E. E. Harris, Fin Off, SISAC, 17 Oct 45. RG 338.

[23] Ltr, Capt G. D. Osburn, Fin Off, 171st FDS, to CO, Base K, APO 72, 2 Jun 45, sub: Unit History, PDF 314.7. RG 338.

sight of American women, esthetic and intellectual diversion. Each
week at Tacloban, Leyte, the information and education officer of
the WAC detachment arranged concerts from recordings of the
great masters. She also conducted a weekly forum on current
events.[24]

Although finance men reveled in planned parties with sufficient women and refreshments, the First FDS had its best break
when it moved into a ready-made party. At the end of hostilities,
the First was billeted in private rooms in the Fuerst Leopold Hotel
in Detmold, Germany. The hotel had a full-sized bar with six beer
spigots. At a local brewery the men could buy a fifteen-gallon keg
of beer for two dollars. Thus the section had a head start on diversion. The unit's standard of living profited further from a successful supply corporal, who, even if he could not get necessary GI
supplies and clothing, would always manage to find something special for the men. His talents ranged to collecting German ski caps,
parachutists' jackets, jump suits, coat liners, and helmets, some of
which obviously had more souvenir than practical value.[25]

Finance men, while overseas, approached both work and recreation with creative enthusiasm. These men who worked hard
and played hard were men of spirit, feeling, and intelligence. Finance units, as primary groups, were close-knit, small groups of
able men, probably having a greater proportion of sensitive individuals than most military organizations. A sensitivity to their environment was evident from various conditions affecting morale. The
most substantial demonstration of this sentience came from their
writing about army life.

Their writing skills derived from recognizing basic truths
emerging from everyday life and translating those truths into terms
another could identify in his own experience. Certainly one can
write sympathetically about any phase of man's activity. The following example displays a gentle, literate wittiness, demonstrating
self-understanding.

> A man gets mighty powerful tired of sitting around day after
> day trying to prove that the gold that glitters in Shakespeare's
> play was a mere twinkle compared with the seat of a finance man's

---

[24] Ltr, Osborn to CO, Base K, 2 Jul 45, sub: Unit History, PKF 314.7.
[25] S/Sgt Glynn E. Hall, "Unit History."

trousers—so we entered the base athletic schedule. It is better that we merely state that the office *participated* in the soft ball league —the actual scores might prove uninteresting. Anyway, who could expect a fifteen-man office to furnish a ten-man team and still round out the roster of the dart and scittles match at the nearby pub?[26]

As his unit left the comparative safety of England and headed toward the Continent, where the Battle of the Bulge would erupt, one finance man expressed universal feelings of nostalgia and melancholy:

> The men stood at the ship's rail watching the white cliffs of England fading from sight; and as they watched, they reminisced of London, Worcester, and Glasgow Red Cross Clubs, theaters, and pubs, and of the ancient castles, churches, universities, and the cities they'd seen. They talked about the phlegmatic English, how they'd struck up friendships they'd probably never renew, how English newspapers appeared very partisan and Empire conscious, and how they would never have it as good as in Malvern Link. They talked of a camp's cook who provided the best food they'd had in the army; of the soft mattresses left behind; of evenings at the Fir Tree, Bakery, and Express Inns; and of the dentist's assistant who chuckled at Bob Hope's radio jokes while the dentist drilled deep into one's tooth. And as they reminisced, the ship passed every conceivable type of ship-in-war. Signals were flickered back and forth and steel harbor nets parted to let the ship pass. England was lost to view and the ship was lone to the world on an uneasy sea.[27]

Besides writing with perceptions of self-understanding and universal emotions, finance men displayed a degree of sensitivity toward the routine business of living, toward the impact of army life on the individual. They reacted quickly to conditions affecting troop morale and made reasonable adjustments to their environment.

An accurate gauge of morale was the amount of time a man could claim as his own. Naturally, military duties had to be fulfilled before anyone could expect spare time, but if time was available and unwarranted restrictions were imposed, morale suffered. While in England in September 1944, the work volume of the

---

[26] Maj Tom C. Hawkins, "Unit History."
[27] T/4 Stanley Mack, "Unit History."

111th FDS decreased to the point that men could have their evenings free and a day off each week. On the surface this seemed a great morale boost, but as soon as time became available, the post commander forced the men to leave the garrison on their days off. That meant that each man had to buy his meals during the day and that no personal correspondence or laundry could be taken care of in camp. A final blow to the 111th's spirits was a thirteen-week military training program outside duty hours. The training schedule allowed Tuesday and Sunday nights off, but Tuesdays were GI party nights when the office and huts were scrubbed down with soap and water. These restrictions put morale at its lowest ebb.[28]

The Eightieth FDS, commanded by Capt. Stanley O. Shea, in May 1945 gave each man one day off during the week. All testified that the relaxation and opportunity to take care of personal business relieved the nervous tension created by office work and resulted in better performance during the rest of the week.[29]

The surest way for a man to have time of his own was to take a pass and get away from his base. Sometimes commanding officers of finance units could grant passes as the work load permitted, but in other cases, the quota of passes was beyond the control of finance officers. Maj. J. A. Stewart, commandant of the Seventy-ninth FDS, granted two passes a month when his unit was located at Marseilles in December 1944 and January 1945. He gave all his men opportunities to go to Paris and enabled them to spend leisure time on the Riviera.[30] A trip to Paris, regardless of label, was usually hailed as a noteworthy event and a tremendous boost for the spirits. Two men of the 119th FDS were put on temporary duty in August 1944 to help move the fiscal director's headquarters to Paris. "The section's adventurers, Francis H. Greeley and George H. Kassner, returned from Paris with tales of great accomplishments against tremendous odds on . . . their own 'D Day.'" The section gratefully accepted their contribution of three bottles of champagne, vintage 1912.[31]

When commanders of finance sections could not grant passes, men were much more likely to feel that they were having to work

28 CWO Merton G. Jefts, "Unit History."
29 Capt Stanley O. Shea, "Unit History."
30 Stewart, "Unit History."
31 Sale, Sutton, and Lesley, "Unit History."

too hard. The complaint of the First FDS that the unit received its first belated pass allocation in May 1945, having landed on Utah Beach on 18 June 1944, evidenced this feeling of imposition. Then the section was further restricted in June when it was attached to a headquarters company in a redeployment area. Not only were finance men again part of another organization's pass quota, but they were subject to all orders issued by the company in connection with garrison duties. Such restriction hardly appealed to men who had grown used to the comforts of private rooms in a hotel that had six spigots for beer![32]

Promotions were another good measure of troop morale. The departure of most of the high-point men in finance units to the States created vacancies that permitted advancement for the men left behind. The Twenty-ninth FDS reported that after twenty-nine months men were ready for another stripe or two.[33] Those doing good work felt keenly the injustice of being unable to be promoted because of an inelastic system. The responsibility of disbursing and accounting for millions of dollars a year should have allowed the possibility of personal advancement.[34] Many finance officers considered it a mistake to send units overseas with a full table of organization, since that left no room for promotion. Since few vacancies occurred in finance sections during the war, men had little chance to advance in rank.[35]

In all overseas locations other constant indicators of morale were food, quarters, mail, and the prospects of returning to the United States. The 119th FDS on its voyage to Europe was in its usual high spirits. It occupied three- and four-man air-conditioned staterooms and dined in style.[36] On its return to the United States on 5 September 1945, the 119th sailed in even greater comfort on the *Queen Mary*. Again, quarters and meals were excellent. The cordial reception in New York—brass bands, blaring whistles, Red

[32] Hall, "Unit History."
[33] Capt C. F. Hathaway, Jr., "Unit History."
[34] Jefts, "Unit History."
[35] Typical of *The American Soldier's* focus on combat arms, Stouffer et al. ignore the lack of promotion opportunities in units without significant personnel change, such as finance disbursing sections. See "Social Mobility in the Army," pp. 230–283.
[36] Sale, Sutton, and Lesley, "Unit History."

Cross doughnuts and fresh milk, steak dinners, and clean sheets—raised spirits immensely.[37] The 111th was not so fortunate. Its men were shipped across in the crowded hold of a British vessel, and their meals were meager. The 111th's officers supplemented the enlisted rations with sandwiches from the officers' mess.[38] In the Pacific during hostilities, chances of having a varied menu were sometimes slim, and morale suffered. But afterward in the Philippines, men were able to get fresh vegetables and ice cream, which eased the inconveniences of waiting to go home.[39]

Finance men, just as any other soldiers away from home, depended on correspondence to maintain ties with family and friends. Whenever mail service was disrupted, morale took a sharp dip, and men thought more longingly of home.[40] A "Dear John" letter likewise shattered a soldier's spirits.

Since redeployment to the United States was the greatest possible fillip for morale, any delay was disheartening. After V-J Day, 2 September 1945, the transportation situation was the surest gauge of spirits. At first those eligible for redeployment and discharge had expected to be back in the States by Christmas. In October the morale of high-point men in the 171st FDS drooped when it appeared that they would be lucky to be on a boat by Christmas. Then the next month many of them got orders for immediate shipment, and morale soared. To most men, the best part of troop life was the thought of going home.[41]

Army life for finance men differed appreciably from what most observers have taken as representative. Without trying to substitute the specialized experience of finance men for the norm, this chapter calls attention to the great variation in the quality of life in the army during World War II. Because the administrative services were much smaller than combat arms, they have heretofore been ignored. Generalizations about troop life have dealt largely—almost exclusively, in fact—with what it was like on the front line, notwithstanding the fact that only a comparatively few soldiers

[37] CWO Edward M. Lesley, "Unit History."
[38] Jefts, "Unit History."
[39] Maj J. L. Ryan, "Unit History."
[40] Shea, "Unit History."
[41] Ryan, "Unit History."

served at the front. To achieve needed balance in assessing the impact of the war on American soldiers, the multiform nature of that experience should be recognized and its differing components analyzed.

Finance men were not a breed apart from other soldiers—probably no better morally nor more patriotic—but their native abilities and specialized assignments resulted in some discernible differences between their troop life and that of combat forces. Those assigned to Finance had greater intellectual abilities than those in most other branches. This ability enabled them to perform tasks efficiently and to have more than ordinary understanding of the situations they faced and well-adjusted reactions to the vicissitudes of army life. Conforming to primary group characteristics, finance units were close knit, mutually supportive, and self-confident. The enthusiasm and aptitude for their work displayed by officers and men was uncommon in the army. The morale of finance men reflected the zest and sentience they brought to their work. Their morale was affected by the same factors that affected all other soldiers, but finance men understood that they enjoyed a protected niche and that their complaints were minor in comparison to those of soldiers who actually faced the enemy. Troop life for finance men and those in other administrative services differed markedly from that of combat soldiers. Recognition of that difference is important for an accurate assessment of the quality of American troop life in World War II.

CHAPTER *11*

Conclusion

The Finance Department's record in World War II was handicapped by inadequate prewar planning. As war clouds gathered over Europe in the late 1930's, military planners in the War Department realized that combat arms should be prepared. They staged extensive maneuvers in Louisiana in 1939 to test the readiness of the infantry, artillery, and cavalry (armor). Although the organic finance units of one cavalry and five infantry divisions provided service for the maneuvers,[1] the Office of the Chief of Finance apparently did not take the cue from the combat arms to devote as much attention to plans for wartime fiscal operations as the combat arms devoted to their manuevers. Nor did the War Department seem to pressure Finance for contingency plans. The result was that when war began the Finance Department had to scramble to meet immediate emergencies and to supply patchwork solutions to a great array of problems. It entered wartime operations with prewar methods, some of which proved adequate and some totally unsuitable.

Then during the war, those in Washington responsible for most kinds of fiscal planning lacked the imagination exhibited by tactical leaders, such as Generals Patton, MacArthur, and Bradley. Financial planners really had little sense of innovation, except for such comparatively routine functions as the personal transfer account, spearhead deposit, and Class X allotment. In the major areas of pay and exchange of currencies, they tried to make inadequate systems work rather than inaugurating new methods. Perhaps the innate conservatism of finance officers was responsible. Those who rose high in the Finance Department may have done so because of their records of circumspection and caution; such caution precluded devising the kind of disbursing systems needed under varying wartime conditions and in diverse locations. Some finance offi-

---

[1] "History of Fiscal Services," p. 66.

cers with command responsibilities did, nevertheless, break out of the mold and devised new organizational units for specialized service, particularly in the Pacific.

The finance organization performed some of its functions commendably, such as fiscal diplomacy, budgeting and accounting, and funding. In facilitating the army's relations with other nations and other branches of the government, Finance contributed to a smoother and more effective prosecution of the war. It demonstrated that money could grease many skids, both foreign and domestic. Those responsible for budgeting understood that prewar procedures were utterly unsuitable for wartime conditions. They simplified operations so that the Comptroller General could tell how the money was spent, without haggling over how much was spent. Nor did budget procedures attempt in any way to limit amounts allocated to various military purposes. Those planners comprehended that wartime exigencies must prevail over a balanced budget, and field budget procedures reflected this streamlined, commonsense approach. Peacetime accounting methods transferred smoothly to wartime operations, differing only in a larger number of appropriation classifications and vaster sums of money. While not limiting the amounts in specific appropriations for the army, Congress still expected a strict accounting for what was spent. Much irony attaches to such concern for army expenses, considering the inevitably immense wastage of materiel and human life.

Finance officers devised funding methods largely under the pressure of overseas operations, for peacetime models offered only skeletal assistance. Except for the government's continuing indecision over using yellow seal dollars in the Mediterranean area, the mechanical aspects of funding proceeded smoothly. With only a few exceptions, disbursing officers usually had the currency they needed.

Those financial services most directly affecting troops were not suitably adapted to wartime conditions overseas. These included the organization of finance offices, their facilities and equipment, pay of military personnel, and exchange of currencies. In matters of Finance administration, Washington provided a single blueprint for the entire structure of theater fiscal offices, without taking into account the different problems that each theater would face. Similarly, architects of T/O&E's for finance disbursing sections, curiously unanticipated early in the war and later provided only as a stopgap, did not foresee and allow for some critical needs, such as currency exchange, the promotion of personnel, or proper office facilities and equipment.

The chief defect in payment procedures was the expectation that, under trying overseas conditions, entitlements be figured to the last penny—just as in the United States during peacetime. The tyranny of the end-of-the-month payday likewise caused serious imbalances in finance routines. Had Finance devised a more flexible pay system and persuaded the War Department and Congress of its desirability, service could have improved greatly. Savings in time and effort in finance offices would have compensated for the imprecision of the system. Even if pay proximations had been always slightly in favor of the payee, the loss to the government would have been miniscule in comparison with the overall costs of the war.

The War Department's decision to exchange foreign currencies for soldiers placed tremendous strains on finance offices—strains they could not wholly absorb. Their inadequate exchange service caused them, as well as their clientele, a morale burden. Despite these obvious deficiencies, Finance did muddle through; for no extended period did its operations break down entirely. Except for the particularly difficult problems of currency control, Finance performed most of the fiscal functions passably, and some well.

Total war, such as World War II, should have implied that all components of the army would adapt themselves to overseas requirements—that they would abandon peacetime procedures designed for a sedentary stateside military establishment. Strategic and tactical leaders understood that they would face new challenges, that they must meet the enemy on his own terms. Finance officers could have followed suit by adapting their activities similarly. With partial payments they did move toward simplifying pay for casuals, hospitalized soldiers, and others separated from their personnel records, but such simplified methods were not widely applied. In all overseas areas procedures for pay and exchanging currencies should have been streamlined and standardized. These transactions could have taken place at the army's convenience—not with the army facing the deadline of payday at the end of each month, regardless of the tactical situation.

That Finance did not streamline and adapt its functions to the demands of overseas operations resulted from understandable decisions to maintain conservative, traditional patterns with obviously smaller risks. The combat arms devised daring new tactics under the pressure of life-and-death situations for great numbers of men. Since Finance operations did not involve such high stakes, it was easier to work within established molds than to try to break out of them. The same aversion to change made cavalrymen reluctant to give up the horse for the tank and made ground and naval strategists slow to accept the capabilities of air power. Because of combat necessities, the army devised new tactics, organizational structures, and equipment. The same imperatives rarely existed for Finance and many other parts of the military, who found it easier to adhere to established routines that were often awkward, obsolete, and inadequate. With few external demands for improved service, Finance hewed to the safety of known procedures and operations rather than striking out boldly on any new paths.

Poor service in paying troops and exchanging currency resulted, not only from the timidity of Finance leadership, but also from more powerful forces in the War Department. The Judge Advocate General, the Chief of the Civil Affairs Division of the War Department special staff, and the War Department budget officer emphatically denied the possibility of restricting pay overseas. Their narrow, legalistic opinions fertilized the collapse of currency control at the end of the war. With no curbs on soldiers' pay and grossly inadequate restrictions on currency exchanges, the army reaped a harvest of a $530,775,440 overdraft.[2] Had those War Department officials whose decisions paved the way for this administrative failure been more imaginative and flexible in their thinking, the army might have avoided this highly embarrassing situation. But those officials, like the Finance leadership in Washington, were cautious and conservative. They thought it would have been more undemocratic to regulate fiscal operations according to the army's convenience than to demand that a man follow

[2] Walter Rundell, Jr., *Black Market Money*, p. 7.

orders and die in battle. In so doing, they missed a chance to prove that administrative aspects of military operations could be updated and galvanized just as the strategic and tactical were. In paying and exchanging money for troops, fiscal planners were unwilling to adopt ideas from the German army, which, with the introduction of Reichskreditkassenscheine, greatly simplified matters of pay and exchange. While outside Germany, the Wehrmacht was paid with this military money, which soldiers had to spend on the local economy, for it could not be exchanged for Reichmarks. This arbitrary simplification of pay procedures by the German army contributed to administrative efficiency. Whether such efficiency would have outweighed the morale problem of GI's lacking absolute control of their money cannot be determined.

The American military obviously drew a line between what was acceptable for an aggressor in war and what a "peace-loving" democratic government would do. Americans now realize that total —and even limited—war destroys some of the behavioral niceties we have espoused as a society. It follows then that when the nation was committed to total war, the army could have geared all its operations—strategic, tactical, technical, and administrative—to the most efficient conduct of that war. Strategically, the U.S. government acknowledged this principle when it dropped the atomic bomb on Hiroshima. That the army's fiscal history in World War II was marked by awkward, obsolete, and inadequate procedures reflects the predicament of a democracy engaged in war, where arbitrary authority works best.

1) List of FDS'?
" " Finance schools?

2) Sixth army Fin Sec

Bibliography

ARCHIVAL MATERIAL

General Archives Division, Washington National Records Center,
 National Archives and Records Service

Records of the Office of the Chief of Finance (Army), Record *1*
  Group 203

Records of United States Army Commands, 1942— , Record *2*
 Group 338

  Bulletins—War Department, Finance Department, Theaters,
  Base Sections

  Cables—War Department, Theaters

  Carrier Sheets—Theater Headquarters

  Charts—Analysis and Disposition of Pay in Foreign Theaters

  Circulars—War Department, Finance Department, Theaters,
  Base Sections

  Circular Letters—Finance Department, Theaters, Base Sections

  Intelligence Reports—Counterintelligence Corps, Attaché

  Interoffice Communications—Treasury Department

  Interstaff Routing Slips—Theater Headquarters

  Letters (Correspondence Files)—War Department, Treasury
  Department, Theaters, Base Sections, Armies, Corps, Divisions, Air Forces, Finance Disbursing Sections

  Memoranda—War Department, Treasury Department, Finance
  Department, Theaters

  Minutes of Meetings—War Department and Treasury Department Committees

  Radiograms—War Department, Theaters

  Reconnaissance Reports

  Special Orders—Theaters

  Staff Studies—War Department

  twx's—Theaters

REPORTS OF OPERATION (Record Group 338)

"After Action Report, Annex no. 217, Finance, U.S. Seventh Army,
 June 1944–May 1945."

Buckingham, E. M., Maj. "Report of Operation," Office of the Finance
 Officer, U.S. Hq Berlin District, 8 May 45–30 Sep 45.

"Historical Report of Operations," Chanor Base Section, Fiscal Station,
 apo 562, V-E Day–20 Feb 46.

Leighton, H. L., Col. "VI Corps History," Hq Sixth Corps, Office of the Finance Officer, 11–31 May 45.

"Operational Report," Finance Section, Hq Sixth Army, 25 Jan 43–24 Jan 46.

"Report of Operations," Berlin District, Jan–Mar 46.

"Report of Operations (Final After Action Report)," Twelfth Army Group, vol. 10.

Report of the Leyte Operation, 20 Oct 44–25 Dec 44. Sixth Army.

"Semi-Annual Report, 1 Jun–31 Dec 1945," AFWESPAC.

Taylor, J. M., 2d Lt. "Monthly Historical Report," Office of the Finance Officer, Hq Base Three, USASOS, APO 923, Jul 44.

"Tenth Army Action Report, Report of Operations in the Ryukyus Campaign, Chapter 11, Staff Section Reports, Section XIX—Finance."

Vance, John R., Col. "Report of Operations, Finance Officer, USFIP, Dec 8, 1941–May 6, 1942," 30 Sep 44.

UNIT HISTORIES (Record Group 338)

Alexander, R. A., Capt. Twenty-fourth FDS, 1 Aug 42–1 Jun 44.

Anon. "Unit History," 237th FDS, 14 May 45–inactivation.

Blanchard, P. L., CWO. 175th FDS, AFWESPAC, APO 920, Jul 45.

Blumberg, A. E., Maj. 113th FDS, 21 Feb 45.

Cavin, W. M., Maj. Seventy-third FDS, 16 Jan–15 Apr 45.

Chilton, Murray J., CWO. 210th FDS, Hq 2d Bombardment Division, Jan 44–Apr 45.

Dame, Samuel, Capt. "Monthly Unit History," 184th FDS, USASOS, APO 75, 1 Jul 45.

Deuchler, Erwin W., T/5. 110th FDS, 9 May–1 Jul 45.

Glazer, Milton, T/4. Twenty-fifth FDS, 15 Jul 42–25 Oct 45.

Goleman, Ocie A., Maj. Fiftieth FDS.

Gragier, R. J., 2d Lt. 184th FDS, USAFUSAPAC, APO 75, 2 Sep–1 Nov 45.

Greenberg, H., 1st Lt. 2974th Finance Detachment (class B) Provisional AAF Station 118, APO 558, 1 Jul–31 Jul 44.

Hall, Glynn E., S/Sgt. First FDS, Apr 45–Jun 45.

Hathaway, C. F., Jr., Capt. Twenty-ninth FDS, May 45.

Hawkins, L. A., Col. Fin Sec, Fifth Corps, 9 Jul 44–3 Feb 45.

Hawkins, Tom C., Maj. 202d Fin Sec ADO (Avn), 1 Apr–30 Nov 44.

Jackson, Robert C., Capt. Twenty-seventh FDS, 7 Aug 42–30 Apr 44.

Jefts, Merton G., CWO. 111th FDS, 25 Mar 44–30 Jun 45.

Jones, Catesby ap R., Lt Col. Twenty-ninth FDS, Feb–May 45.

Lesley, Edward M., CWO. 119th FDS, 1 Sep–13 Oct 45.

Lord, W. H., Capt. Sixteenth FDS, 15 Jan 43–30 Jun 44.

Mack, Stanley, T/4. 106th FDS, 1 Mar 44–13 Jul 45.

O'Brien, W. J., 2d Lt. "Historical Report," 253d FDS, 28 Aug 45.
Ryan, J. L., Maj. 171st FDS, AFWESPAC, APO 72, Oct 45.
Sale, Nathan, T/3; T/5 Paul N. Sutton; and WOJG Edward M. Lesley. 119th FDS, 25 Mar 44–13 Oct 45.
Schuman, Ivy J., Lt Col. Thirty-second FDS, Jun 43–Aug 45.
Shea, Stanley O., Capt. Eightieth FDS, Oct 44–May 45.
Shugart, G. W., CWO. Sixty-seventh FDS, Jul 44.
Stewart, James A., Maj. Seventy-ninth FDS, 1 Nov 43–9 Oct 45.
Taylor, J. M., 2d Lt. Office of the Finance Officer, Hq Base Three, USASOS, APO 923, 1 Jun 44.
Thompson, H. M., Capt. "Historical Report," 138th FDS, Jan 46.
———. Sixty-fourth FDS, Mar 46.
Walker, David B., Fifty-second FDS, 5 Jul 43–30 Apr 46.
Wegman, L. J., Maj. Disbursing Division, Office of the Fiscal Director, USAFWESPAC, APO 707, 6 Dec 45.
Westgaard, Elve T., CWO. Ninetieth FDS, 22 Feb 44–9 Oct 45.
Williams, Alan O., WOJG. 230th FDS, 17 Jan 46.
Wilson, Edward S., T/5. 100th FDS, 1 Mar 44–25 Aug 45.
Wood, J. W., Maj. 109th FDS, Apr 45.

PERSONAL INTERVIEWS (Notes in the author's files)

Archer, T. W., Lt Col. 3 Feb 54.
Ashworth, T. D., Col. 26 Jul 55.
Barnhill, Paul P., Capt. 3 May 55.
Benton, D. E., Maj. 21 Dec 56.
Campbell, William P., Brig Gen (Ret). 27 Apr 54.
Clos, Delavan C., Lt Col. 15 Feb 54.
Coakley, Robert W., Dr. 31 Mar 54.
Feyereisen, Paul A., Col. 24 Aug 55.
Graham, Raymond E., Lt Col. 17 May 53 and 8 Feb 54.
Gretser, George R., Col. 30 Mar 54.
Jenks, Royal G., Col (Ret). 17 Aug 55.
Kennedy, Robert A., 9 Nov 54.
Koch, Ralph A., Col. 12 Jul 54.
McClellan, Wayland. 29 Sep 72.
Melton, E. R., Lt Col. 15 May 53.
Metzger, Ralph A., Lt Col. 26 Jul 55.
Miller, A. H., Col. 15 Aug 56.
Nelson, Merlin, Lt Col. 29 Oct 54.
Osborn, Gordon D. 24 Jun 55.
Rogers, B. M., Maj. 16 May 53.
Routh, Ross H., Col. 24 Jun 54.
Tullington, B. J., Col. 2 Aug 55.

GOVERNMENT DOCUMENTS

Annual Report of the Secretary of Treasury on the State of the Finances for the Fiscal Year Ended June 30, 1944. Washington: Government Printing Office, 1945.

Foreign Claims Settlement Commission of the United States, *Annual Report to the Congress for the Period January 1–December 1968.*

History and Organization of the Finance Corps. St14–160, 25 Sep 51.

Occupation Currency Transactions. Hearings before the committees on Appropriations, Armed Services, and Banking and Currency, U.S. Senate, 80th Cong, 1st sess. Washington: Government Printing Office, 1947.

Report on House Resolution 150, Appendix A, signed by Henry L. Stimson, Secretary of War, 28 Apr 45.

Sixth Annual Report of the United States High Commissioner to the Philippine Islands to the President and Congress of the United States covering the Fiscal Year July 1, 1941 to June 30, 1942. Washington: Government Printing Office, 1942.

UNPUBLISHED SECONDARY SOURCES

"Administrative History, Office of the Fiscal Director," CGQ, USAFPAC, 6 Apr 45–31 Dec 46. CMH.

"Budgetary and Financial Aspects of the Occupation, 1946–1947." Occupation Forces in Europe Series, 1946–1947. Office of the Chief Historian, European Command, Frankfurt-am-Main, Germany, 1947. CMH.

Cobbs, N. H., Brig Gen (Ret). "Finance Department, European Theater of Operations," Jan 46. RG 338.

"Final History of Base Section No. One, SOS IBT, Karachi, India, 25 Oct 44 to 15 May 45." CMH.

"The First Year of the Occupation." Occupation Forces in Europe Series, 1945–1946. CMH.

"Historical Record of Headquarters Service Command, APO 502, 10 Nov 42–30 Sep 43." RG 338.

"Historical Report," Detachment Finance Section, Alaska Department. RG 338.

"Historical Report of Shangai Base Command," 1 Feb 46. RG 338.

"History of Base Section Two, SOS IBT," 21 May 45–31 Dec 45. CMH.

"History of CPBC During World War II, vol. 5, Historical Review Covering Activities of Construction Service," 15 Sep 45. RG 338.

"History of Fiscal and Finance Activities in the Middle Pacific from 7 Dec 1941 to 2 Sep 1945." CMH.

"History of Fiscal and Finance Operations, Services of Supply, China-Burma-India, from Activation thru 31 Dec 1944," 15 Jan 45. CMH.

"History of the Fiscal Section," Hq Advance Section, Communications Zone, Office of the Finance Officer, APO 113, U.S. Army. CMH.

"History of the Fiscal Services, 1940–1945." CMH.

"History of India-Burma Theater, Appendix 8, Fiscal and Finance Operations, 21 May 45–25 May 46." CMH.

"History of the Peninsular Base Section, NATOUSA, 28 Aug 1943 to 31 Jan 1944." RG 338.

"History of the Services of Supply, CBI, Appendix 13, Fiscal and Finance Operations, 28 Feb 1942 to 24 Oct 1944." CMH.

"History of Services of Supply, India-Burma Theater, Appendix 15, Fiscal Section, 25 Oct 44–20 May 45." CMH.

"History of the United States Army Forces in the Far East, 1943–1945." CMH.

Jacobs, Fenton S., Col. "History of the Western Base Section, APO 515." RG 338.

Koch, Ralph A., Col; Lt Col Harold W. Uhrbrock; and Lt Col Maynard N. Levenick. "The Activities of the Finance Department in the European Theater of Operations." Study 75, Report of the General Board, USFET, File R 013/1, 46. RG 338.

"Narrative History of the Mediterranean Base Section, for the Period September 1942 to 1 May 1944." CMH.

"Organizational History, Services of Supply, South Pacific Area, 1 Oct 43 to 31 Mar 44." CMH.

"Organizational History, Services of Supply, South Pacific Area, 1 Apr to 30 Jun 44." CMH.

Van Riper, Wendell J., Maj. "Logistical Support by the Army Finance Corps, 1940–1945," for Military Science #151, Aug 51. OCF.

PUBLISHED SECONDARY SOURCES

Books

Banque de France. *Compte Rendu des Operations*. Paris: Imprimeries Paul Dupont, 1947.

Carroll, Berenice A. *Design for Total War: Arms and Economics in the Third Reich*. The Hague: Mouton, 1968.

Chang, Kia-Ngau. *The Inflationary Spiral: The Experience in China, 1939–1950*. Cambridge: The Technology Press of Massachusetts Institute of Technology, and New York: John Wiley and Sons, Inc., 1958.

Clark, Mark W. *Calculated Risk*. New York: Harper and Brothers, 1950.

Coakley, Robert W., and Richard M. Leighton. *Global Logistics and Strategy, 1943–1945*. United States Army in World War II. Washington: Office of the Chief of Military History, 1968.

Donn, Albert I. *World War II Prisoner of War Scrip of the United States.* Iola, Wis.: Krause Publications, 1970.

Dougherty, James J. *The Politics of Wartime Aid: American Economic Assistance to France and French Northwest Africa, 1940–1946.* Westport, Conn.: Greenwood Press, 1978.

Dulles, Eleanor Lansing. *The French Franc, 1914–1928: The Facts and Their Interpretation.* New York: The Macmillan Company, 1929.

Edgeworth, E. Y. *Currency and Finance in Time of War.* London: Oxford University Press, 1918.

————. *On the Relations of Political Economy to War.* London: Oxford University Press, n.d.

Ellis, Howard S. *Exchange Control in Central Europe.* Cambridge: Harvard University Press, 1941.

Feilchenfeld, Ernst H. *The International Economic Law of Belligerent Occupation.* Washington: Carnegie Endowment for International Peace, 1942.

Feis, Herbert. *Churchill, Roosevelt, Stalin: The War They Waged and the Peace They Sought.* 2d ed. Princeton: Princeton University Press, 1967.

Funk, Arthur L. *Charles de Gaulle: The Crucial Years, 1943–1944.* Norman: University of Oklahoma Press, 1959.

Howe, George F. *Northwest Africa: Seizing the Initiative in the West.* United States Army in World War II. Washington: Office of the Chief of Military History, 1957.

Hunt, I. L., Col. *American Military Government of Occupied Germany, 1919–1920, Report of the Officer in Charge of Civil Affairs, Third Army and American Forces in Germany,* N.p., n.p., 1920.

Kasten, Helmut. *Wahrung und Reichskreditkassen in den Besetzien Gebieten.* Berlin: Bank-Verlag, 1941.

Kimball, Warren F. *The Most Unsordid Act: Lend-Lease, 1939–1941.* Baltimore: Johns Hopkins Press, 1969.

Lagrenée, Jacques. *Le Problème Monétaire en France après les Guerres de 1870–1871 et 1914–1918.* Paris: Les Presses Universitaires de France, 1923.

Lee, Ulysses. *The Employment of Negro Troops.* United States Army in World War II. Washington: Office of the Chief of Military History, 1966.

Leighton, Richard M., and Robert W. Coakley. *Global Logistics and Strategy, 1940–1943.* United States Army in World War II. Washington: Office of the Chief of Military History, 1955.

Logistical History of NATOUSA-MTOUSA. Naples: G. Montanino, 1945.

Loria, Achille. *Le Peripezie Monetarie Della Guerra.* Milano: Fratelli Treves Editori, 1920.

Matloff, Maurice, and Edwin M. Snell. *Strategic Planning for Coalition Warfare, 1941–1942.* United States Army in World War II. Washington: Office of the Chief of Military History, 1959.

Merton, Robert K., and Paul F. Lazarsfeld, eds. *Continuities in Social Research: Studies in the Scope and Method of "The American Soldier".* Glencoe, Ill.: The Free Press, 1950.

Millett, John D. *The Organization and Role of the Army Service Forces.* United States Army in World War II. Washington: Office of the Chief of Military History, 1954.

Milward, Alan S. *The German Economy at War.* London: Athlone Press, 1965.

Ouchi, Hyoye. *Financial and Monetary Situation in Post-War Japan.* New York: Institute of Pacific Relations, 1947.

Palmer, Robert R.; Bell I. Wiley; and William R. Keast. *The Procurement and Training of Ground Combat Troops.* United States Army in World War II. Washington: Historical Division, Department of the Army, 1948.

Paxton, Robert O. *Vichy France: Old Guard and New Order, 1940–1944.* New York: Alfred A. Knopf, 1972.

Petrov, Vladimir. *Money and Conquest: Allied Occupation Currencies in World War II.* Baltimore: Johns Hopkins Press, 1967.

Pogue, Forrest C. *George Marshall: Organizer of Victory.* New York: Viking Press, 1973.

Popovics, Alexander. *Das Geldwesen im Kriege.* Wien: Holder-Pilcher-Tempsky, 1925.

Reveille, Thomas. *The Spoil of Europe: The Nazi Technique in Political and Economic Conquest.* New York: W. W. Norton and Company, 1941.

Risch, Erna. *Quartermaster Support of the Army: A History of the Corps, 1775–1939.* Washington: Office of the Quartermaster General, 1962.

Rogers, James Harvey. *The Process of Inflation in France, 1914–1927.* New York: Columbia University Press, 1929.

Romanus, Charles F., and Riley Sunderland. *Stilwell's Command Problems.* United States Army in World War II. Washington: Office of the Chief of Military History, 1955.

Rundell, Walter, Jr. *Black Market Money: The Collapse of U.S. Military Currency Control in World War II.* Baton Rouge: Louisiana State University Press, 1964.

Rutlader, James. *Allied Military Currency: [Issues of Military Payment Certificates from World War II—to Date and Emergency Issues Caused by a War].* Kansas City: Bill Johnson Creative Printers, 1968.

Schwan, C. Frederick, and Joseph E. Bolling. *World War II Military Currency*. Portage, O.: BNR Press, 1978.

Sherwin, Stephen F. *Monetary Policy in Continental Western Europe, 1944–1952*. Wisconsin Commerce Studies, vol. 2, no. 2. Madison: University of Wisconsin, 1956.

Shugg, Roger W., and Maj H. A. DeWeerd. *World War II*. Washington: The Infantry Journal, 1946.

Southard, Frank A., Jr. *The Finances of European Liberation*. New York: King's Crown Press, 1946.

Spahr, Walter E. *Allied Military Currency*. New York: Economists' National Committee on Monetary Policy, 1943.

Stamp, Sir Josiah C. *The Financial Aftermath of War*. London: Ernest Benn, Ltd., 1932.

Stettinius, Edward R., Jr. *Lend-Lease: Weapon for Victory*. New York: The Macmillan Company, 1944.

Stouffer, Samuel A., Louis Guttman, Edward A. Suchman, Paul F. Lazarsfeld, Shirley A. Star, and John A. Clausen. *Studies in Social Psychology in World War II*. 4 vols. Princeton: Princeton University Press, 1949–50.

Swails, Alfred J. *Military Currency, World War II: U.S. and Allies*. Tucson: Monitor Printing Company, 1961.

Toy, Raymond S. *All Known Issues of World War II and Post War (U.S. and Allies) Military Currency Are Listed*. 3rd illus. ed. Tucson: Monitor Offset Printing Company, 1969.

————, and Bob Meyer. *Axis Military Currency: All Known Issues of World War II are Listed*. Tucson: Monitor Offset Printing Company, 1967.

Tuchman, Barbara W. *Stilwell and the American Experience in China, 1911–45*. Bantam Books. New York: The Macmillan Company, 1971.

Wright, Gordon. *The Ordeal of Total War, 1939–45*. New York: Harper and Row, 1968.

Young, Arthur N. *China and the Helping Hand*. Cambridge: Harvard University Press, 1963.

Articles

Abbott, Alfred A., Maj. "The Army as Banker." *Army Information Digest* 2 (August 1947): 37–44.

Bell, Harry H. "Monetary Problems of Military Occupation." *Military Affairs* 6 (Summer 1942): 77–88.

Bratter, Herbert. "Invasion Currency." *Banking* 36 (November 1943): 28, 84.

Bressett, K. E., and Neil Shafer. "Allied Military Currency: A Reappraisal." *Whitman Numismatic Journal* 5 (November 1968): 621–652.

Buhite, Russell D. "Soviet-American Relations and the Repatriation of Prisoners of War, 1945." *The Historian* 35 (May 1973): 384–397.

"Fixing the Lira Rate." *The Economist* (London) 145 (10 July 1943): 54.

Kemmerer, Donald L., and T. Eugene Beattie. "Allied Military Currency in Italy." *Commercial and Financial Chronicle* 160 (21 Sep 44): 1241, 1268–1269.

Lester, Richard A. "International Aspects of Wartime Monetary Experience." *Essays in International Finance* 3 (August 1944): 1–22.

Rundell, Walter, Jr. "Invasion Currency: A U.S. Army Fiscal Problem in World War II." *Southwestern Social Science Quarterly* 43 (September 1962): 143–151.

———. "Paying the POW in World War II." *Military Affairs* 22 (Fall 1958): 121–134.

———. "Troop Life: The Finance Department in World War II." *The Historian* 41 (November 1978): 94–106.

Southard, Frank A., Jr. "Some European Currency and Exchange Experiences: 1943–1946." *Essays in International Finance* 7 (Summer 1946): 1–23.

Tamagna, Frank M. "The Fixing of Foreign Exchange Rates." *Journal of Political Economy* 53 (March 1945): 57–72.

Index

CPSIA information can be obtained at www.ICGtesting.com
Printed in the USA
BVOW031113100612

292203BV00001B/61/A